CONTENTS

D1358294

INTRODUCTION

The sport of basketball is unique because it blends both power and finesse. Even though strength and power are desirable traits, a basketball player so often fears losing quickness or fluidity of movement, that he will avoid strength and power exercises, commonly associated with traditional resistance training. The ball handling and shooting skills of basketball are so finely tuned that the temporary muscle fatigue and tightness associated with resistance training often keep young basketball players from including resistance training into their physical conditioning programs. Understanding these attitudes toward physical preparation was a motivating factor in the creation of this book. As a strength-coach, it was important for me to provide a workout plan that considered the validity of those player's fears. If a player is afraid of losing his skills due to a poorly designed program, then regardless of how good the program is, it will not provide that player any true benefit.

Accordingly, agility, mobility and basketball skill retention, therefore, must be considered to be of the utmost importance to the basketball athlete when designing a complete conditioning program. Having a player's performance hindered by a lack of strength, or the onset of fatigue are correctable problems that can be remedied through a proper year-round physical conditioning program. The athlete, however, must believe that the program will help him. Flexibility training, resistance training, cardiorespiratory conditioning, speed development, and the control of body composition are all exercise variables that can improve a basketball athlete's ability to perform.

This book is unique in that it provides you with a complete 52-week exercise plan for high-performance basketball. The plan is built upon a typical college academic and athletic calendar and, with only slight variations, can be used by any high school program in the country. By using periodization principles that modulate intensity, you'll promote maximum muscle strength and stability, and most importantly, proper muscle recovery.

A well-designed workout plan mimics or parallels specific activities that occur during the actual sporting event, such as blocking out an opponent, dunking the basketball or sprinting up-court between players or obstacles. By understanding and considering the specificity of training, the workouts in this book are exclusively designed to enhance the physical abilities of the basketball athlete.

Due to the lean body structures and height of most basketball athletes, strength is often a problem. Long arms and legs provide less leverage potential for these athletes, thus reducing their power output. Many exercises have been provided in this book that help empower the basketball athlete by mobilizing his own body weight through a wide variety of activities. These exercises, in turn, strengthen the torso and hips to aid in the production of power and thus provide a chance for the arms and legs to be extensions of that power. A good basketball strength and conditioning program must consider the requirements for absolute power versus the need for absolute endurance that basketball requires.

This balance of power versus endurance within the sport determines everything about the conditioning program; how long to work out; how long to rest between sets of an exercise; how much weight lifting versus running to do; and how far or how long to run. If an athlete does not consider the balance of power versus endurance, he may not perform up to his potential.

This book neatly lays out a year-round system of physical training that balances both the variables of power and endurance in the exercise elements of resistance training, as well as, overall conditioning, fitness, and skill abilities. Part I provides you with detailed resistance training, conditioning, and skills workouts for a full year of training from postseason training, which begins at the end of your basketball season (chapter 1), to the following fall's in-season training (chapter 5). Part II then provides you with illustrated instructions to help you perform the flexibility exercises (chapter 6), resistance training exercises (chapter 7), speed and power drills (chapter 8) and basketball-specific agility drills (chapter 9).

Because basketball is a sport that can be played at any time during the year, under a variety of playing environments and competitive levels, it is often difficult for the basketball athlete to know on which phase of the training cycle he should actually concentrate. Although the workout plan in this book is based on what an athlete might experience at the Division I level of college basketball, it also provides scenarios on how to arrange the plan to best suit your workout and playing needs.

Physical training alone, however, will not totally prepare you to succeed in your sport. You must also consider other important factors that go beyond the scope of this book, but still demand mentioning.

Nutrition: Proper nutrition is a critical element in the promotion of muscle recovery. Without taking in the proper numbers of calories in the appropriate percentages of the required nutrients, the muscles you have worked so diligently to train will fail to properly heal. Each workout thereafter will only promote further fatigue, and eventually overtraining will result in a loss of strength and performance. Therefore, you should be equally concerned about the amount and type of food that you are providing your body. Recovery is the key to success in any workout plan, and proper nutrition and rest constitute a plan of recovery. Remember, when you work out, you are creating microscopic damage at the cellular level of the muscles. Failing to sleep and eat properly will result in an inability to re-build this muscle.

Mental Preparation: Another important factor to consider is the mental training that parallels physical training. Physical success is virtually impossible unless the mental desire to succeed accompanies one's physical efforts. Most every athlete believes that he can perform a physical task until he fails the first time. Each failure thereafter only solidifies the athlete's doubt in his ability to succeed. Therefore, you must create planned workouts that promote achievement rather than failure. Structured achievement is where constructive goal setting is applied.

Goal Setting: Setting a goal can be motivational. Setting an objective for yourself that is realistically obtainable can often act as a stimulus to prove yourself. Goals can be simple, such as getting out of bed in the morning when the alarm rings. Goals can be difficult as well, such as scoring 1000 points in a career, or being a leading shot blocker for a single season. Whatever you choose as your goals, make plans to obtain them realistically and systematically.

In a physical conditioning program, it is important that you set specific goals that can be divided into smaller steps. These steps are small goals within themselves. These small goals should lead to the ultimate goal. Using this step-by-step approach may take months or even years to reach the ultimate goal, but as a result of proper planning and the confidence gained from completing each small step, you can more easily obtain your ultimate or long range goal. You can do this a number of ways, depending upon the individual athlete and the athlete's trainer as to how that goal is approached. Adopt a plan that the athlete is comfortable with and has taken some part in designing. In this way, the goal will be approached with more enthusiasm. Confidence is an athlete's biggest weapon against defeat. With successful goal setting, an athlete can gain that all so important confidence, making the goal more easily obtainable.

From this workout, exercise format and order should be observed. However, because the workout is designed and laid out before you, exercise order and format is not the most important consideration. If you come away with nothing else, you should adhere to these three rules:

- Be consistent and train on a regular basis. To respond maximally, your body must be continually challenged.

- Work hard and smart. Hard work with intelligent regard for recovery during the post exercise period will produce greater results.

- Rest thoroughly when it is time to rest. Workouts only serve to break you down. Resting builds you back up.

Your biggest enemy preventing you from being successful is yourself. Only through consistent, structured training and by adopting an unflinching desire to be the best, will your goals be met. So what are you waiting for? Get out there and get started!!!

PART 1

Five Phases
of
Year-Round Basketball Conditioning

Year-Round Training for Basketball

The 52-week basketball conditioning plan presented in this book is just one possible example of how to set up a complete exercise training plan for basketball players. The primary purpose of the program presented is to show you, whether you're an athlete or a coach, how to incorporate all the aspects of your daily workouts into a consolidated and structured routine. Consider this program to be just one of many methods of exercise planning. Every athlete is an individual who knows his or her own body best. Some workout methods produce better results for some athletes and teams than others because of how the program is constructed. The times of the year when certain training elements are applied, and the different practice and game schedules of the team the athlete plays for are important factors. The workout plan presented in this book fully considers the various factors attendant to the basketball player, his team, and the stresses he might encounter on and off the basketball court.

Program Structure

The following program, a 52-week macrocycle, was designed around a typical collegiate basketball athletic and academic calendar. The macrocycle is a method of structuring and viewing a workout plan. This workout is based on a year-long observation and goal-setting period. For a basketball player, a year-by-year observation period is advised. An Olympic-caliber athlete may choose to structure his macrocycle based on a four-year observation period, because he is attempting to maximize his goals by the time of the next Olympic trials or games This basketball workout is realistic in regard to schedule restraints at the collegiate level, but can also be easily adapted for high school student athletes whose busy schedule can be similar to that of collegiate players. Each peak in intensity during the training year is controlled by the academic schedule and the time of year in relation to the sport season.

The macrocycle is constructed around the basketball season and is divided into in-season, post-season, and pre-season periods. These three distinct periods impact every variable of the exercise plan. For example, a basketball player's training becomes more specific to basketball as he approaches the in-season period. This way, he can convert the basic strength he acquired in the weight room during the post-season and pre-season periods to more functional strength that can be applied to his skills on the basketball court.

The number of days per week of training (frequency) and the length of the training session (duration) are all determined by these three primary training periods and can be further broken down into phases called mesocycles. The five mesocycles (phases) of year-round training are shown in Figure 1.1. Each

Figure 1.1. The five mesocycles (phases) of year-round training

Phase 1 Postseason	Phase 2 Early Summer	Phase 3 Late Summer	Phase 4 Preseason	Phase 5 In-season
Mar. Apr.	May Jun.	Jul. Aug.	Sep. Oct.	Nov. Dec. Jan. Feb. Mar

mesocycle is covered separately in chapters 1 through 5. Each mesocycle is further broken down into 8 to 12 microcycles. The program presented in this book has 52 separate microcycles that comprise one macrocycle.

The in-season, post-season, and pre-season phase divisions mark points in time en route to the upcoming basketball season and provide observations of progress made during that portion of the training. Some phases flow right into others with little, if any, break in the workout. Other phases are separated by a planned week off.

This 52-week plan also considers breaks in the academic calendar that occur in the in-season, post-season, and pre-season periods. Academic breaks create periods when athletes may be away from the training environment. However, planning these breaks into the training program helps the athlete maintain consistency in his fitness even while he is away from school. Either breaks can be planned as time off for recovery, or workouts can be provided for the athletes to take home. Take-home workouts can prevent a loss in the physical improvements already achieved.

Program Components

Each workout in Part 2 is made up of six main components:

- Warming up and flexibility: Designed to prepare your muscles for the workout, increase your range of motion, and reduce the risk of injury (Chapter 6).

- Resistance training: Designed to increase muscle stability to protect you from injury, as well as increase muscular endurance, size, and power (Chapter 7).

- Power and speed: Designed to take the raw muscular strength you have gained from resistance training and convert it to powerful movements that can be applied on the basketball court (Chapter 8).

- Agility and foot speed: Designed to improve your mobility and body control (Chapter 9).

- Running and conditioning: Designed to promote aerobic and anaerobic fitness, thereby improving the ability of the heart, lungs, endocrine, and vascular systems to better support your muscular work (Chapter 10).

- Skill training: Designed to improve your ability to perform at a maximum level on the court through practice and your enhanced level of fitness (Chapter 11).

Before beginning your workout, it is important to understand several considerations that can assist in accelerating your progress. This book provides you with the structure of the workout, the types and order of exercises, the number of sets and repetitions for each exercise, and the amount of rest to be taken between each exercise. Each chapter in Part 1 details one of the five mesocycles of the 52-week plan and provides weekly workout programs for that mesocycle. Each week in the mesocycle divides the workouts into three parts: resistance training, conditioning, and applied skill training. Part 2 of this text explains and illustrates the specific exercises you will use throughout the 52-week program.

At some point in time, as you become more experienced, you may desire to create your own workout. Understanding the structural components of a workout will help you in your endeavors.

Warming Up

Warming up briefly, prior to a workout, is beneficial in several ways.

- It prepares the muscle tissue for more intense activity by gradually warming up the muscle. This factor ensures that your muscles will adapt to more intense exercise.

Figure 1.2. Warming up prior to a workout prepares the muscle tissue for more intense activity.

- Warming up prior to exercise has been shown to increase nerve activity in the working muscles, resulting in an increased contraction speed of the muscle fibers, as well as an increase in the amount of force or power output of the muscle. This type of response is especially beneficial for power and strength athletes.

- Warming up prior to exercise may also reduce the potential for injury by increasing muscle flexibility. This can assist in the reduction of strains and tears in the muscles and connective tissues.

- Warming up prior to exercise can reduce a sharp rise in blood pressure and thus, place less stress on the athlete's heart – a factor that is particularly important since an athlete's blood pressure naturally rises at the beginning of exercise. This can be important to an athlete who might already have high blood pressure, as well as to all athletes who are naturally concerned about their health.

- In general, research has shown that performance can increase in athletes who warm-up prior to exercise.

If the athlete is about to perform flexibility training and no other physical exercise, then a passive warm-up is suggested (see Flexibility Exercises, Chapter 6). For activities that involve substantial muscular contractions, like playing basketball or resistance training, it is suggested that you perform a 5-to-10 minute overall body warm-up performed at a sub-maximal effort, such as calisthenics or light physical activities, like jogging or jumping rope. Table I-1 lists several examples of sample overall-body warm-up exercises. An overall body stretch can also be incorporated into the warm-up. Next, perform one to two sets of a more specific warm-up for the activity that is about to be performed, such as a warm-up set on the bench press if you are weight training. The more specific warm-up will help you increase your body temperature in the area of the body that you will be exercising.

As a rule, warming up is recommended primarily before the conditioning workouts. The flexibility portion of the workout is referred to as either a "dynamic warm-up" or a "static stretch". The dynamic warm-up is described along with the plyometric section in Chapter 8. The static stretch can consist of the pre-practice stretching warm-up routine described in Chapter 6, or any combination of stretching exercise to promote a more permanent state of flexibility. Even though a warm-up period is not indicated prior to the resistance training portion of the workout, you should warm up by doing light, full-body movements and light sets of the exercise about to be performed. Light stretching can be included. However, over-stretching of the muscle prior to a resistance training session can result in muscle instability, and can cause an inability to safely stabilize the weight during the movement. If you like to stretch before or between resistance training exercises, keep the stretches light in intensity. It is probably best to avoid stretching before an exercise that requires high muscular stability, like a

Specific	Overall Body
Push Ups (for arm work)	Jogging in place
Pull-ups	Jumping jacks
Deep knee bends	Jumping rope
Stretching	Stationary cycling
Very light single set of the exercise to be performed.	

Table 1.1. Sample warm-up exercises

bench press or squats. Instead, reserve your stretches for periods before and between the less-demanding, supporting exercises.

Resistance Training

Resistance training is an important part of any workout plan. By overloading the muscles during a workout with an amount of resistance well over that of the athlete's body weight, the athlete will find his body weight to seem far less of a burden while playing his sport. Resistance, for this reason, is highly important to the basketball athlete. In order to gain ultimate control of his body weight when playing and to achieve meaningful increases in muscular size, resistance training must always be a part of the basketball athlete's workout plan. The emphasis of the resistance training portion of the workout is to maximize the muscle to its fullest strength and power capability. The strength and power obtained by the muscle in the weight room can then be fine tuned on the practice court and, through the conditioning and applied skills sections of his workout, can assist the player in becoming a stronger and more powerful athlete.

A standard resistance workout should be created for all basketball athletes regardless of their position on the court. The resistance training should only address each player's physical weaknesses, not directly attempt to make them better basketball players. It is important to keep in mind that basketball players are made on the court, while athletes are made stronger in the weight room. Therefore, resistance training routines should address every conceivable body movement and apply resistance to those movements. In the process, the athletes will develop a balanced level of strength, and will, therefore, be safer on the court.

If an athlete is having a problem with a particular exercise and is unsafe because of his mechanics or body structure, the workout should then be changed to meet his needs. Since only fifteen or so athletes will be working out at one time, no problem should exist with the flow of the workout and how the weight room is used. If you have a small workout facility, then consider breaking your team down into workout groups. As a last result, you may have to create two or three different workouts. On the other hand, performing multiple workouts can become very confusing, thereby making spotting and safety an issue. If multiple workouts are your only option, then construct the workouts so that each group of athletes moves through the weight-room at conflicting exercise stations. This can help keep the athletes from running into one another, or wasting time waiting to get on a bench or machine. Athletes are first and foremost students and don't want to be in the weight room all day or night. They have class to attend, papers to write, and tests to study for. The workout should work for them.

How to Read the Resistance Training Workout

Each week starts by noting the amount of rest you should take between repetitions of a particular exercise, and, where applicable, sets of exercises, as well as the amount of rest between the actual exercises in minutes and seconds. To the right of each exercise name, you'll see the number of repetitions to be performed for each set and the amount of weight (noted as a specific percentage of the athlete's one-repetition maximum – 1 RM – for that exercise). For example:

- Bench press 8 \x\ 70%, 8 \x\ 75%, and 8 \x\ 80%.

This means you are doing 3 sets of 8 repetitions of the bench press at 70%, 75%, and 80% of your 1 RM. If your 1 RM on the bench press is 200, you would lift:

70% of 200 (.70 \x\ 200) or 140 pounds on the first set,

75% of 200 (.75 \x\ 200) or 150 pounds on the second set, and

80% of 200 (.80 \x\ 200) or 160 pounds on the third set.

Determining Your 1 RM Max

To determine your one repetition maximum (1 RM) – the most weight you can lift for a particular exercise a singe time – determine your 1 RM for selected exercises. Subsequently, this information will be used as the basis of your resistance training program. Keep in mind that not every exercise has to be tested for maximal ability. By using the maximums from several core lifts, other exercises maximums can be estimated. In this regard, three core lifts are suggested:

- Bench press (upper-body, push exercises)

- Close-grip lat (upper-body, pull exercises)

- Leg press or squat (lower-body exercises)

Then, using week-to-week observations of the athlete's workout sheets or logbooks, the coach or athlete can fine-tune the estimated exercises to near perfect resistance levels. For the high school freshman or younger athletes, 1RM attempts are ill-advised. All factors considered, a repetition maximum of the core lifts can serve as the standard upon which to base the workout resistance levels. The high school athlete can choose a manageable weight and perform a number of repetitions just short of complete muscular failure. He can then examine the weight percentage charts included in this book, and determine what the number of repetitions at that weight corresponds to as a 1RM.

These corresponding percentages are the approximate levels of resistance that should be used. This means that 60% is lighter than 90%, and because of this, on a day when you see 60%, you should consider that day a lighter-resistance workout. That is not to say that the workout should be easy, just that the resistance should be less. The lighter resistance will allow the athlete to concentrate more on strict adherence to the proper way that each repetition should be performed, allowing for higher repetitions or combination sets. As such, even light workouts can be really difficult.

Use the percentages indicated on the workouts as guidelines, but do not be afraid to adjust your 1 RM on a lift as your strength improves. For example, maybe Michael has made an improvement on the bench press exercise, and he's ready to increase his last set of the exercise by five pounds on his next workout. But when looking at the exercise plan, his last set of bench press is scheduled to be 80%. In fact, he's scheduled to lift 80% on the last set for the next four weeks. The weight Michael is currently using is too easy for him, but he needs to continue progressing. Just because the workout says to use 80% for the next four weeks, Michael does not need to lift the same weight all four weeks.

Let's say Michael's previous 1 RM for the bench press was 200 pounds (80% of 200 pounds is 160). The workout suggests using 160 pounds for the next four weeks regardless of whether Michael has improved or not. The way to address strength improvement using the workout plan is to increase the 1 RM by about five pounds. (When using free weights, the most common increase is to add a 2-1/2 lb. plate to each side of the bar.) This adjustment will make Michael's new 1 RM 205 pounds, and his workout weight (80% of 205) will be bumped to 164 pounds. Rounded to the nearest five pounds, Michael's new workout weight is 165 pounds.

This method of increasing an individual's 1 RM is very useful because it projects the athlete upward all the way to the end of the training cycle. Come test time, instead of the athlete working with a weight that is too easy, he can work out with a weight closer to that of his new 1 RM. If this method of increasing weight is too difficult, the athlete can simply keep records of his weekly progress in each lift. Having the athlete keep records can lead to poorly kept data and lost record sheets, but this may be the only method you can use. You may be asking why even keep records? Why not simply go in, work hard in the weight room, and kick butt? That's all that matters, right? You may choose to run your program this way, however, the gains you make, if any, will come early in the training, and in the long haul, you will probably become less productive and fall short of your long-term goals. This situation occurs because athletes without a structured plan may often acquire fatigue-related injuries or burnout.

Table 1.2. Weight percentage chart

Max%	95	90	85	80	75	70	65	60	55	50	45	40	35	30	25
245	233	221	208	196	184	172	159	147	135	123	110	98	86	74	61
250	238	225	213	200	188	175	163	150	138	125	113	100	88	75	63
255	242	230	217	204	191	179	166	153	140	128	115	102	89	77	64
260	247	234	221	208	195	182	169	156	143	130	117	104	91	78	65
265	252	239	225	212	199	186	172	159	146	133	119	106	93	80	66
270	257	243	230	216	203	189	176	162	149	135	122	108	95	81	68
275	261	248	234	220	206	193	179	165	151	138	124	110	96	83	69
280	266	252	238	224	210	196	182	168	154	140	126	112	98	84	70
285	271	257	242	228	214	200	185	171	157	143	128	114	100	86	71
290	276	261	247	232	218	203	189	174	160	145	131	116	102	87	73
295	280	266	251	236	221	207	192	177	162	148	133	118	103	89	74
300	285	270	255	240	225	210	195	180	165	150	135	120	105	90	75
305	290	275	259	244	229	214	198	183	168	153	137	122	107	92	76
310	295	279	264	248	233	217	202	186	171	155	140	124	109	93	78
315	299	284	268	252	236	221	205	189	173	158	142	126	110	95	79
320	304	288	272	256	240	224	208	192	176	160	144	128	112	96	80
325	309	293	276	260	244	228	211	195	179	163	146	130	114	98	81
330	314	297	281	264	248	231	215	198	182	165	149	132	116	99	83
335	318	302	285	268	251	235	218	201	184	168	151	134	117	101	84
340	323	306	289	272	255	238	221	204	187	170	153	136	119	102	85
345	328	311	293	276	259	242	224	207	190	173	155	138	121	104	86
350	333	315	298	280	263	245	228	210	193	175	158	140	123	105	88
355	337	320	302	284	266	249	231	213	195	178	160	142	124	107	89
360	342	324	306	288	270	252	234	216	198	180	162	144	126	108	90
365	347	329	310	292	274	256	237	219	201	183	164	146	128	110	91
370	352	333	315	296	278	259	241	222	204	185	167	148	130	111	93
375	356	338	319	300	281	263	244	225	206	188	169	150	131	113	94
380	361	342	323	304	285	266	247	228	209	190	171	152	133	114	95
385	366	347	327	308	289	270	250	231	212	193	173	154	135	116	96
390	371	351	332	312	293	273	254	234	215	195	176	156	137	117	98
395	375	356	336	316	296	277	257	237	217	198	178	158	138	119	99
400	380	360	340	320	300	280	260	240	220	200	180	160	140	120	100
405	385	365	344	324	304	284	263	243	223	203	182	162	142	122	101
410	390	369	349	328	308	287	267	246	226	205	185	164	144	123	103
415	394	374	353	332	311	291	270	249	228	208	187	166	145	125	104
420	399	378	357	336	315	294	273	252	231	210	189	168	147	126	105
425	404	383	361	340	319	298	276	255	234	213	191	170	149	128	106
430	409	387	366	344	323	301	280	258	237	215	194	172	151	129	108
435	413	392	370	348	326	305	283	261	239	218	196	174	152	131	109
440	418	396	374	352	330	308	286	264	242	220	198	176	154	132	110
445	423	401	378	356	334	312	289	267	245	223	200	178	156	134	111
450	428	405	383	360	338	315	293	270	248	225	203	180	158	135	113
455	432	410	387	364	341	319	296	273	250	228	205	182	159	137	114
460	437	414	391	368	345	322	299	276	253	230	207	184	161	138	115

Table 1.2. Weight percentage chart (continued)

Max%	95	90	85	80	75	70	65	60	55	50	45	40	35	30	25
465	442	419	395	372	349	326	302	279	256	233	209	186	163	140	116
470	447	423	400	376	353	329	306	282	259	235	212	188	165	141	118
475	451	428	404	380	356	333	309	285	261	238	214	190	166	143	119
480	456	432	408	384	360	336	312	288	264	240	216	192	168	144	120
485	461	437	412	388	364	340	315	291	267	243	218	194	170	146	121
490	466	441	417	392	368	343	319	294	270	245	221	196	172	147	123
495	470	446	421	396	371	347	322	297	272	248	223	198	173	149	124
500	475	450	425	400	375	350	325	300	275	250	225	200	175	150	125
505	480	455	429	404	379	354	328	303	278	253	227	202	177	152	126
510	485	459	434	408	383	357	332	306	281	255	230	204	179	153	128
515	489	464	438	412	386	361	335	309	283	258	232	206	180	155	129
520	494	468	442	416	390	364	338	312	286	260	234	208	182	156	130
525	499	473	446	420	394	368	341	315	289	263	236	210	184	158	131
530	504	477	451	424	398	371	345	318	292	265	239	212	186	159	133
535	508	482	455	428	401	375	348	321	294	268	241	214	187	161	134
540	513	486	459	432	405	378	351	324	297	270	243	216	189	162	135
545	518	491	463	436	409	382	354	327	300	273	245	218	191	164	136
550	523	495	468	440	413	385	358	330	303	275	248	220	193	165	138
555	527	500	472	444	416	389	361	333	305	278	250	222	194	167	139
560	532	504	476	448	420	392	364	336	308	280	252	224	196	168	140
565	537	509	480	452	424	396	367	339	311	283	254	226	198	170	141
570	542	513	485	456	428	399	371	342	314	285	257	228	200	171	143
575	546	518	489	460	431	403	374	345	316	288	259	230	201	173	144
580	551	522	493	464	435	406	377	348	319	290	261	232	203	174	145
585	556	527	497	468	439	410	380	351	322	293	263	234	205	176	146
590	561	531	502	472	443	413	384	354	325	295	266	236	207	177	148
595	565	536	506	476	446	417	387	357	327	298	268	238	208	179	149
600	570	540	510	480	450	420	390	360	330	300	270	240	210	180	150
605	575	545	514	484	454	424	393	363	333	303	272	242	212	182	151
610	580	549	519	488	458	427	397	366	336	305	275	244	214	183	153
615	584	554	523	492	461	431	400	369	338	308	277	246	215	185	154
620	589	558	527	496	465	434	403	372	341	310	279	248	217	186	155
625	594	563	531	500	469	438	406	375	344	313	281	250	219	188	156
630	599	567	536	504	473	441	410	378	347	315	284	252	221	189	158
635	603	572	540	508	476	445	413	381	349	318	286	254	222	191	159
640	608	576	544	512	480	448	416	384	352	320	288	256	224	192	160
645	613	581	548	516	484	452	419	387	355	323	290	258	226	194	161
650	618	585	553	520	488	455	423	390	358	325	293	260	228	195	163
655	622	590	557	524	491	459	426	393	360	328	295	262	229	197	164
660	627	594	561	528	495	462	429	396	363	330	297	264	231	198	165
665	632	599	565	532	499	466	432	399	366	333	299	266	233	200	166
670	637	603	570	536	503	469	436	402	369	335	302	268	235	201	168
675	641	608	574	540	506	473	439	405	371	338	304	270	236	203	169

Table 1.2. Weight percentage chart (continued)

Max%	95	90	85	80	75	70	65	60	55	50	45	40	35	30	25
680	646	612	578	544	510	476	442	408	374	340	306	272	238	204	170
685	651	617	582	548	514	480	445	411	377	343	308	274	240	206	171
690	656	621	587	552	518	483	449	414	380	345	311	276	242	207	173
695	660	626	591	556	521	487	452	417	382	348	313	278	243	209	174
700	665	630	595	560	525	490	455	420	385	350	315	280	245	210	175
705	670	635	599	564	529	494	458	423	388	353	317	282	247	212	176
710	675	639	604	568	533	497	462	426	391	355	320	284	249	213	178
715	679	644	608	572	536	501	465	429	393	358	322	286	250	215	179
720	684	648	612	576	540	504	468	432	396	360	324	288	252	216	180
725	689	653	616	580	544	508	471	435	399	363	326	290	254	218	181
730	694	657	621	584	548	511	475	438	402	365	329	292	256	219	183
735	698	662	625	588	551	515	478	441	404	368	331	294	257	221	184
740	703	666	629	592	555	518	481	444	407	370	333	296	259	222	185
745	708	671	633	596	559	522	484	447	410	373	335	298	261	224	186
750	713	675	638	600	563	525	488	450	413	375	338	300	263	225	188
755	717	680	642	604	566	529	491	453	415	378	340	302	264	227	189
760	722	684	646	608	570	532	494	456	418	380	342	304	266	228	190
765	727	689	650	612	574	536	497	459	421	383	344	306	268	230	191
770	732	693	655	616	578	539	501	462	424	385	347	308	270	231	193
775	736	698	659	620	581	543	504	465	426	388	349	310	271	233	194
780	741	702	663	624	585	546	507	468	429	390	351	312	273	234	195
785	746	707	667	628	589	550	510	471	432	393	353	314	275	236	196
790	751	711	672	632	593	553	514	474	435	395	356	316	277	237	198
795	755	716	676	636	596	557	517	477	437	398	358	318	278	239	199
800	760	720	680	640	600	560	520	480	440	400	360	320	280	240	200
805	765	725	684	644	604	564	523	483	443	403	362	322	282	242	201
810	770	729	689	648	608	567	527	486	446	405	365	324	284	243	203
815	774	734	693	652	611	571	530	489	448	408	367	326	285	245	204
820	779	738	697	656	615	574	533	492	451	410	369	328	287	246	205
825	784	743	701	660	619	578	536	495	454	413	371	330	289	248	206
830	789	747	706	664	623	581	540	498	457	415	374	332	291	249	208
835	793	752	710	668	626	585	543	501	459	418	376	334	292	251	209
840	798	756	714	672	630	588	546	504	462	420	378	336	294	252	210
845	803	761	718	676	634	592	549	507	465	423	380	338	296	254	211
850	808	765	723	680	638	595	553	510	468	425	383	340	298	255	213
855	812	770	727	684	641	599	556	513	470	428	385	342	299	257	214
860	817	774	731	688	645	602	559	516	473	430	387	344	301	258	215
865	822	779	735	692	649	606	562	519	476	433	389	346	303	260	216
870	827	783	740	696	653	609	566	522	479	435	392	348	305	261	218
875	831	788	744	700	656	613	569	525	481	438	394	350	306	263	219
880	836	792	748	704	660	616	572	528	484	440	396	352	308	264	220
885	841	797	752	708	664	620	575	531	487	443	398	354	310	266	221
890	846	801	757	712	668	623	579	534	490	445	401	356	312	267	223
895	850	806	761	716	671	627	582	537	492	448	403	358	313	269	224
900	855	810	765	720	675	630	585	540	495	450	405	360	315	270	225
905	860	815	769	724	679	634	588	543	498	453	407	362	317	272	226

Using the Weight Charts

This section includes a weight percentage chart to assist you in assigning appropriate weight amounts. Simply read along the top row of each page to note the desired percentages, and the column to the right of your maximum lift to find how much weight (percentage-wise) of your 1 RM you should lift.

Other Notations to Consider

Information is sometimes noted beside the resistance training exercises. These notes are designed to provide you with some details on how the exercise should be performed. The following list presents examples of notations as they might appear in your workouts and what they mean:

- (seated) – The exercise should be performed while sitting down.

- (standing) – The exercise should be performed while standing up.

- (w/##lb vest) – The exercise should be performed while wearing a weighted vest.

- (w/##lb DB's) – The exercise should be performed while holding dumbbells.

- (light) – The exercise is performed more for the movement, rather than the muscular stress.

- (w/res) – Some type of resistance (manual, budgie cords, or rubber bands) is applied to an exercise that is usually done with just the individual's body weight or weight of his arms or legs.

- (w/neg) – An eccentric force (negative force) is applied during the lowering of the resistance or body part.

Breathing During Resistance Training

When doing resistance training, breathing correctly is very important for both the success of the lift, and your immediate and long-term health. If you can breath normally during a lift, then do so by breathing in when lowering the resistance and breathing out during the exertion of the lift. As the resistance you lift increases, you will be tempted to hold your breath to create a sense of stability and control over the weight. If you are tempted to hold your breath, the following method is recommended for breathing during the course of a resistance exercise:

- Remove the bar from the resting position and stabilize.

- Take a deep breath.

- Hold your breath and begin the exercise movement.

- Begin to return the weight to the starting point.

- Release your breath during the last 1/2 or 2/3 of the movement.

- Repeat the cycle.

This method of breathing in and then holding your breath can contribute to the success of the movement. Holding your breath can increase the level of pressure in the abdominal area. This increase in pressure can help stabilize your spine, which in turn, can stabilize your shoulders and rib cage.

If you hold your breath too long during the lift, however, the pressure may become excessive, resulting in some potentially harmful side effects, including:

- Blood pressure increases (places stress on heart and circulatory system).

- Pressure in the upper chest area can rise to 200 mg/Hg.

- This build-up in pressure in the upper chest area (thoracic cavity) can branch outwardly to the working muscles, which can result in pressure being placed on your veins and arteries. This can alter the flow of blood being pumped from the heart (cardiac output), which in turn can result in the athlete fainting.

- Releasing of the breath can result in a rapid fall in blood pressure, which can result in the athlete fainting also. This fainting occurs because the fall in blood pressure prevents the blood from returning to the heart as quickly as it should. This factor is known as a valsalva effect.

A healthy athlete's vascular system should not be damaged by such breath-holding techniques. However, to ensure that any risks are minimized, remember to release the breath during the last 1/2 to 2/3 of the exercise movement. Heavy weight training can produce hypertrophy of the heart's ventricles.

Running and Conditioning

Running and conditioning refer to anaerobic and aerobic training through wind sprints, combination running (sprint and jog), and any variations of a running format that can place a constructive demand on the cardiorespiratory system. Perform cardiorespiratory conditioning three to four times per week. You can do your cardiorespiratory conditioning before or after the resistance-training portion of the workout. If you perform cardiorespiratory training first in your workout, you should realize that the fatigue resulting from such training will adversely effect your weight room performance. The reverse holds true as well. Arrange ample recovery time between these types of workouts. For example, schedule your running in the morning, and your resistance training in the afternoon to effect full recovery.

A good running and conditioning workout includes a 10-minute flexibility and warm-up session. Flexibility training consists of a warm-up stretch and a combination of form runs, low-level plyometrics, and agility drills. The total time of your conditioning workout should be flexible. The workouts can be extended or reduced depending on how your athletes are feeling and performing.

For each running and conditioning workout, interval times are provided for three groups: the #1 and #2 players, #3 and #4 players, and the #5 players (1&2, 3&4, 5). The times listed on the workouts are based on the 94-foot college court and the abilities of the average male college player. For the high-school court (84 feet) and player, or the female basketball player, the recommended interval times may have to be adjusted (see Chapter 10). You should attempt to perform all repetitions of each exercise within the times noted for your position.

Dividing the times between player positions makes the workouts more personalized, while still accommodating a large group. This division of groups also allows one group to recovery between exercise bouts while another group is running. If you are capable of running in a faster group, then do so. Consider, however, even though the times may be easier on the first couple of sprints or runs, these first bouts are serving as moderately intense warm-ups, and as fatigue sets in, the bouts will become more exhausting by the end of your workout. If you want to move to the faster running group, wait until you have performed several running sessions to see how well you are doing at the end of the session. As the weeks go by, you will begin to add more and more yardage to your sprint workouts. This step is another way to introduce and apply an overload to your workout.

Skill Training

Skill training should also be an essential part of an athlete's workout plan. Foot speed, agility, balance, and position-specific drills are what differentiate a successful basketball player from other athletes. The resistance training program produces explosive, powerful, and quick muscular ability. Raw muscular ability, however, is useless in a controlled athletic environment. Skill training refines and shapes the athlete with raw muscular ability into a basketball player.

Skill training is blended into the workout plan on various days during the week. You work on some skills in the skills section called "on your own." Other drills are performed with teammates. These drills act as bridges that connect your newly acquired weight-room strength to a more functional and athletic activity. The strength and conditioning exercises are focused on the common goal of producing highly conditioned basketball players, not simply highly conditioned individuals.

Your coach may also suggest some drills that would assist you in developing the fundamentals and techniques involved with your position. Subsequent chapters include suggested days and times to include these drills in your workout. Your off-season work, performed with your teammates, will hopefully strengthen the bond with your teammates, and remind you that you are not an individual. Instead, you are a team player. It requires five men working toward the same goal to win in basketball. Always work toward strengthening the team, while you strengthen yourself. Details on how to perform these "on your own" drills are included in Chapter 11.

Athlete Evaluation

Evaluate your performance each week to see if you made progress in physical conditioning within your microcycle:

- Were all the repetitions assigned for a particular exercise achieved?

- Was it easy or hard to complete all the assigned repetitions?

If you achieved all the work assigned, then it's time to increase the exercise resistance for the next microcycle. At the end of each week, note any decrease or increase in the workout resistance or running times. A decrease in performance in one exercise, or during one day of training, should not necessarily raise a warning flag since any number of variables can cause a decrease in productivity. If an entire week of exercises shows declines, however, then you need to ask why. It could be anything from a common cold coming on, to a fatigue, or a overtraining problem. If warranted, you may require several (i.e., three) days off from your training routine for constructive recovery.

At the end of each week, the resistance exercises may need subtle adjustments. Reducing or increasing the resistance can promote gradual increases along the entire course of the workout plan. If the weight lifted is not monitored, you may prematurely burnout from having worked too heavy, too soon, thus dowsing any hopes of reaching your full potential. Working out with too light a load, on the other hand, would place an insufficient level of stress to challenge your muscles into responding favorably to the workout. In evaluating the microcycle this way, you maintain a constant interactive approach to your training. By having an interactive training plan, the workout is more personal, and you can avoid overestimating or underestimating your potential. This, in turn, will produce the best results by the time you are scheduled to undertake the in-season portion of your training program.

With good fortune, your team's basketball season will be extended beyond the regular season. This extension will delay you in starting your post-season conditioning program. If post-season play is your destiny, just continue to work out under the in-season format. The last week of your in-season workout can be repeated as often as needed to complete the extended period, or if three weeks are added to the season, you can repeat the last three weeks of your in-season workouts. After the last game is played, you should take a week off. This interruption from working out will allow you to be a regular student for a short while, and to release your mind from basketball-related responsibilities. While this will delay the start of your off-season routines, this delay is not critical for the workout program.

Just prior to the in-season period, Phase 5, each athlete undertakes a battery of physical tests. These tests are designed to assess your improvements and the effectiveness of the workout program. Additional mesocycles or phases can be considered to determine how effective the workouts have been. However, these periods should only be observed, rather than subjected to physical testing. Before overanalyzing the workout or yourself, however, remember, that overtesting can actually result in a reduction in performance. In fact, excessive pressure to perform better and better on each test can promote failure rather than success. By observing the workout log from one month to the next, you can determine if resistance exercises and running times are improving. Remember that you can crunch numbers and statistics to create any outcome desired. The ultimate test is whether you and your teammates win basketball games.

Testing is performed to determine how effective the training program has been in the production of power and endurance. The tests consist of lifts to determine the amount of raw power gained, and more functional activities to determine how effectively the transition has been made from the gains achieved by performing resistance exercises to your improved ability to perform specific athletic movements.

Recommended Tests:

Resistance exercises (to test muscular strength and endurance):
- Dips — performed for maximal repetitions
- Pull-ups — performed for maximal repetitions

Speed and quickness (to assess specific motor skills):

- 30-second step slide — (explained in Chapter 9, under *foot-speed package #3*)

- 20-yard shuttle — (explained in Chapter 10)

Athletic power (to test your ability to generate force):

- In-place vertical jump

Conditioning (to assess anaerobic/aerobic fitness):

	1&2	3&4	5
• 2 x 32 court crosses	3:45	3:55	4:05

If you run as a team, even though each position has its own running time, run the test with only two groups. Place the 3,4, and 5 players all together in one group. This step reduces the necessary rest time to a one-to-one ratio. You must make all assigned transitions under the allotted times or perform extra work until the minimal times are achieved.

As a rule, testing resistance exercises is not recommended for basketball players. In this instance, dips and pull-ups are employed, because if an athlete can be a master over his own body weight, he can probably be more athletic when his body weight is the primary obstacle to overcome (such as in the sport of basketball). If the coach needs information on a player's lifting strength, the coach can see how the player has progressed on certain lifts from the player's log book. Assigning certain lifts as tests means that you will need to concentrate on those lifts during the year to prove your success. That can make your workouts very one-sided and can lead to possible muscular imbalances. Not surprisingly, most coaches would rather their athletes be safe, have muscular balance, and prove their worth on the basketball court than in the weight room. However, if you wish, you can always use weight-training test exercises as an assessment measure.

Keeping a Training Log

This book provides you with the foundation of the training log, the 52-week program itself. When using this book, your responsibility is to record your daily workout weights and times, as well as jotting down notes as to how you felt during a particular workout session. By doing this, you help make the prescribed workout your personal routine.

Consistency is crucial to successful training. Working out regularly in a planned fashion creates the foundation for continuous improvement. Keeping records will serve as a map, reminding you of what you have accomplished in previous workouts. The records will keep you on the track with your goals. Keeping this information in a training log will help you and your coach examine your assigned training program to determine if you are achieving the desired results. In your training log, you should keep a record of the following information:

- Date of workout.

- What exercises should be performed (in order).

- How much weight or resistance should be used.

- Number of sets and repetitions of each exercise that should be performed.

- How much rest should be taken between sets of an exercise.

- How you felt during the workout.

- Whether your aerobic conditioning was performed before or after weight training.

- Any other piece of data or information that may have an impact on your level of success.

CHAPTER 2

PHASE 1
(Beginning of the
Post-Season)

PHASE 1 ANALYSIS

Resistance Training

Phase 1 begins during the third week of March and lasts through the second week of May. The start time of this collegiate-level workout plan is conservative, because if you're doing this particular phase in March, this means that your team went to the NCAA tournament, but did not make it to the "Final Four." If your team did not make the tournament, then you can start this phase of training one week after any post-season play in which your team was involved. If you were in the "Final Four," then you would just continue the In-season phase for two to three more weeks. This macrocycle is created on a loop, so when you finish phase 5, you return to phase 1 and begin the loop over again. This plan is based on a collegiate academic schedule, and is designed to proceed through the end of the academic semester. The first two weeks of this phase are very intense. Since the athletes will normally get tired and sore, use precaution in order to avoid injury.

Purpose: The initial purpose of this phase is to create a muscular base (hypertrophy). As the phase progresses, the intensity level of the workouts will gradually increase toward a peak in power output some weeks ahead. If the periodization model is considered, this phase is the hypertrophy stage, and the beginning of the basic strength stage.

Goal of the workout: In the first two weeks, the primary objective is to get the athlete to experience momentary muscular fatigue as often as possible during his workouts. Begin a gradual and steady increase in resistance to promote initial strength building.

Exercises: The exercises during the early part of this phase consist of some core lifts and many supporting and assisting exercises. The core lifts are always present throughout the macrocycle. In order to basically maintain or build a power base for the athlete. The supporting and assisting exercises are utilized more so in the early part of this phase of training. The use of these exercises places higher levels of stress on the individual muscles. This, in turn, will hopefully lead to a greater level of hypertrophy in those muscle areas. If the muscle can be increased in size, more joint stability can be achieved. Thus, as the amount of resistance lifted increases later in this stage and in later stages of the macrocycle, less potential for injury is present. Many exercises are performed manually. These exercises are very strenuous if performed correctly and are excellent for inducing extreme fatigue or momentary muscular failure (MMF). Other exercises are performed using cable devices and machines. The use of the cables and machines allows the athlete to worry less about just moving the weight through the "up" (concentric) phase of the exercise, and enables him to focus on properly using the designated muscle group to perform the work.

Exercise order: The order in which the exercises should be performed is traditional in that it addresses the larger muscle groups first in the workout and then the smaller muscle groups later. One factor that is unique to the first two weeks of this phase is the use of pre-exhaustion sets, super-sets, and circuits that are designed to produce a greater level of muscular fatigue.

Rest between sets (b/s on comment): The amount of rest between the sets of an exercise is relatively low. Some exercises have a "B" before them on the workout sheet, while the other exercises have an "S" before them. Look in the comment section at the top of the workout sheet. You will see :55 b/s B exercises and :40 b/s S exercises. This simply means that for any exercise marked with a B, the athlete should rest 55 seconds between the sets of that exercise. The relatively low amount of rest is just an added measure of insurance to help ensure that the athlete will efficiently fatigue the muscle.

Rest between exercises (b/e on comment): The amount of rest between exercises is indicated in the comment section of the workout. During a particular section of the workout, one minute of rest may be allowed.

Number of sets and repetitions: The number of sets and repetitions in early phase 1 workouts is high. This high *volume* is another method of increasing the overall level of fatigue during the workout. Later in the phase, the number of repetitions is slightly reduced to begin the promotion of power production and a reduction in endurance.

Special sets or repetitions: Super-sets and manual exercises were mentioned previously as a unique aspect of this phase. In the third week, circuit routines are included. No rest between exercises is allowed during the circuit.

Repetition style and speed: During the first three weeks of phase 1, the style of repetition is very strict. Each repetition of an exercise should be performed deliberately and more slowly than normal. While performing a repetition, the athlete should attempt to imagine squeezing the muscle. To help an athlete learn to deliberately flex the muscle, the bench press can be employed. For example, tell the athlete to imagine a coin sitting on the center of his chest (don't put a coin on his chest, however, since an injury could occur). Then, have the athlete imagine the two portions of his pectorals coming together in the center, and folding the coin in half. This imagery technique can be applied to any area of the body.

Another method of insuring proper flexion of the muscle during this phase is to have the athlete isometrically push his hands toward one anther during a pushing exercise, and isometrically pull his hands apart during a pulling exercise. (The athlete's hands will not actually move on the apparatus or bar. The athlete's hands are just squeezing.) Make sure the athlete breathes properly while using these techniques. After the third week, the athlete can relax his style of repetition and perform a faster repetition. By the end of the phase, the athlete can add some controlled "cheat" repetitions to ensure that he performs the required number of repetitions.

Tempo or cadence of movement (repetitions): The tempo or cadence of the repetitions should be constant during the early part of the phase. The repetition should not stop at the bottom or the top of the movement. The only reason during this phase for the movement to stop is so the athlete can flex the muscle even more intensely. After the third week, all repetitions in this phase should be executed with a pausing tempo. This suggestion refers to the fact that some repetitions can be performed without pause. However, as the resistance training begins to cause fatigue, the athlete should pause for an instant in a locked-out position to allow for momentary recovery. This step will help insure that each repetition is a powerful repetition. Repetitions should become more explosive as the phase progresses.

Running and Conditioning

During the first two weeks of this phase, no running or conditioning is planned. This is not to say that the athlete is not encouraged to run on his own. What is suggested, even more strongly, is that the athletes participate in other sports that involve aerobic fitness, like soccer, volleyball, tennis, swimming, etc. This undertaking can serve as an active rest period away from basketball. These other sports activities require the use of slightly different muscle motor patterns than those required in basketball. The development of these motor patterns can provide for a stronger muscle motor unit base. At the same time, the mental stress of having to succeed in these sports is not present. In this way, while the athlete stays physically active, he often perceives the activity to be less stressful.

Conditioning begins at a low level during the third week of this phase, consisting of some low-yardage transitional sprints on Mondays. These sprints should never exceed 1000 yards. Other conditioning activities are intentionally diverse. This diversity is another method of reducing the emphasis on traditional basketball-sprint workouts. For example, engaging in a boxing bout can be an excellent way to get the athlete breathing hard, while sparing his legs to some degree.

Heavy play is a series of transitions up and down the basketball court while wearing a weighted vest. When first beginning heavy play, only put two pounds in the vest and, over a period of weeks, you can increase the weight in the vest. *Never exceed ten pounds of weight in the vest. If you do, you may cause more stress to the joints than necessary.* Hill running is a running specific strength builder that is performed on Thursdays.

Applied Skills

Applied skills are exercises performed to help the athlete take the muscle that he has been stressing in the weight room, and teach those newly developed muscle fibers to perform athletically. Keep in mind that in the weight room, the best result you can achieve is broad specificity for the sport for which you are training. You must train the muscle to perform specific motor (athletic) skills such as speed, quickness, and agility. You should work to improve your level of balance and reaction time as well. Only by performing drills related to your sport can you become better at that sport. A stronger muscle can make you a better athlete, but only if you teach the muscle the movements you would like it to perform. Reaction drills, balance drills, foot-speed and quickness drills, and sports related drills are discussed in detail in Chapter 11 (Applied and Basketball-specific Drills).

Chapter 11 also includes a section on "personal drills and play" – a designated area of the workout where you can work on those basketball skills that you feel are personally underdeveloped. This period of your workout program also includes "constructive free play" – a time when you and your teammates can get together and play pick-up games. During these games, it is important to work on new moves and incorporate those skills that you have performed piecemeal during your personal routines.

Table 2.1. Phase 1 – Week #1

Name:

Comment: :55 b/s B excercises, :40 sec b/s S excercises, :55 b/ excercises

Resistance Training	Week #1	Conditioning Training & Applied Skills	3rd Week of March

Monday:
B) Bench press — 10 x 60 10 x 60 10 x 60 10 x 60
S) Middle chest flex — 2 x 10
Super Set Next 2, 3x
B) Close incline press — 10 x 60 10 x 60 10 x 60
S) Incline dumbbell fly — 12 x 55 12 x 55 12 x 55
Super Set Next 2, 3x
S) Manual side raise — 10 x __ 10 x __ 10 x __
B) Smith Military — 10 x 60 10 x 60 10 x 60
S) Triceps push-down — 12 x 55 12 x 55
S) Reverse dip — 10 x __ 10 x __
Cylinder Circuit #1 — 15 x each

Tuesday:
S) High lat front — 12 x 55 12 x 55 12 x 55 12 x 55
S) Close low lat — 10 x 60 10 x 60 10 x 60
Super Set Next 2, 3x
S) Cable upright row — 10 x 60 10 x 60 10 x 60
S) Cable shrug — 40 sec. 40 sec. 40 sec.
S) Bent dumbbell raise — 10 x 60 10 x 60 10 x 60
S) Straight dumbell pullover — 15 x 55 15 x 55 15 x 55
Circuit Next 3 x 1
S) Wrist flex — 100 x __
S) 21 Blaster (biceps)
S) Concentration curl — 12 x 55
S) Alternating dumbbell curl (seated) — 12 x 55

Thursday:
S) Incline dumbbell press — 10 x 60 10 x 60 10 x 60 10 x 60
Super Set Next 2, 3x
B) Ham decline — 12 x 55 12 x 55 12 x 55
S) Lower chest flex — 12 x __ 12 x __ 12 x __
S) Push up — 20 x __
Super Set Next 2, 3x
S) Shoulder fly — 12 x 55 12 x 55 12 x 55 12 x 55
S) Two-arm dumbbell press (seated) — 10 x 60 10 x 60 10 x 60
S) Smith behind neck — 10 x 60 10 x 60
S) Kickback — 12 x 55 12 x 55
Cylinder Circuit #1 — 15 x each

Friday:
S) High lat rear — 12 x 55 12 x 55 12 x 55 12 x 55
Super Set Next 2, 3x
S) Dumbbell upright row — 10 x 60 10 x 60 10 x 60
S) Split dumbbell pullover — 15 x 55 15 x 55 15 x 55
S) Preacher curl — 12 x 55 12 x 55
S) Dumbbell squat — 10 x 60 10 x 60 10 x 60
S) Box squat — 15 x __ 15 x __
S) Lunge—3 pumps — 10 x __
S) Side lunge — 15 x __
S) Step-up — 30 x __
S) Single leg hops — 25 x __

Conditioning Training & Applied Skills — 3rd Week of March

Monday:
Static Stretch Routine
NO CONDITIONING

Tuesday:
Static Stretch Routine
NO CONDITIONING

Thursday:
Static Stretch Routine
NO CONDITIONING

Friday:
Static Stretch Routine
NO CONDITIONING

Table 2.2. Phase 1 – Week #2

Name: _____

Comment: :55 b/s B excercises, :40 sec b/s S excercises, :55 b/ excercises

Resistance Training

Monday:
B) Bench press — 10 x 60 10 x 60 10 x 60 10 x 60
S) Middle chest flex — 3 x 10
Super Set Next 2, 3x
B) Close incline press — 10 x 60 10 x 60 10 x 60
S) Incline dumbbell fly — 12 x 55 12 x 55 12 x 55
Super Set Next 2, 3x
S) Manual side raise — 10 x ___ 10 x ___ 10 x ___
B) Behind neck press — 10 x 60 10 x 60 10 x 60
S) Triceps push-down — 12 x 55 12 x 55
S) Reverse dip — 12 x ___ 12 x ___
Cylinder Circuit #1 — 15 x each

Thursday:
S) Incline dumbbell press — 10 x 60 10 x 60 10 x 60 10 x 60
Super Set Next 2, 3x
B) Ham decline — 12 x 55 12 x 55 12 x 55
S) Lower chest flex — 12 x ___ 12 x ___ 12 x ___
S) Push up — 20 x ___
Super Set Next 2, 3x
S) Shoulder fly — 12 x 55 12 x 55 12 x 55 12 x 55
S) Two-arm dumbbell press (seated) — 10 x 60 10 x 60 10 x 60
S) Smith behind neck — 10 x 60 10 x 60
S) Kickback — 12 x 55 12 x 55
Cylinder Circuit #1 — 15 x each

Week #2

Tuesday:
S) High lat front — 12 x 55 12 x 55 12 x 55 12 x 55
S) Close low lat — 10 x 60 10 x 60 10 x 60
Super Set Next 2, 3x
S) Cable upright row — 10 x 60 10 x 60 10 x 60
S) Cable shrug — 40 sec. 40 sec. 40 sec.
S) Bent dumbbell raise — 10 x 60 10 x 60 10 x 60
S) Straight dumbbell pullover — 15 x 55 15 x 55 15 x 55
Circuit Next 3 x 1
S) Wrist flex — 100 x ___
S) 21 Blaster (biceps)
S) Concentration curl — 12 x 55
S) Alternating dumbbell curl (seated) — 12 x 55

Friday:
S) High lat rear — 12 x 55 12 x 55 12 x 55 12 x 55
Super Set Next 2, 3x
S) Dumbbell upright row — 10 x 60 10 x 60 10 x 60 10 x 60
S) Split dumbbell pullover — 15 x 55 15 x 55 15 x 55 15 x 55
S) Preacher curl — 12 x 55 12 x 55
S) Dumbell squat — 10 x 60 10 x 60 10 x 60
S) Box squat — 15 x ___ 15 x ___
S) Lunge—3 pumps — 10 x ___
S) Side lunge — 15 x ___
S) Step-up — 30 x ___
S) Single leg hops — 25 x ___

Conditioning Training & Applied Skills

4th Week of March

Monday:
Static Stretch Routine
NO CONDITIONING

Tuesday:
Static Stretch Routine
NO CONDITIONING

Thursday:
Static Stretch Routine
NO CONDITIONING

Friday:
Static Stretch Routine
NO CONDITIONING

Table 2.3. Phase 1 – Week #3

Name:

Comment: 1:00 b/s B exercises, :45 sec b/s S exercises, NO TIME b/s C exercises, 1:00 b/exercises

Week #3

1st Week of April

Resistance Training

Monday:
B) Bench press — 10 x 60 10 x 60 10 x 60 10 x 60
Circuit Next 4, 2 x (go through each exercise once, then repeat)
C) Ham 10 chest — 12 x 55 12 x 55
C) Incline dumbbell press — 12 x 55 12 x 55
C) Medicine ball, push-up — 10 x __ 10 x __
C) Ham decline — 15 x 55 15 x 55
Super Set Next 2, 3x
S) Manual side raise — 10 x 70 10 x 70 10 x 70
S) Behind neck press — 10 x __ 10 x __ 10 x __
S) Triceps push-down — 10 x 70 10 x 70 10 x 70
S) Reverse dip — 10 x 70 10 x 70 10 x 70
Cylinder Circuit #1 — 15 x each

Tuesday:
S) High lat front — 10 x 60 10 x 60 10 x 60 10 x 60
S) Close low lat — 10 x 60 10 x 60 10 x 60
S) Dumbbell shrug — 40 sec. 40 sec. 40 sec.
S) Manual rear deltoid — 10 x __ 10 x __ 10 x __
S) Kickback — 10 x 60 10 x 60 10 x 60
S) Smith Squat — 10 x 65 10 x 65 10 x 65 10 x 65
S) Baby Squat — 1.5 minute 1.5 minute 1.5 minute
S) Side lunge — 10 x __ 10 x __ 10 x __
S) Two-leg curl — 10 x 60 10 x 60 10 x 60 10 x 60
S) Single leg hops — 25 x
Cylinder Circuit #1 — 15 x each

Thursday:
B) Smith incline press — 10 x 60 10 x 65 8 x 70 8 x 75
B) Flat dumbbell press — 10 x 60 10 x 65 10 x 70
B) Dips — max reps max reps max reps
B) Smith behind neck — 10 x 60 10 x 65 8 x 70 8 x 75
Circuit Next 3, 1x
C) Shoulder fly — 15 x 55
C) Two-arm dumbbell press (seated) — 12 x 55
C) Front dumbbell raise — 10 x 60
S) Alternating dumbbell curl (seated) — 10 x 70 10 x 70 10 x 70
S) Wrist flex — 100 x __
Cylinder Circuit #1 — 15 x each

Friday:
S) High lat rear — 10 x 60 10 x 60 10 x 65 10 x 65
S) Manual shrug — 20 x __ 20 x __ 20 x __
S) Manual upright row — 8 x __ 8 x __ 8 x __
S) Triceps push-down — 12 x 60 12 x 60
S) Reverse dip — 10 x __ 10 x __
S) Box squat — 15 x __ 15 x __ 15 x __
S) Hip Flex — 25 x __ 25 x __
S) Two leg curls — 10 x 65 10 x 65 10 x 65
Cylinder Circuit #1 — 15 x each

Conditioning Training

Monday:
Dynamic Warm-up

	1&2	3&4	5
1) 2 x 10 court crosses	:58	:59	1:00 (313 yds)

Rest: 1:55 b/s — 626 yards

Thursday:
Dynamic Warm-up
1) Jump rope bouts — 5 x 3 minute rounds

Applied Skills

Monday:
Static Stretch Routine
NO CONDITIONING

Tuesday:
Static Stretch Routine
NO CONDITIONING

Thursday:
Static Stretch Routine
NO CONDITIONING

Friday:
Static Stretch Routine
NO CONDITIONING

Table 2.4. Phase 1 – Week #4

Name:

Comment: 1:00 b/s B exercises, :45 sec b/s S exercises, 1:00 b/exercises

	Week #4	2nd Week of April
Resistance Training	**Conditioning Training**	**Applied Skills**

Resistance Training

Monday:
B) Bench press — 8 x 60 8 x 65 8 x 70 8 x 75
B) Incline dumbbell press — 10 x 65 8 x 70 8 x 75
S) Incline dumbbell fly — 10 x 70 10 x 70 10 x 70
B) Smith Military — 10 x 60 8 x 70 8 x 70 8 x 75
S) Alternating dumbbell press (seated) — 10 x 70 8 x 75 8 x 75
S) Side dumbbell raise — 10 x 60 10 x 60 10 x 60
S) Preacher curl — 10 x 70 8 x 75 8 x 75
S) Concentration curl — 10 x 70 8 x 75 8 x 75
Cylinder Circuit #2 — 15 x each

Tuesday:
S) High lat front — 10 x 60 8 x 70 8 x 70 8 x 75
S) Close high lat — 10 x 60 8 x 70 8 x 70 8 x 75
S) Dumbbell shrug — 20 x 60 20 x 60 20 x 60
S) Manual rear deltoid — 10 x __ 10 x __ 10 x __
S) Two arm dumbbell triceps extension — 15 x 55 15 x 55
S) Smith Squat — 10 x 60 8 x 70 8 x 70 8 x 75
S) Baby squat — 1.5 minute 1.5 minute 1.5 minute
S) Side lunge — 10 x __ 10 x __
S) Two-leg curl — 10 x 60 10 x 60 10 x 60 10 x 60
S) Single leg hops — 25 x __
Cylinder Circuit #2 — 15 x each

Thursday:
B) Smith incline press — 10 x 60 10 x 65 8 x 70 8 x 75
B) Flat dumbbell press — 10 x 65 8 x 70 8 x 75
S) Ham 10 chest — 10 x 70 10 x 70 10 x 70
B) Smith behind neck — 10 x 60 10 x 65 8 x 70 8 x 75
S) Alternating dumbbell press — 10 x 70 10 x 70 10 x 70
S) Shoulder fly — 10 x 55 10 x 55 10 x 55
S) Alternating dumbbell curl (seated) — 10 x 70 10 x 70 10 x 70
S) Wrist flex — 100 x __
Cylinder Circuit #1 — 15 x each

Friday:
S) High lat rear — 10 x 60 10 x 65 8 x 70 8 x 70
S) Manual shrug — 20 x __ 20 x __ 20 x __
S) Manual upright row — 8 x __ 8 x __ 8 x __
S) Triceps push-down — 12 x 60 12 x 60
S) Reverse dip — 12 x __ 12 x __
S) Box squat — 15 x __ 15 x __
S) Hip Flex — 30 x __ 30 x __
S) Two leg curls — 10 x 65 10 x 65 10 x 65
Cylinder Circuit #1 — 15 x each

Conditioning Training

Monday:
Dynamic Warm-up

	1&2	3&4	5
1) 3 x 12 sideline crosses	:43	:44	:45 (200 yds)
Rest: 1:25 b/s			600 yards

Thursday:
Dynamic Warm-up

1) Heavy play (w/5 lb) — 5 x 3 minute rounds

Applied Skills

Monday:
1) One Leg Plyometrics
   a) 25 in place hops (each leg)
   b) 25 horizontal hops (each leg)
2) Static Stretch
3) Personal Drills and Play

Tuesday:
1) Foot-speed Package #1
2) Static Stretch
3) Personal Drills and Play

Thursday:
1) Static Stretch Routine
2) Personal Drills and Play

Friday:
1) Balance Package #1
2) Static Stretch Routine
3) Personal Drills and Play

Table 2.5. Phase 1 – Week #5

Name:

Comment: 1:00 b/s B excercises, :45 sec b/s S exercises, 1:00 b/exercises

Week #5 — 3rd Week of April

Resistance Training

Monday:
B) Bench press — 8 x 60 8 x 65 8 x 70 8 x 75
B) Incline dumbbell press — 10 x 65 8 x 70 8 x 75
S) Close incline press — 10 x 70 10 x 70 10 x 70
B) Military press — 10 x 60 8 x 70 8 x 70 8 x 75
B) Two-arm dumbbell press (standing) — 10 x 70 8 x 75 8 x 75
S) Side dumbbell raise — 10 x 60 10 x 60 10 x 60
B) Incline curl — 10 x 70 8 x 75 8 x 75
Cylinder Circuit #2 — 10 x 70 8 x 75 8 x 75
  15 x each

Tuesday:
B) Close-grip lat — 8 x 70 8 x 70 8 x 70 8 x 75
S) Close high lat — 8 x 70 8 x 70 8 x 70 8 x 75
S) Dumbbell shrug — 20 x 65 20 x 65 20 x 65
S) Rear deltoid swim — 10 x ___ 10 x ___
S) Two-arm dumbbell triceps extension — 12 x 55 12 x 55 12 x 55
B) Squat — 10 x 60 8 x 70 8 x 70 8 x 75
S) Box squat — 15 x ___ 15 x ___ 15 x ___
S) Donkey kicks — 30 x ___ 30 x ___ 30 x ___
S) Two-leg curl — 8 x 75 8 x 75 8 x 75
Cylinder Circuit #3 — 15 x each

Thursday:
B) Smith incline press — 10 x 60 8 x 70 8 x 75 8 x 75
B) Flat dumbbell press — 10 x 65 8 x 70 8 x 75
S) Ham 10 chest — 8 x 70 8 x 70 8 x 70
B) Smith behind neck — 8 x 70 8 x 70 8 x 70 8 x 75
S) Alternating dumbbell press (standing) — 8 x 75 8 x 75 8 x 75
S) front dumbbell raise — 10 x 60 10 x 60 10 x 60
S) Alternating dumbbell curl (seated) — 8 x 75 8 x 75 8 x 75
Cylinder Circuit #1 — 15 x each

Friday:
S) High lat rear — 10 x 60 10 x 65 8 x 70 8 x 70
S) Manual shrug — 8 x 75 8 x 75 8 x 75
S) Straight dumbbell pullover — 12 x 75 12 x 75 12 x 75
S) Triceps push-down — 10 x 60 10 x 60
S) Reverse dip — 12 x ___ 12 x ___
S) Two-leg press — 8 x 70 8 x 70 8 x 70 8 x 75
S) Slideboard — 2 x 30 crosses
Cylinder Circuit #5 — 15 x each

Conditioning Training

Monday:
Dynamic Warm-up

	1&2	3&4	5
1) 1 x 6. 50 yard crosses	:56	:57	:58 (300 yds)
Rest: 1:55 b/s			
2) 2 x 4. 50 yard crosses	:35	:36	:37 (200 yds)
Rest: 1:00 b/s			

700 yards

Thursday:
Dynamic Warm-up

1) Up-hill sprints (30 yards) 45% Grade
   3 x sprints at 1/2 speed
   8 x sprints at 3/4 speed
   3 x sprints at 1/2 speed

Applied Skills

Monday:
1) 2 x 100 small jumps (both legs) Perform a big jump on every 10th rep.
2) Static Stretch Routine
3) Personal Drills and Play

Tuesday:
1) Static Stretch
2) Personal Drills and Play

Thursday:
1) Snake, T and Box #1 Agility drills Do each drill 3 times each for time
2) Static Stretch Routine
3) Personal Drills and Play

Friday:
1) Balance Package #2
2) Static Stretch Routine
3) Personal Drills and Play

Table 2.6. Phase 1 – Week #6

Name:

Comment: 1:05 b/s B excercises, :50 sec b/s S exercises, 1:05 b/exercises

Resistance Training

Monday:
B) Bench press — 8 x 65 8 x 70 8 x 75 8 x 80
B) Incline dumbbell press — 8 x 70 8 x 75 6 x 80
S) Close incline press — 8 x 70 8 x 75 6 x 80
B) Military press — 8 x 65 8 x 70 8 x 75 8 x 80
B) Two-arm dumbbell press (standing) — 8 x 75 8 x 75 8 x 75
S) Side dumbbell raise — 8 x 70 8 x 70 8 x 70
B) Straight-bar curl — 8 x 70 8 x 70 8 x 70
B) Incline curl — 8 x 70 8 x 70 8 x 70
Cylinder Circuit #2 — 15 x each

Tuesday:
B) Close-grip lat — 8 x 70 8 x 70 8 x 75 8 x 75
S) Two-arm dumbbell row — 8 x 70 8 x 70 8 x 75 8 x 75
S) Rear deltoid swim — 20 x __ 20 x __
B) Free-weight upright row — 8 x 75 8 x 75 8 x 75
B) Dumbbell french press — 8 x 75 8 x 75 8 x 75
S) Squat — 8 x 70 8 x 70 8 x 70 8 x 75
S) Box squat (w 10 lb vest) — 15 x __ 15 x __ 15 x __
S) Donkey kicks — 30 x __ 30 x __
S) Two-leg curl — 8 x 75 8 x 75 8 x 75
Cylinder Circuit #3 — 15 x each

Thursday:
B) Incline bench press — 10 x 60 8 x 70 8 x 75 8 x 75
B) Flat dumbbell press — 8 x 70 8 x 75 6 x 80
S) Ham 10 chest — 10 x 70 10 x 70 10 x 70
B) Dumbbell push press — 8 x 75 8 x 75 8 x 75
S) Moon push-up — 8 x __ 8 x __ 8 x __
S) Hammer curl — 10 x 70 10 x 70 10 x 70
Cylinder Circuit #1 — 15 x each

Friday:
S) High lat rear — 8 x 70 8 x 70 8 x 75 8 x 75
S) Close low lat — 10 x 60 8 x 70 8 x 70 8 x 75
S) Dumbbell upright row — 8 x 75 8 x 75 8 x 75
S) Straight dumbbell pulloever — 12 x 75 12 x 75 12 x 75
S) Reverse dip (w/ 10 lb vest) — 10 x __ 10 x __
S) Two-arm dumbbell triceps extension — 12 x 55 12 x 55
B) Two-leg press — 8 x 70 8 x 70 8 x 75 8 x 75
S) Slideboard — 3 x 30 crosses
Cylinder Circuit #5 — 15 x each

Week #6

Conditioning Training

Monday:
Dynamic Warm-up

	1&2	3&4	5
1) 2 x Double court ladder Rest: 2:05 b/s	1:04	1:06	1:08 (313 yds)
2) 2 x gassers Rest: :45 b/s	ALL OUT		(63 yds)

752 yards

Tuesday:
Dynamic Warm-up

1) Shadow boxing bouts 3 x 3 minute rounds
Rest 1:00 b/s

Thursday:
Dynamic Warm-up

1) Heavy play (w/ 5 lb vest) 6 x 3 minute rounds
Rest: 1:00 b/s

4th Week of April

Applied Skills

Monday:
1) Foot-speed Package #2
2) Static Stretch Routine
3) Personal Drills and Play

Tuesday:
1) Static Stretch
2) Personal Drills and Play

Thursday:
1) S, W and Box #2 - Agility drills
Do each drill 3 times each for time
2) Static Stretch Routine
3) Personal Drills and Play

Friday:
1) Balance Package #2
2) Static Stretch Routine
3) Personal Drills and Play

Table 2.7. Phase 1 – Week #7

Name:

Comment: 1:05 b/s B exercises, :50 sec b/s S exercises, 1:05 b/exercises

	Week #7	1st Week of May
Resistance Training	**Conditioning Training**	**Applied Skills**

Resistance Training

Monday:
B) Bench press — 8 x 65 8 x 70 8 x 75 6 x 80
B) Dips — max reps max reps max reps
S) Feet on balance ball, push up — 20 x ___ 20 x ___
B) Push press — 8 x 75 8 x 75 8 x 75
B) Two-arm dumbell press (standing) — 8 x 75 8 x 75 8 x 75
B) Medicine ball circuit — 10 x each exercise
B) EZ-bar curl — 8 x 75 8 x 75 8 x 75
Cylinder Circuit #2 — 20 x each

Tuesday:
B) Pull up — max reps max reps max reps
S) Two-arm dumbbell row — 8 x 70 8 x 70 8 x 75 8 x 75
S) Free-weight upright row — 8 x 75 8 x 75 8 x 75
B) Bent dumbbell raise — 10 x 60 10 x 60 10 x 60
B) Dumbbell french press — 8 x 75 8 x 75 8 x 75
B) Squat — 8 x 70 8 x 70 8 x 75 8 x 75
S) Step-up — 30 x ___ 30 x ___
S) Backward lunge — 20 x ___ 20 x ___
S) Two-leg curl — 8 x 75 8 x 75 8 x 80
Cylinder Circuit #3 — 20 x each

Thursday:
B) Incline bench press — 8 x 60 8 x 70 8 x 75 8 x 75
B) Flat dumbbell press — 8 x 70 8 x 75 6 x 80
B) Dumbbell push press — 8 x 75 8 x 75 8 x 75
S) Moon push-up — 10 x ___ 10 x ___ 10 x ___
S) Shoulder fly — 10 x 60 10 x 60 10 x 60
S) Hammer curl — 10 x 70 10 x 70 10 x 70
Cylinder Circuit #4 — 20 x each

Friday:
S) High lat rear — 8 x 70 8 x 70 8 x 75 8 x 75
S) Close low lat — 10 x 60 8 x 70 8 x 70 8 x 70 8 x 75
S) Dumbbell hang clean — 8 x 75 8 x 75 8 x 70
S) Split dumbbell pullover — 12 x 70 12 x 70 12 x 70
S) Two-arm dumbbell triceps extension — 10 x 65 10 x 65 10 x 65
S) Close grip push-up — 10 x ___ 10 x ___
B) Two-leg press — 8 x 70 8 x 70 8 x 75 8 x 75
S) Slideboard — 4 x 30 crosses
Cylinder Circuit #5 — 20 x each

Conditioning Training

Monday:
Dynamic Warm-up

	1&2	3&4	5	
1) 2 x 6. 50 yard crosses	:56	:57	:58	(300 yds)
Rest: 1:55 b/s				
2) 1 x 4 50 yard crosses	:35	:36	:37	(200 yds)

800 yards

Tuesday:
Dynamic Warm-up
1) Jump rope bouts 5 x 3 minute rounds
Rest 1:00 b/s

Thursday:
Dynamic Warm-up
1) Up-hill sprints 3 x sprints at 1/2 speed
(30 yards) 3 x hops on one leg
25% grade 3 x sprints at 3/4 speed
3 x hops on one leg

Applied Skills

Monday:
1) Foot-speed Package #3
2) Static Stretch Routine
3) Personal Drills and Play

Tuesday:
1) 3-cone reaction drill. 5 times
2) Static Stretch
3) Personal Drills and Play

Thursday:
1) Static Stretch Routine

Friday:
1) Balance Package #4
2) Static Stretch Routine
3) Personal Drills and Play

Table 2.8. Phase 1 – Week #8

Name:

Comment: 1:05 b/s B excercises, :50 sec b/s S exercises, 1:05 b/exercises

	Week #8	2nd Week of May
Resistance Training	**Conditioning Training**	**Applied Skills**

Resistance Training

Monday:
- B) Bench press — 8 x 65 8 x 70 8 x 75 6 x 80
- B) Dips — max reps max reps max reps
- S) Feet on balance ball, push up — 20 x __ 20 x __
- B) Push press — 8 x 75 8 x 75 8 x 75
- B) Two-arm dumbell press (standing) — 8 x 75 8 x 75 8 x 75
- B) Medicine ball circuit — 10 x each exercise
- B) EZ-bar curl — 8 x 75 8 x 75 8 x 75
- Cylinder Circuit #2 — 20 x each

Tuesday:
- B) Pull up — max reps max reps max reps
- S) Two-arm dumbbell row — 8 x 70 8 x 70 8 x 75 8 x 75
- B) Free-weight upright row — 8 x 75 8 x 75 8 x 75
- B) Bent dumbbell raise — 10 x 60 10 x 60 10 x 60
- B) Dumbbell french press — 8 x 75 8 x 75 8 x 75
- B) Squat — 8 x 70 8 x 70 8 x 75 8 x 75
- S) Step-up — 30 x __ 30 x __
- S) Backward lunge — 20 x __ 20 x __
- S) Two-leg curl — 8 x 75 8 x 75 8 x 80
- Cylinder Circuit #3 — 20 x each

Thursday:
- B) Incline bench press — 8 x 60 8 x 70 8 x 75 8 x 75
- B) Flat dumbbell press — 8 x 70 8 x 75 6 x 80
- B) Dumbbell push press — 8 x 75 8 x 75 8 x 75
- S) Moon push-up — 10 x __ 10 x __
- S) Shoulder fly — 10 x 60 10 x 60 10 x 60
- S) Hammer curl — 10 x 70 10 x 70 10 x 70
- Cylinder Circuit #4 — 20 x each

Friday:
- S) High lat rear — 8 x 70 8 x 70 8 x 75 8 x 75
- S) Close low lat — 10 x 60 8 x 70 8 x 70 8 x 75
- S) Dumbbell hang clean — 8 x 75 8 x 75 8 x 70
- S) Split dumbbell pullover — 12 x 70 12 x 70 12 x 70
- S) Two-arm dumbbell triceps extension — 10 x 65 10 x 65 10 x 65
- S) Close grip push-up — 10 x __ 10 x __
- B) Two-leg press — 8 x 70 8 x 70 8 x 75 8 x 75
- S) Slideboard — 4 x 30 crosses
- Cylinder Circuit #5 — 20 x each

Conditioning Training

Monday:
Dynamic Warm-up

	1&2	3&4	5
1) 2 x Double court ladder	1:04	1:06	1:08 (313 yds)
Rest: 2:05 b/s			
2) 3 x 2. 50 yard crosses	:15	:16	:17 (100 yds)
			926 yards

Tuesday:
Dynamic Warm-up

	1&2	3&4	5
1) 1 x 32 court crosses	3:45	3:50	3:55 (1003 yds)

Thursday:
Dynamic Warm-up

1) Plyometric Package #1
2) Shadow boxing bouts   3 x 3 minute records

Applied Skills

Monday:
1) Static Stretch Routine
2) Personal Drills and Play

Tuesday:
1) Static Stretch
2) Personal Drills and Play

Thursday:
1) Foot-speed Package #3
2) Static Stretch Routine
3) Personal Drills and Play

Friday:
1) Balance Package #2
2) Static Stretch Routine
3) Personal Drills and Play

Table 2.9. Phase 1 – Week #9

Name:

Comment: _____

Week #9	3rd Week of May

WEEK OFF
(end of Spring Academic Term)

PHASE 2
(Early Summer Workouts)

PHASE 2 ANALYSIS

Resistance Training

Phase 2 begins during the fourth week of May and continues through the fourth week in June. This workout plan progresses from week 10 through week 15 of the 52–week macrocycle. This phase is a continuation of Phase 1 where the athlete is still increasing the amount of resistance he lifts and reducing the number of repetitions he performs. Some critics may argue that this slow reduction in repetitions over the last 15 weeks provides less of a shock to the neuro-muscular unit, thus resulting in less power potential by the athlete. Personally, I have seen better results achieved by a stair-step decent in repetitions. As such, the success of the program is governed by the close supervision of the strength coach. The strength coach must impress upon the athletes in his charge to avoid working to momentary muscular failure after the first three weeks of Phase 1. The stress must increase gradually toward all-out intensity. If the athlete progresses too rapidly, he will sacrifice power.

Purpose: The basic purpose of this phase is to gradually, over a period of weeks, increase the athlete's level of nerve activity and excitability. To a point, muscle mass will continue to be increased, but less from a fatigue-related response, and more from the load increases planned during the exercises.

Goal of the workout: In this phase, the primary objective is to increase nerve activity and excitability by gradually increasing the intensity of the resistance on each exercise (mostly core and any super core exercise).

Exercises: The exercises during this phase consist of core, supporting, and assisting exercises. During the early part of this stage, the use of dumbbells make up a majority of the upper-body exercises. Because basketball players have longer limbs than most athletes, stability and balance of the limb sections often require extra attention. The use of dumbbells early on requires a greater emphasis on balance and stability of the joint than those exercises performed with barbells. Barbell exercises are used more toward the end of this phase.

Exercise order: In this phase, as in phase 1, the order of the exercises is traditional in that it addresses the larger muscle groups first in the workout, and the smaller muscle groups later. The use of super-sets and decreasing resistance sets is discontinued.

Rest between sets (b/s on comment): The amount of rest between the sets of an exercise increases as the phase progresses. As phase 2 begins, 1:10 is allowed between the sets of B exercises, and :55 is allowed between sets of S exercises. By week 15, 1:20 is allowed for b/s B exercises, while S exercises still have :55. The increased amount of rest as the weeks of training progress is an adjustment which compensates for the ever-increasing load of the resistance during the workout. This added recovery time between sets insures that with each and every repetition, the athlete will efficiently excite the nerve pathways that activate the muscle.

Rest between exercises (b/e on comment:): The amount of rest between exercises remains at 1:10.

Number of sets and repetitions: The number of sets and repetitions in phase 2 workouts begins to gradually decrease over the 5-week period. This *lowered* volume is another method of heightening the overall level of nerve activity and excitability, which will result in greater power output.

Special sets or repetitions: This phase includes no special sets. All of the sets are straight forward. Some transitional set schemes are employed during weeks 10 and 11. For example, 8 x 65%, 8 x 70%, 6 x 75%, 6 x 85% are used to assist the athlete in making the transition from straight sets of eight repetitions to straight sets of six repetitions.

Repetition style and speed: During this phase, the style of repetition is less strict. Each repetition should be intelligently performed with good form to avoid injury. More speed can be incorporated into the movement to allow for greater resistance to be used. By week 15, the athlete should be pushing with everything he's got to move the resistance, while maintaining good exercise form.

Tempo or cadence of movement (repetitions): All repetitions in this phase should be executed with a pausing tempo. In other words, some repetitions can be performed without pause. However, as the resistance used begins to cause the individual to fatigue, the athlete should pause for an instant in a locked-out position to allow for momentary recovery. This will help insure that each repetition is a powerful repetition. Repetitions should become more explosive as the phase progresses.

Running and Conditioning

Conditioning during this phase is structured much like that of phase 1. As the phase progresses, the work becomes more diverse. What you hope to create is a work atmosphere that will address as many of the physiological needs of the athlete as possible. At the same time, you must remember the physical requirements of basketball. During this phase, the number of conditioning workouts increases to three times per week in order to cover all the areas necessary to improve performance. Mondays are still interval-sprint days, with a slight increase in yardage occurring each week. Early in the phase, Thursdays are reserved for longer, less intense runs to build and maintain an endurance base. As the phase progresses, Thursdays become agility days that incorporate tag games and movement courses. Fridays involve incorporating combination training into the formula.

Basketball players should only condition three days per week. You should factor in that they will be involved in summer leagues and play. Because of this factor, more rest is needed. Some athletes will play more than others in the summer. You must consider their energy expenditure outside the conditioning and resistance workouts. If they look or feel fatigued, then you might need to reduce the workout load for that athlete.

Table 3.1. Phase 2 – Week #10

Name: Week #10   4th Week of May

Comment: 1:10 b/s B exercises, :55 sec b/s S exercises, 1:10 b/ exercises

Resistance Training

Monday:
B) Flat dumbbell press	8 x 70	8 x 75	6 x 80	6 x 80
B) Two-arm dumbbell row	8 x 70	8 x 70	8 x 75	8 x 75
S) Close incline press	8 x 75	8 x 75	8 x 75	
S) Close low lat	8 x 70	8 x 70	8 x 75	
B) Push press	8 x 75	8 x 75	8 x 75	
B) Free-weight upright row	8 x 75	8 x 75	8 x 75	
S) Split dumbbell pullover	8 x 70	8 x 70	8 x 70	
S) Side dumbbell raise	8 x 70	8 x 70	8 x 70	
Cylinder Circuit #2	25 x each			

Tuesday:
B) Squat	8 x 70	8 x 75	6 x 80	6 x 80
S) Hip flex	30 x __	30 x __	8 x __	
S) Step-up (w/ 10 lb DB's)	8 x __	8 x __	10 x __	
S) Side lunge	10 x __	10 x __	10 x __	
S) Donkey kicks	30 x __	30 x __		
S) Hamstring on balance ball	10 x __	10 x __	10 x __	
S) BW one-leg calf	30 x __	30 x __		

Thursday:
B) Incline dumbbell press	8 x 75	8 x 75	8 x 75
S) One-arm dumbbell row	8 x 70	8 x 70	8 x 75
B) Military press	8 x 70	8 x 75	8 x 75
B) Dumbbell upright row	8 x 75	8 x 75	8 x 75
B) Medicine ball underhand backward throw	10 x __	10 x __	
S) EZ-bar curl	8 x 75	8 x 75	
S) Shooters french press	8 x 60	8 x 60	
Cylinder Circuit #4	25 x each		

Friday:
B) Two-leg press	8 x 70	8 x 70	8 x 75	8 x 75
S) Power Skip	10 x __	10 x __		
S) Hip flex	30 x __	30 x __		
S) Musketeer lunge	10 x __	10 x __		
S) Around the world legs	1 x around the basketball court			
S) Calf raise leg press	30 x __	30 x __		

Conditioning Training

Monday:
Dynamic Warm-up
1) 3 x 10 court crosses
Rest: 1:55 b/s

1&2	3&4	5	
:58	:59	1:00	(313 yds)
			939 yds

Thursday:
Dynamic Warm-up
1) 3 x 1/2 mile
Rest 5:00 b/s
2) 2 x 1/4 mile
Rest 3:00 b/s

1&2	3&4	5	
2:30	2:33	2:36	(880 yds)
1:30	1:32	1:34	(440 yds)
			3520 yds

Friday:
Dynamic Warm-up
1) 2 x 32 court crosses
Rest 5:00 b/s

1&2	3&4	5	
3:45	3:50	3:55	(1003 yds)
			2006 yds

Applied Skills

ON YOUR OWN:

Every Day: Shoot at least 100 game simulated shots, with at least 50 free throws added at various times between shots.

Tuesday: Footspeed Package #1
Thursday: Agility Package #1
Friday: Balance Package #1

BY POSITION:

Tuesday:

1&2	-	Applied Skills #1
3&4	-	Applied Skills #1
5	-	Applied Skills #1

Table 3.2. Phase 2 – Week #11

Name:

Comment: 1:10 b/s B exercises, :55 sec b/s S exercises, 1:10 b/ exercises

	Week #11	5th Week of May
Resistance Training	Conditioning Training	Applied Skills

Resistance Training

Monday:

B) Flat dumbbell press	8 x 70	6 x 80	6 x 80	6 x 80 6 x 80
B) Two-arm dumbbell row	8 x 70	8 x 70	8 x 75	6 x 80
S) Close incline press	8 x 75	8 x 75	6 x 80	
S) Close low lat	8 x 70	8 x 70	8 x 75	
B) Push press	8 x 75	8 x 75	8 x 75	
B) Free-weight upright row	8 x 75	8 x 75	8 x 75	
S) Split dumbbell pullover	8 x 70	8 x 70	8 x 70	
S) Side dumbbell raise	8 x 70	8 x 70	8 x 70	
Cylinder Circuit #3	25 x each			

Tuesday:

B) Squat	8 x 65	8 x 70	6 x 75	6 x 85
S) Hip flex	30 x __	30 x __		
S) Step-up (w/ 10, 15, 15 lb DB's)	8 x __	8 x __	8 x __	
S) Side lunge	10 x __	10 x __	10 x __	
S) Donkey kicks	30 x __	30 x __		
S) Hamstring on balance ball	10 x __	10 x __	10 x __	
S) BW one-leg calf	30 x __	30 x __		

Thursday:

B) Incline dumbbell press	8 x 75	8 x 70	8 x 75
B) One-arm dumbbell row	8 x 70	8 x 70	8 x 75
B) Military press	8 x 70	8 x 70	8 x 75
B) Dumbbell upright row	8 x 75	8 x 75	8 x 75
B) Medicine ball underhand backward throw	10 x __	10 x __	
S) EZ-bar curl	8 x 75	8 x 75	
S) Shooters french press	8 x 60	8 x 60	
Cylinder Circuit #5	25 x each		

Friday:

B) Two-leg press	8 x 70	8 x 70	8 x 75	8 x 75
S) Power Skip	10 x __	10 x __	10 x __	
S) Hip flex	30 x __	30 x __		
S) Musketeer lunge	10 x __	10 x __	10 x __	
S) Around the world legs	1 x around the basketball court			
S) Calf raise leg press	30 x __	30 x __		

Conditioning Training

Dynamic Warm-up

	1&2	3&4	5
1) 5 x 12 Sideline crosses	:43	:44	:45

Rest 1:25 b/s

(200 yds)
1000 yds

Thursday:

Dynamic Warm-up

10% Grade	Muscular Strength Building
1) Up Hill Sprints	3 x sprints at 1/2 speed
	8 x sprints at full speed
	3 x sprints at 1/2 speed

Friday:

Dynamic Warm-up

	1&2	3&4	5
1) 2 Mile Fun Run		NO TIME	

Applied Skills

ON YOUR OWN:

Every Day: Shoot at least 100 game simulated shots, with at least 50 free throws added at various times between shots.

Tuesday: Agility Package #2
          Thursday: Foot-speed Package #2
Friday: Balance Package #2

BY POSITION:

Tuesday:

1&2 - Applied Skills #2
3&4 - Applied Skills #2
5   - Applied Skills #2

Table 3.3. Phase 2 – Week #12

Name: | **Week #12** | **1st Week of June**

Comment: 1:20 b/s B exercises, :55 sec b/s S exercises, 1:10 b/ exercises

Resistance Training

Monday:

Exercise				
B) Flat dumbbell press	6 x 70	6 x 80	6 x 80	6 x 80
B) Pull-up	max reps	max reps	max reps	max reps
B) Dips	max reps	max reps	max reps	max reps
B) Dumbbell pull press	8 x 70	8x 70	8 x 70	
S) Side dumbbell raise	8 x 25	8 x 25	8 x 25	
B) Medicine ball underhand backward throw	12 x __	12 x __		
S) Straight dumbbell pullover	15 x 75	15 x 75		
Cylinder Circuit #3	25 x each			

Tuesday:

Exercise					
B) Squat	8 x 65	8 x 70	6 x 75	6 x 75	6 x 85
S) Hip flex	30 x __	30 x __	8 x __		
S) Step-up (w/ 10, 15, 15 lb DB's)	8 x __	8 x __	8 x __		
S) Alternating leg lunge	30 x __				
S) Two-leg curl	8 x 70	8 x 70	8 x 70	8 x 70	
S) Calf raise leg press	30 x __	30 x __			

Thursday:

Exercise			
B) Incline dumbbell press	8 x 75	8 x 75	8 x 80
B) High lat rear	8 x 70	8 x 70	8 x 75
B) Military press	6 x 70	6 x 75	6 x 80
B) Power row	8 x 75	8 x 75	8 x 75
S) Roll-out	10 x __	10 x __	
S) Hammer curl	8 x 75	8 x 75	
S) Reverse dip	10 x __	10 x __	
Cylinder Circuit #6	20 x each		

Friday:

Exercise			
B) Two-leg press	8 x 70	8 x 70	8 x 75	8 x 80
S) Box squat (w/ 10 lb vest)	10 x __	10 x __	10 x __
S) Lunge – 3 pumps			
B) Dead lift (light)	8 x 65	8 x 60	8 x 60
S) BW one-leg calf	30 x __	30 x __	

Conditioning Training

Monday:
Dynamic Warm-up

	1&2	3&4	5	
1) 2 x 10 court crosses	:58	:59	1:00	(313 yds)
Rest: 1:55 b/s				
2) 1 x 2, 50 yard crosses	:15	:16	:17	(100 yds)
Rest :30 b/s				
3) 1 x 10 court crosses	:58	:59	1:00	(313 yds)
				1039 yds

Thursday:
Dynamic Warm-up

Plyometric Package #1

Friday:
Dynamic Warm-up

1) 4 Section Fartlek   10:00

Applied Skills

ON YOUR OWN:

Every Day: Shoot at least 100 game simulated shots, with at least 50 free throws added at various times between shots.

Tuesday: Agility Package #3

Friday: Balance Package #3

BY POSITION:

Tuesday:

1&2	-	Applied Skills #3
3&4	-	Applied Skills #3
5	-	Applied Skills #3

Table 3.4. Phase 2 – Week #13

Name:

Comment: 1:20 b/s B exercises, :55 sec b/s S exercises, 1:10 b/ exercises

Resistance Training

Monday:
B) Flat dumbbell press	6 x 75	6 x 80	6 x 80	6 x 80
B) Pull-up	max reps	max reps	max reps	max reps
S) Dips	max reps	max reps	max reps	max reps
B) Dumbbell pull press	8 x 70	8x 70	8 x 70	
S) Shoulder fly	8 x 70	8x 70	8 x 70	
B) Medicine ball underhand backward throw	15 x __	15 x __		
S) Straight dumbbell pullover	15 x 75	15 x 75		
Cylinder Circuit #4	25 x each			

Tuesday:
B) Squat	8 x 65	8 x 70	6 x 75	6 x 85
S) Hip flex	30 x __	30 x __		
S) Step-up (w/ 10, 15, 20 lb DB's)	8 x __	8 x __	8 x __	
S) Alternating leg lunge	30 x __	30x		
S) Two-leg curl	8 x 70	8 x 70	8 x 70	8 x 70
S) Calf raise leg press	30 x __	30 x __		

Thursday:
B) Incline dumbbell press	8 x 75	8 x 75	8 x 80	
S) High lat rear	8 x 70	8 x 70	8 x 75	
B) Military press	6 x 70	6 x 75	6 x 80	
B) Power row	8 x 75	8 x 75	8 x 75	
S) Roll-out	10 x __	10 x __		
S) Hammer curl	8 x 75	8 x 75		
S) Reverse dip	10 x __	10 x __		
Cylinder Circuit #6	20 x each			

Friday:
B) Two-leg press	8 x 70	6 x 75	6 x 80	6 x 85
S) Box squat (w/ 10 lb vest)	10 x __	10 x __	10 x __	
S) Slideboard (w/ 15 lb vest)	3 x 30 crosses			
B) Dead lift (light)	8 x 65	8 x 65	8 x 70	
C) Standing calf raise	30 x __	30 x __		

Week #13

Conditioning Training

Monday:
Dynamic Warm-up

	1&2	3&4	5	
1) 4 x 6, 50 yard crosses	:56	:57	:58	(300 yds)
Rest: 1:55 b/s				1200 yds

Thursday:
Dynamic Warm-up

Plyometric Package #2

Friday:
Dynamic Warm-up

1) 2 Section Fartlek — 10:00

2nd Week of June

Applied Skills

ON YOUR OWN:

Every Day: Shoot at least 100 game simulated shots, with at least 50 free throws added at various times between shots.

Tuesday: Agility Package #4

Friday: Balance Package #4

BY POSITION:

Tuesday:

1&2 - Applied Skills #1
3&4 - Applied Skills #1
5 - Applied Skills #1

Table 3.5. Phase 2 – Week #14

Name:

Comment: 1:20 b/s B exercises, :55 sec b/s S exercises, 1:10 b/ exercises

Resistance Training	Conditioning Training	Applied Skills
	Week #14	3rd Week of June

Resistance Training

Monday:
B) Bench press   6 x 75   6 x 80   6 x 80   6 x 80
B) Pull-up   max reps max reps max reps
S) Dips   max reps max reps
B) Dumbbell pull press   8 x 70   8 x 70   8 x 70
S) Shoulder fly   8 x 70   8 x 70   8 x 70
B) Medicine ball underhand backward throw   15 x __   15 x __
S) Straight dumbbell pullover 15 x 75 15 x 75
Cylinder Circuit #5   25 x each

Tuesday:
B) Squat   8 x 65   8 x 70   6 x 75   6 x 85
S) One-leg extension   20 x 65 20 x 65 20 x 65
S) 30-second step slide   30 sec   30 sec   30 sec
S) Two-leg curl   8 x 70   8 x 70   8 x 70   8 x 70
S) BW one-leg calf   30 x __ 30 x __

Thursday:
B) Incline bench press   8 x 70   8 x 70   8 x 75
S) High lat rear   8 x 70   8 x 70   8 x 75
B) Dumbbell push press   6 x 70   6 x 75   6 x 80
Movement Course #1

DO ONLY 1 OF NEXT 2
B) Hang clean (light)   8 x 60   8 x 60   8 x 60
B) Power row   8 x 60   8 x 60   8 x 60

S) Roll-out   10 x __   10 x __
S) Preacher curl   8 x 75   8 x 75
S) Close grip push-up   10 x __   10 x __
Cylinder Circuit #6   20 x each

Friday:
B) Two-leg press   8 x 70   6 x 75   6 x 80   6 x 85
S) Power Skip   10 x __   10 x __   10 x __
S) Slideboard (w/ 15 lb vest) 3 x 30 crosses
B) Dead lift (light)   8 x 65   8 x 70   8 x 70
C) Standing calf raise   30 x __   30 x __

Conditioning Training

Monday:
Dynamic Warm-up
    1&2   3&4   5
1) 4 x 6, 50 yard crosses   :56   :57   :58   (300 yds)
Rest 1:55 b/s   1200 yds

Thursday:
Dynamic Warm-up

Friday:
Dynamic Warm-up
1) 12 Minute Run

Applied Skills

ON YOUR OWN:

Every Day: Shoot at least 100 game simulated shots, with at least 50 free throws added at various times between shots.

Monday: 10 Quality Depth Jumps (off 2 foot height)

Friday: 10 Quality Jump Ups (onto 4 ft box)

BY POSITION:

Tuesday:

1&2 - Applied Skills #2
3&4 - Applied Skills #2
5   - Applied Skills #2

Table 3.6. Phase 2 – Week #15

Name: Week #15   4th Week of June

Comment: 1:20 b/s B exercises, :55 sec b/s S exercises, 1:10 b/ exercises

Resistance Training

Monday:
B) Bench press	6 x 75	6 x 80	6 x 80	6 x 80
B) Pull-up	max reps	max reps	max reps	
S) Dips	max reps	max reps		
B) Dumbbell snatch, Dumbbell push press	8 x 70	8 x 70		
S) Shoulder fly	8 x 70	8x 70	8 x 70	
B) Medicine ball underhand backward throw	20 x __	20 x __		
S) Straight dumbbell pullover	15 x 75	15 x 75		
Cylinder Circuit #2	25 x each			

Tuesday:
B) Squat	8 x 65	8 x 70	6 x 75	6 x 85
S) One-leg extension	20 x 65	20 x 65	20 x 65	
S) 30-second step slide	30 sec	30 sec	30 sec	30 sec
S) Two-leg curl	8 x 70	8 x 70	8 x 70	8 x 70
S) BW one-leg calf	30 x __	30 x __		

Thursday:
B) Incline bench press	8 x 70	8 x 70	8 x 75
S) High lat rear	8 x 70	8 x 75	8 x 75
B) Dumbbell push press	6 x 70	6 x 75	6 x 80

DO ONLY 1 OF NEXT 2
B) Hang clean (light)	8 x 70	8 x 70	8 x 70
B) Power row	8 x 60	8 x 60	8 x 60

S) Roll-out	10 x __	10 x __
S) Preacher curl	8 x 75	8 x 75
S) Close grip push-up	10 x __	10 x __
Cylinder Circuit #6	25 x each	

Friday:
B) Two-leg press	6 x 70	6 x 75	6 x 80	6 x 85
S) Power Skip	10 x __	10 x __	10 x __
S) Slideboard (w/ 20 lb vest)	3 x 30 crosses		
B) Dead lift (light)	8 x 65	8 x 70	8 x 70
C) Standing calf raise	30 x __	30 x __	

Conditioning Training

Monday:
Dynamic Warm-up

	1&2	3&4	5
1) 3 x 10 court crosses	:58	:59	1:00

Rest 1:55 b/s   (313 yds)

930 yds

Thursday:
Dynamic Warm-up

Movement Course #2

Friday:
Dynamic Warm-up

1) Game Simulation Sprints

Applied Skills

ON YOUR OWN:

Every Day: Shoot at least 100 game simulated shots, with at least 50 free throws added at various times between shots.

Monday: 10 Quality Depth Jumps (off 2 foot height)
10 Quality Jump Ups (onto 4 ft box)
Friday: Foot-speed Package #3

BY POSITION:

Tuesday:

1&2 - Applied Skills #3
3&4 - Applied Skills #3
5 - Applied Skills #3

PHASE 3

(Late Summer Workouts)

PHASE 3 ANALYSIS

Resistance Training

Phase 3 begins at the start of the second session of summer school, during the first week of July. This workout plan progresses from week 16 through week 24 of the 52-week macrocycle. This phase begins with a period of reduced load intensity. This reduction of weight being used allows the athlete an opportunity to recover fully from the demands of the progression of the second phase. The reduction in weight also allows for higher repetitions to be used again. This increase in repetitions can shock the muscle to some degree, thereby stimulating a measure of muscle hypotrophy (enlargement). Any increase in muscle mass gained will help the athlete as he attempts to lift more and more weight near the end of the phase. Workout resistance increases are added throughout the phase until week 23, when several pre-test measures are taken to assess the progress of the athlete. This phase carries the athlete through summer's end and into the first week of the fall semester. A week off is given at the end of this phase to allow the athlete time to recover and to settle into his academic schedule.

Purpose: The purpose of this phase is to increase the levels of peak power. This phase is an extension of phase 2. It is a bridge that leads to the pre-season workout period, when the emphasis on power will be decreased. In phase 4, the emphasis will shift slightly toward muscular endurance and functional strength.

Goal of the workout: In this phase, the primary objective is to work as hard as possible, assisting the athlete toward slowly increasing the amount of resistance lifted on the core exercises each week whenever possible. You want to fully optimize peak-power outputs.

Exercises: The exercises during this phase consist of core lifts, and supporting and assisting exercises.

Exercise order: In this phase, as in phase 1 and 2, the order of the exercises is traditional in that it addresses the larger muscle groups first in the workout, and the smaller muscle groups later.

Rest between sets (b/s on comment): The amount of rest between the sets of an exercise increases as the phase progresses. In the beginning of the phase, 1:00 is allowed between the sets of B exercises, and :45 is permitted between sets of S exercises. At the end of the phase, 1:25 is allowed between the sets of B exercises, and :55 is permitted between sets of S exercises. More time is allowed between sets as the load intensity increases. The amount of rest time permitted at the highest load period is less for basketball, however, than it would be for a sport like football. This factor is attributed to a basketball player's slightly higher requirement for muscular endurance and power, rather than of raw power alone.

Rest between exercises (b/e on comment): The amount of rest between exercises remains at 1:10 to 1:25.

Number of sets and repetitions: The number of sets and repetitions in phase-3 workouts are varied. In the beginning of the phase, more repetitions are prescribed for core and supporting exercises. As the phase progresses, the number of repetitions is reduced in both types of exercises. The reduction of repetitions falls as far as a single repetition on some exercises

Special sets or repetitions: Circuits are included in the early weeks of this phase to enhance the level of fatigue and to again promote growth in the muscles. Also, a circuit allows an athlete to move quickly through the workout, thereby saving him time while, still pushing up the intensity.

Repetition style and speed: During this phase, the style of how a repetition should be performed should be more strict in the early part of the phase and less strict near the end of the phase. Throughout the entire phase, the repetitions can be less strict on the core lifts, but more strict on the supporting lifts. This combination of repetition styles will insure that both muscular power and endurance needs are maintained.

Tempo or cadence of movement (repetitions): During the early part of the phase, the repetitions should be executed with a pausing tempo on the core lifts, and a more constant tempo on the supporting lifts. This combination of movement tempo will insure that both power and endurance needs are maintained. As the weight lifted becomes heavier as the phase progresses, a pausing tempo can be applied to all repetitions, if needed. The pausing tempo will insure that each repetition is a powerful one.

Running and Conditioning

Similar to previous phases, conditioning during this phase consists of interval sprints on Mondays. Doing interval sprints is a steady feature of the conditioning workouts. Interval sprints are done on Mondays to allow the athlete to run on fresh legs. After a weekend long rest, the athlete's legs should be prepared for the highest-intensity, conditioning workout of that week. Once again, on Thursdays and Fridays, a mixture of activity is utilized to condition the basketball athlete. During the early part of the phase, tag games, heavy play, and movement courses are employed to provide a mode of agility training and functional strength training that help promote a high degree of variety. The use of fartlek training and a game simulator are included during this phase to provide combination training and game-situation training. By week 21 of the phase, the agility work is replaced with longer, slower intervals on Thursdays and Fridays to help the athlete prepare for the pre-conditioning test that is conducted on week 23. In week 22, the amount of conditioning work is reduced somewhat to help the athlete recover to some degree before the pre-conditioning test.

Table 4.1. Phase 3 – Week #16

Name:

Comment: 1:00 b/s B exercises, :45 sec b/s S exercises, NO TIME b/s C exercises, 1:10 b/ exercises

	Week #16	1st Week of July
Resistance Training	**Conditioning Training**	**Application Training**

Resistance Training

Monday:
Push/Pull

B) Bench press	8 x 60	8 x 65	8 x 70	8 x 75
B) Close-grip lat	8 x 70	8 x 70	8 x 70	8 x 75
S) Zigzag push-up	10 x __	10 x __		
S) Close low lat	8 x 75	8 x 75	8 x 75	
B) Military press	8 x 70	8 x 70	8 x 75	
B) Free-weight upright row	8 x 65	8 x 70	8 x 75	
B) Two-arm dumbbell press (standing)	8 x 75	8 x 75	8 x 75	
S) Straight dumbbell pullover	15 x 75	15 x 75	15 x 75	
Cylinder Circuit #2	30 x each			

Tuesday:
B) Squat 10 x 60 8 x 70 8 x 70 8 x 75
Circuit Next 6, 2 x

C) One-leg extension	20 x 65	20 x 65
C) Hip flex	20 x __	20 x __
C) Box squat	15 x __	15 x __
C) Step-up (w/ 10 lb DB's)	15 x __	15 x __
C) Hamstring on balance ball	30 x __	30 x __
C) Donkey kicks	30 x __	30 x __
C) One stiff leg dead	10 x __	10 x __
C) Standing calf raise	30 x __	30 x __

Thursday:
Push/Pull

B) Incline bench press	10 x 60	8 x 70	8 x 70	8 x 75
B) High lat rear	10 x 65	8 x 65	8 x 70	
B) Smith behind neck	8 x 70	8 x 70	8 x 70	
S) Dumbbell upright row	8 x 75	8 x 75	8 x 75	
S) Shoulder fly	10 x 55	10 x 55	10 x 55	
S) Dumbbell stroll (w/ 40 lb DB's)	100 yds			
S) Alternating dumbbell curl (standing)	8 x 75	8 x 75	8 x 75	
S) Shooters french press	8 x 60	8 x 60	8 x 60	
Cylinder Circuit #4	30 x each			

Friday:

B) Two-leg press	8 x 70	8 x 70	8 x 70	8 x 75
B) Dead lift (light)	8 x 70	8 x 70	8 x 70	
S) 30-second step slide	30 sec	30 sec	30 sec	
B) Medicine ball underhand backward throw	12 x __	12 x __	(heavier ball)	
S) Calf raise leg press	30 x __	30 x __		

Conditioning Training

Monday:
Dynamic Warm-up

	1&2	3&4	5
1) 2 x 6, 50 yard crosses	:56	:57	:58	(300 yds)
Rest 1:55 b/s			
2) 2 x 4, 50 yard crosses	:35	:36	:37	(200 yds)
Rest 1:00 b/s			(1000 yds)

Thursday:
Dynamic Warm-up

1) Plyometric Package #3

2) Shadow boxing bouts   3 x   3 minute rounds
Rest 1:00 b/s

Friday:
Dynamic Warm-up

1)   Heavy play   6 x 3 minute rounds

Application Training

ON YOUR OWN:

Every Day: Shoot at least 100 game simulated shots, with at least 50 free throws added at various times between shots.

Monday: 10 vertical jumps (w/ 2 lb vest)
10 Quality Jump Ups
(onto 4 ft box or higher)

Friday: Foot-speed Package #2

BY POSITION:

Tuesday:

1&2	-	Applied Skills #4
3&4	-	Applied Skills #4
5	-	Applied Skills #4

Table 4.2. Phase 3 – Week #17

Week #17

2nd Week of July

Comment: 1:00 b/s B exercises, :45 sec b/s S exercises, NO TIME b/s C exercises, 1:10 b/ exercises

Resistance Training

Monday:
Push/Pull

B) Bench press	8 x 60	8 x 65	8 x 70	8 x 70	8 x 75
B) Close-grip lat	8 x 70	8 x 70	8 x 70	8 x 75	
S) Zigzag push-up	10 x —	10 x —			
S) Close low lat	8 x 75	8 x 75	8 x 75		
B) Military press	8 x 70	8 x 70	8 x 75		
B) Free-weight upright row	8 x 65	8 x 70	8 x 75		
B) Two-arm dumbbell press (standing)	8 x 75	8 x 75	8 x 75		
S) Straight dumbbell pullover	15 x 75	15 x 75	15 x 75		
Cylinder Circuit #3	30 x each				

Tuesday:

B) Squat 1	0 x 60	8 x 70	8 x 70	8 x 75

Circuit Next 6, 2 x

C) One-leg extension	20 x 65	20 x 65
C) Box squat	15 x —	15 x —
C) Step-up (w/ 15 lb DB's)	15 x —	15 x —
C) Hip flex	30 x —	30 x —
C) Donkey kicks	30 x —	30 x —
C) One stiff leg dead	10 x —	10 x —
C) Standing calf raise	30 x —	30 x —

Thursday:
Push/Pull

B) Incline bench press	10 x 60	8 x 70	8 x 70	8 x 75
S) High lat rear	10 x 60	8 x 65	8 x 70	
S) Smith behind neck	8 x 70	8 x 70	8 x 70	
S) Dumbbell upright row	8 x 75	8 x 75	8 x 75	
S) Shoulder fly	10 x 55	10 x 55	10 x 55	
S) Dumbbell stroll (w/ 45 lb DB's)	100 yds			
S) Alternating dumbbell curl (standing)	8 x 75	8 x 75	8 x 75	
S) Shooters french press	8 x 60	8 x 60	8 x 60	
Cylinder Circuit #5	30 x each			

Friday:

B) Two-leg press	8 x 70	8 x 70	8 x 70	8 x 75
B) Dead lift (light)	8 x 70	8 x 70	8 x 70	8 x 70
S) 30-second step slide	30 sec	30 sec	30 sec	
B) Medicine ball underhand backward throw	12 x —	12 x —		
S) Calf raise leg press	30 x —	30 x —		

Conditioning Training

Monday:
Dynamic Warm-up

	1&2	3&4	5	
1) 2 x Double court ladder	1:04	1:06	1:08	(313 yds)
Rest: 2:05 b/s				
2) 2x 8 court crosses	:44	:45	:46	(250 yds)
Rest: 1:25 b/s				
				(1126 yds)

Thursday:
Dynamic Warm-up

1) Movement Course #3

Friday:
Dynamic Warm-up

	1&2	3&4	5	
1) 3 x 1/2 mile	2:30	2:33	2:36	(880 yds)
Rest 5:00 b/s				
				2640 yds

Application Training

ON YOUR OWN:

Every Day: Shoot 50 three pointers, 50 twos off a penatration move, and 50 free throws.

Monday: 10 Quality Jump Ups (onto 4 ft box or higher)

Thursday: Foot-speed Package #3

BY POSITION:

Tuesday:

1&2 - Applied Skills #5
3&4 - Applied Skills #5
5   - Applied Skills #5

Table 4.3. Phase 3 – Week #18

Name: _____   Week #18   3rd Week of July

Comment: 1:00 b/s B exercises, :45 sec b/s S exercises, NO TIME b/s C exercises, 1:10 b/ exercises

Resistance Training

Monday:
Push/Pull

B) Bench press	8 x 60	8 x 65	8 x 70	8 x 75
B) Close-grip lat	8 x 70	8 x 70	8 x 70	8 x 75
S) Zigzag push-up	10 x __	10 x __		
S) Close low lat	8 x 75	8 x 75	8 x 75	
B) Push press	8 x 70	8 x 70	8 x 75	
B) Free-weight upright row	8 x 65	8 x 75	8 x 80	
B) Two-arm dumbbell press (standing)	8 x 75	8 x 75	8 x 75	
S) Straight dumbbell pullover	15 x 70	15 x 70	15 x 70	
Cylinder Circuit #1	35 x each			

Tuesday:

B) Squat	10 x 60	8 x 70	8 x 70	8 x 70	8 x 75

Circuit Next 6, 2 x

C) One-leg extension	20 x 65	20 x 65	
C) Box squat	15 x __	15 x __	
C) Step-up (w/ 15 lb DB's)	10 x __	10 x __	10 x __
C) Hip flex (w/ neg)	30 x __	30 x __	
C) Donkey kicks (w/ res)	30 x __	30 x __	
C) One-leg curl	10 x __	10 x 70	70
C) Single leg hops	30 x __	30 x __	

Thursday:
Push/Pull

B) Incline bench press	10 x 60	8 x 70	8 x 75
S) High lat front	10 x 60	8 x 65	8 x 70
B) Smith behind neck	8 x 70	8 x 70	8 x 70
B) Dumbbell upright row	8 x 75	8 x 75	8 x 75
S) Shoulder fly	10 x 55	10 x 55	10 x 55
S) Dumbbell stroll (w/ 50 lb DB's)	100 yds		
B) Straight-bar curl	8 x 75	8 x 75	8 x 75
S) Shooters french press	8 x 60	8 x 60	8 x 60
Cylinder Circuit #4	30 x each		

Friday:
Push/Pull

B) Two-leg press	8 x 70	8 x 70	8 x 70	8 x 75
B) Dead lift (light)	8 x 70	8 x 70	8 x 70	
S) Slideboard (w/ 20 lb vest)	30 sec	30 sec	30 sec	
B) Dunk with medicine ball	12 x __	12 x __		
Jump Rope	200 x __			

Conditioning Training

Monday:
Dynamic Warm-up

1) 5 x 12 Sideline crosses
Rest: 1:25 b/s

	1&2	3&4	5	
	:43	:44	:45	(200 yds)
				(1000 yds)

Thursday:
Dynamic Warm-up

1) Plyometric Package #5

Friday:
Dynamic Warm-up

1) 2 Section Fartlek   10:00

Application Training

ON YOUR OWN:

Every Day: Shoot 50 three pointers, 50 twos off a penatration move, and 50 free throws.

Monday: 10 quality running jumps off each leg.
Thursday: Balance Package #4
Friday: Foot-speed Package #2

BY POSITION:

Tuesday:

1&2 - Applied Skills #6
3&4 - Applied Skills #6
5   - Applied Skills #6

Table 4.4. Phase 3 – Week #19

Name:

Comment: 1:20 b/s B exercises, :55 sec b/s S exercises, 1:10 b/ exercises

Resistance Training / Conditioning Training

Monday:

B) Bench press	6 x 75	6 x 80	6 x 80	6 x 80
B) Pull-up	max reps	max reps	max reps	
S) Ham decline	6 x 75	6 x 80	6 x 80	
B) Dumbbell snatch, Dumbbell push press	8 x 70	8x 70		
S) Shoulder fly	8 x 70	8x 70	8 x 70	
B) Medicine ball underhand backward throw	10 x __	10 x __		
S) Straight dumbbell pullover	15 x _ 75	15 x 75		
Cylinder Circuit #1	35 x each			

Tuesday:

B) Squat	8 x 65	8 x 70	6 x 75	6 x 80
S) One-leg extension	20 x 65	20 x 65		
S) Hamstring on balance ball	30 x __	30 x __		
S) Baby squat	30 x __	30 x __		
S) Lunge—3 pumps	5 x __	5 x __		
B) Dead lift (light)	8 x 75	8 x 75	8 x 75	
S) One-leg curl	8 x 75	8 x 75	8 x 75	
S) Single leg hops	30 x __			

Thursday:

B) Incline bench press	8 x 70	8 x 75	8 x 80
S) High lat front	8 x 70	8 x 70	8 x 75
B) Push press	6 x 70	6 x 75	6 x 80
B) Power row	8 x 75	8 x 75	8 x 75
S) Roll-out	10 x __	10 x __	
S) Straight-bar curl	8 x 75	8 x 75	
S) Reverse dip	10 x __	10 x __	
Cylinder Circuit #6	25 x each		

Friday:

B) Two-leg press	8 x 70	6 x 75	6 x 80	6 x 85
S) Box squat (w/ 15 lb vest)	10 x __	10 x __	10 x __	
S) Slideboard (w/ 20 lb vest)	3 x 30 crosses			
S) Alternating leg lunge	12 x __	12 x __	12 x __	
Jump Rope	200 x __			

Application Training — Week #19

Monday:

Dynamic Warm-up

1) 4 x 6, 50 yard crosses

	1&2	3&4	5
	:56	:57	:58

Rest **1:55 b/s**

(300 yds)
—————
1200 yds

Thursday:

Dynamic Warm-up

1) Agility Package #1

Friday:

Dynamic Warm-up

1) 12 Minute Run

4th Week of July

ON YOUR OWN:

Every Day: Shoot 50 three pointers, 50 twos off a penatration move, and 50 free throws.

Monday: 10 vertical jumps (w/ 2 lb vest) 10 quality running jumps off each leg.

Thursday: Foot-speed Package #3

BY POSITION:

Tuesday:

1&2	-	Applied Skills #4
3&4	-	Applied Skills #4
5	-	Applied Skills #4

Table 4.5. Phase 3 – Week #20

Name:	Week #20	5th Week of July

Comment: 1:20 b/s B exercises, :55 sec b/s S exercises, 1:10 b/ exercises

Resistance Training

Monday:
B) Bench press — 6 x 75 6 x 80 6 x 80 6 x 80
B) Pull-up — max reps max reps max reps
S) Ham decline — 6 x 75 6 x 80 6 x 80
B) Dumbbell snatch, Dumbbell push press — 8 x 70 8x 70
S) Shoulder fly — 8 x 70 8x 70 8 x 70
B) Medicine ball underhand backward throw — 10 x __ 10 x __
S) Split dumbbell pullover — 15 x 75 15 x 75
Cylinder Circuit #2 — 30 x __

Tuesday:
B) Squat — 6 x 65 6 x 70 6 x 75 6 x 85
S) Baby squat — 20 x 65 20 x 65 20 x 65
S) Step-up (w/ 10, 15, 20 lb DB's) — 8 x __ 8 x __ 8 x __
S) Lunge—3 pumps — 5 x __ 5 x __
B) Dead lift — 8 x 75 8 x 75 8 x 75
S) One-leg curl — 8 x 75 8 x 75 8 x 75
Cylinder Circuit #3 — 30 x __

Thursday:
B) Incline bench press — 6 x 70 6 x 75 6 x 80
S) High lat front — 8 x 70 8 x 70 8 x 75
B) Dumbbell push press — 6 x 70 6 x 75 6 x 80

DO ONLY 1 OF NEXT 2
B) Hang clean (light) — 8 x 70 8 x 75 8 x 75
B) Power row — 8 x 70 8 x 75 8 x 75

S) Roll-out — 10 x __ 10 x __
S) Hammer curl — 10 x __ 8 x 75
S) Reverse dip — 10 x __ 10 x __
Cylinder Circuit #4 — 30 x __

Friday:
B) Two-leg press — 8 x 70 6 x 75 6 x 80 6 x 85
S) Box squat(w/ 20 lb vest) — 10 x __ 10 x __ 10 x __
S) Slideboard (w/ 20 lb vest) — 3 x 30 crosses
S) Alternating leg lunge — 12 x __ 12 x __ 12 x __
Cylinder Circuit #5 — 30 x __

Conditioning Training

Monday:
Dynamic Warm-up

	1&2	3&4	5	
1) 2 x 10 court crosses	:58	:59	1:00	(313 yds)
Rest 1:55 b/s				
2) 2 x 12 Sideline crosses	:43	:44	:45	(200 yds)
Rest: 1:25 b/s				
3) 2 x 2, 50 yard crosses	:15	:16	:17	(100 yds)
Rest: :30 b/s				
				1226 yds

Thursday:
Dynamic Warm-up
Movement Course #1

Friday:
Dynamic Warm-up
1) Game Simulation Sprints

Application Training

ON YOUR OWN:

Every Day: Shoot at least 100 game simulated shots, with at least 50 free throws added at various times between shots.

Monday: Balance Package #2

BY POSITION:

Tuesday:

1&2	-	Applied Skills #5
3&4	-	Applied Skills #5
5	-	Applied Skills #5

Table 4.6. Phase 3 – Week #21

Name:

Comment: 1:25 b/s B exercises, :55 sec b/s S exercises, 1:25 b/ exercises

	Week #21	1st Week of August
Resistance Training	**Conditioning Training**	**Application Training**

Resistance Training

Monday:

Exercise					
B) Bench press	5 x 75	5 x 80	5 x 80	5 x 80	5 x 85
B) Pull-up	max reps	max reps	max reps		
S) Spider push-up	10 x __	10 x __			
B) Free-weight upright row	8 x 75	8 x 75	8 x 75		
B) Alternating dumbbell press (standing)	6 x 70	6 x 75	6 x 80		
S) Split dumbbell pullover	15 x 75	15 x 75	15 x 75		
B) Dumbbell french press	8 x 75	8 x 75	8 x 75		
Cylinder Circuit #2	30 x __				

Tuesday:

Exercise				
B) Squat	5 x 70	5 x 75	5 x 80	5 x 85
S) Baby squat	1 minute	1 minute		
S) Step-up (w/ 10, 15, 20 lb DB's)	8 x __	8 x __	8 x __	
S) Ski Jumps	10 x __	10 x __		
S) One-leg curl	8 x 75	8 x 75	8 x 75	
Cylinder Circuit #3	30 x __			

Thursday:

Exercise			
B) Incline bench press	6 x 70	6 x 75	6 x 80
S) High lat front	8 x 70	8 x 70	8 x 75
B) Dumbbell push press	6 x 70	5 x 75	6x 80
Rest 5:00 b/s			

DO ONLY 1 OF NEXT 2

Exercise			
B) Hang clean (light)	6 x 70	6 x 75	6 x 80
B) Power row	6 x 70	6 x 75	6 x 80
B) Bar Shrug	20 x 65	20 x 65	
S) Roll-out	10 x __	10 x __	
S) Hammer curl	8 x 75	8 x 75	
S) Close grip bench	8 x 65	8 x 70	8 x 75
Cylinder Circuit #4	30 x __		

Friday:

Exercise				
B) Two-leg press	6 x 75	6 x 75	6 x 80	6 x 85
S) Box squat (w/ 20 lb vest)	10 x __	10 x __	10 x __	
S) 30-second step slide	30 sec	30 sec		
S) Alternating leg lunge	12 x __	12 x __	12 x __	
S) Wrist flex	100 x __			
Cylinder Circuit #5	30 x __			

Conditioning Training

Monday:
Dynamic Warm-up

	1&2	3&4	5	
1) 4 x 6 court crosses	:32	:33	:34	(188 yds)
Rest 1:00 b/s				
2) 4 x 4 court crosses	:22	:23	:24	(125 yds)
Rest :40 b/s				
3) 5 x 2 court crosses	:09	:09	:10	(62 yds)
Rest :25b/s				
				1562 yds

Thursday:
Dynamic Warm-up

	1&2	3&4	5	
1) 3 x 1/2 mile	2:30	2:33	2:36	(880 yds)
				2640 yds

Friday:
Dynamic Warm-up

	1&2	3&4	5	
1) 2 x Double court ladder	1:04	1:06	1:08	(313 yds)
Rest 2:05 b/s				
				626 yds

Application Training

[TAKE HOME]

ON YOUR OWN:

Monday: 10 vertical jumps use vertical jump tester to test height. On each of the first eight jumps, move a key on the tester. On the last two jumps, go all out

Friday: 10 quality running jumps off each leg.

BY POSITION:

Tuesday:

1&2 - Applied Skills #1
3&4 - Applied Skills #1
5   - Applied Skills #1

Table 4.7. Phase 3 – Week #22

Name: _____ Week #22   1st Week of August

Comment: 1:25 b/s B exercises, :55 sec b/s S exercises, 1:25 b/ exercises

[TAKE HOME]

Resistance Training	Conditioning Training	Application Training

Resistance Training

Monday:
B) Bench press — 5 x 75   5 x 80   4 x 85   4 x 90
B) Pull-up — max reps   max reps   max reps
S) Spider push-up — 10 x __   10 x __   —
B) Free-weight upright row — 6 x 75   6 x 80   6 x 85
B) Alternating dumbbell press (standing) — 6 x 70   6 x 75   6 x 80
S) Split dumbbell pullover — 15 x 75   15 x 75   15 x 75
B) Dumbbell french press — 8 x 75   8 x 75   8 x 75
Cylinder Circuit #2 — 30 x __

Tuesday:
B) Squat — 5 x 70   5 x 75   4 x 85   4 x 90
S) One-leg extension — 20 x 65   20 x 65   20 x 65
S) Hamstring on balance ball — 30 x __   30 x __
S) Baby squat — 1 minute   1 minute
S) Ski Jumps — 10 x __   10 x __
S) One stiff leg dead — 10 x __   10 x __
Cylinder Circuit #3 — 30 x __

Thursday:
B) Incline bench press — 6 x 70   6 x 75   6 x 80
S) High lat rear — 8 x 70   8 x 70   8 x 75
S) Medicine ball, balance ball push-up — 10 x __   10 x __
B) Dumbbell push press — 5 x 75   5 x 80   5 x 85

DO ONLY 1 OF NEXT 2
B) Hang clean (light) — 6 x 70   6 x 75   6 x 80
B) Power row — 6 x 70   6 x 75   6 x 80

B) Bar Shrug — 20 x 65   20 x 65
S) Roll-out — 10 x __   10 x __
S) Straight-bar curl — 6 x 80   6 x 80
S) Close grip bench — 8 x 65   8 x 70   8 x 75
Cylinder Circuit #4 — 30 x __

Friday:
B) Two-leg press — 5 x 75   5 x 80   5 x 85   5 x 90
S) Power Skip — 10 x __   10 x __   10 x __
S) Box squat (w/ 20 lb vest) — 10 x __   10 x __   10 x __
S) 30-second step slide — 30 sec   30 sec
S) Alternating leg lunge — 10 x __   10 x __   10 x __
S) Wrist flex — 100 x __
Cylinder Circuit #5 — 30 x __

Conditioning Training

Monday:
Dynamic Warm-up

	1&2	3&4	5	
1) 4 x 6 court crosses	:32	:33	:34	(188 yds)
Rest 1:00 b/s				
2) 5 x 4 court crosses	:22	:23	:24	(125 yds)
Rest :40 b/s				
3) 5 x 2 court crosses	:09	:09	:10	(62 yds)
Rest :25b/s				

          1687 yds

Dynamic Warm-up
1) 12 Minute Run

Application Training

ON YOUR OWN:

Monday: 10 vertical jumps use vertical jump tester to test height. On each of the first six jumps, move a key on the tester. On the last four jumps, go all out

Friday: 10 vertical jumps use vertical jump tester to test height. On each of the first five jumps, move a key on the tester. On the last five jumps, go all out

BY POSITION:

Tuesday:

1&2 - Applied Skills #2
3&4 - Applied Skills #2
5 - Applied Skills #2

Table 4.8. Phase 3 – Week #23

Name:

Comment: 1:25 b/s B exercises, :55 sec b/s S exercises, 1:25 b/ exercises

	Week #23	3rd Week of August
Resistance Training	**Conditioning Training**	**Application Training**

Resistance Training

Monday:
B) Bench press	5 x 75	5 x 80	max reps	3 x 85	max reps 1 x 100
B) Pull-up	max reps				
B) Dips (w/ 10 lb vest)	max reps				
B) Free-weight upright row	6 x 80	6 x 80	6 x 80		
B) Alternating dumbbell press (standing)	6 x 70	6 x 75	6 x 80		
S) Split dumbbell pullover	15 x 75	15 x 75			
B) Reverse dip	10 x —	10 x —	10 x —		
Cylinder Circuit #2	30 x —				

Tuesday:
B) Squat	5 x 70	5 x 75	4 x 85	4 x 90
S) One-leg extension	20 x 65	20 x 65	20 x 65	
S) Hamstring on balance ball	30 x —	30 x —		
S) Ski Jumps	15 x —	15 x —		
S) One stiff leg dead	10 x —	10 x —		
Cylinder Circuit #3	30 x —			

Thursday:
DIP MAX TEST	max reps		
S) High lat rear	8 x 70	8 x 70	8 x 75
S) Medicine ball, balance ball push-up	10 x —	10 x —	
B) Dumbbell push press	5 x 75	5 x 80	5 x 85

DO ONLY 1 OF NEXT 2
B) Hang clean (light)	6 x 70	6 x 75	6 x 80
B) Power row	6 x 70	6 x 75	6 x 80

B) Bar Shrug	20 x 65	20 x 65	
S) Straight-bar curl	6 x 80	6 x 80	
S) Close grip bench	8 x 65	8 x 70	8 x 75
Cylinder Circuit #4	30 x —		

Friday:
B) Two-leg press	5 x 75	5 x 80	5 x 85	5 x 90
PULL-UP MAX TEST	max reps			
S) 30-second step slide	10 x —	10 x —	10 x —	
S) Box squat (w/ 20 lb vest)	30 sec	30 sec		
S) Wrist flex	100 x —			
Cylinder Circuit #5	30 x —			

Conditioning Training

Monday:
Dynamic Warm-up

	1&2	3&4	5	
1) 4 x 6, 50 yard crosses				(300 yds)
Rest 1:55 b/s	:56	:57	:58	
2) 3 x 4 court crosses	:22	:23	:24	(125 yds)
Rest :40 b/s				
3) 1 x 12 Sideline crosses	:43	:44	:45	(200 yds)
				1779 yds

Thursday:
Dynamic Warm-up

CONDITIONING PRE-TEST

	1&2	3&4	5	
1) 2 x 32 court crosses				(1003 yds)
Rest 4:00 b/s	3:45	3:50	3:55	
				1003 yds

Application Training

ON YOUR OWN:

Monday: 10 vertical jumps use vertical jump tester to test height. On each of the first five jumps, move a key on the tester. On the last five jumps, go all out

Thursday:
Vertical jump TEST
20 yd shuttle TEST
30-second step slide TEST

BY POSITION:

Tuesday:
1&2	-	Applied Skills	#3
3&4	-	Applied Skills	#3
5	-	Applied Skills	#3

Table 4.9. Phase 3 – Week #24

Name:

Comment:

Week #24

4th Week of August

WEEK OFF

(FIRST WEEK OF CLASS- ACADEMIC ORIENTATION)

PHASE 4
(Pre-Season Workouts)

PHASE 4 ANALYSIS

Resistance Training

Phase 4 features a unique workout approach that addresses the time restraints placed on the athlete by the fall academic schedule. A major concern during this time of the training year is to provide enough muscular work to produce continued gains in muscular strength (power and endurance), while at the same time, not interfere with the athlete's studies. During this time of the year, because of school and team meetings, many basketball athletes often feel (and tell their coaches) that, "I've got time for this, but I do not have time for that." As such, the workout program in phase 4 has been designed to incorporate the resistance training, along with the conditioning and agility drills, into a part of the macrocycle that can be referred to as "Basic Training." While the workouts in this phase do not create the best power-producing conditions, due to the short rest periods and the general lack of recovery between sets, the conditioning aspects of the workouts are very much like that of basketball. The rapid changes in intensity throughout the workout mimic the undulations of intensity that occur during a basketball game.

The resistance training portions of the workout can be compared to periods of jumping, sprinting, and playing tough man-to-man defense. The running portions of the workout can be equated to the transitions up and down the floor during the course of the game. Because this workout is much more intense than a true game situation, keep a close eye on your athletes. Allow time outs, if needed, to avoid overstressing the athletes. Although these workouts are tough, they show the athlete what they can do when they set their mind to it. The workout can also serve as a method of re-kindling team unity prior to the new basketball season.

The last two weeks of the phase return to a traditional resistance training format to allow for some active recovery prior to the season. The last week's resistance training is optional to those athletes who feel they need additional recuperation time. The conditioning training during the last week is still required, however.

Purpose: The basic purpose of this phase is to heighten the level of over-all physical fitness prior to the new basketball season.

Goal of the workout: In this phase, the primary objective is to incorporate all the elements of the workout into a complete, but concise workout format. Another goal is to promote complete physical preparedness prior to the new basketball season.

Exercises: The exercises during this phase consist of core lifts, and supporting and assisting exercises. Body weight exercises, such as push-ups, pull-ups, dips, etc. are also frequently incorporated during this phase. All factors considered, if the athlete can move his own body weight, he will be a more functional athlete. Combination movements are also included to incorporate a higher degree of variety and movement into the workout. An example of one such combination movement is a dumbbell upright row/lunge. This exercise is a combination of performing a lunge, followed by a dumbbell upright row on the up phase of the lunge.

Exercise order: In this phase, as in all phases of the training plan, the order of the resistance training is traditional in that it addresses the larger muscle groups first in the workout, and the smaller muscle groups later. However, a unique feature of this phase involves the fact that a conditioning or applied-skill exercise is performed between sets of resistance training exercises.

Rest between sets (b/s on comment): The amount of rest between the sets of an exercise remains the same throughout the phase. 1:00 is allowed between sets of any B exercise, and :45 seconds is permitted between sets of any S exercise. During the basic training portion of the week, :45 seconds is suggested between O exercises. "O" is the sign for basic training exercise combinations. This step is only suggested if the athlete looks like he is under distress. If he is, then allow for a greater rest period.

Rest between exercises (b/e on comment:): The amount of rest between exercises is :55 seconds.

Number of sets and repetitions: The number of sets that the resistance training exercises should be performed is lowered to allow for time restraints placed on the workout by team meetings and academic responsibilities. The number of repetitions are higher on the first day of the week to promote an endurance stress on the muscle. At the end of the week, the repetitions are lower, and the resistance is higher in order to address the power needs of the muscle.

Special sets or repetitions: This phase involves no special resistance training sets. All of the sets are straightforward.

Repetition style and speed: During this phase, the style of repetition is less strict. However, each repetition should be intelligently performed with good form to avoid injury. A higher level of speed can be incorporated into the movement to allow for the use of higher resistance.

Tempo or cadence of movement (repetitions): The repetitions in this phase should be executed with a pausing tempo. In other words, some repetitions can be performed without pause. However, as the resistance begins to cause the individual to fatigue, the athlete should pause for an instant in a locked-out position to allow momentary recuperation. This step will help insure that each repetition is a powerful repetition, and that each repetition assigned is completed prior to momentary muscular failure.

Running and Conditioning

Conditioning during this phase is unique, because it is interwoven between sets of resistance exercise. The entire workout should provide enough cardiorespiratory fatigue to promote conditioning. Agility and plyometric movements are incorporated into movement courses and skill-related exercises. These courses and exercises are conducted between the sets of resistance-training exercises.

Applied Skills

Additional applied skills, in the form of shooting games, are included in this phase (see Chapter 12). These games offer a means of having fun, while still getting all your shots in for that day. If the athlete chooses not to play the game, but would rather perform his own shooting routine, that is fine. It is critically important during all phases of training that the basketball athlete devotes a substantial amount of energy and time on his applied skills. The athlete's body is growing and changing as a result of the resistance training and conditioning. As his body grows, he must allow his basketball skills to grow along with it.

Table 5.1. Phase 4 – Week #25

Week #25   1st Week of September

Name: _____

Comment: 1:00 b/s B exercises, :45 sec b/s S exercises, :45 sec b/s O exercises, :55 b/ exercises

Resistance Training / Conditioning Training

Monday:

Exercise				
DIP MAX TEST	max reps			
S) High lat front	8 x 70	8 x 70	8 x 75	
S) Medicine ball, balance ball push-up	10 x __	10 x __		
S) Dumbbell stroll (w/ 50 lb DB's)	100 yds			
S) Dumbbell snatch	5 x 75	5 x 80	5 x 85	
B) Dumbbell snatch	6 x 80	6 x 80		
S) Straight-bar curl	8 x 75	8 x 75		
S) Triceps push-down	30 x __			
Cylinder Circuit #3				

Tuesday:

Exercise				
B) Two-leg press	5 x 75	5 x 80	5 x 85	5 x 90
PULL-UP MAX TEST	max reps			
B) Dumbbell squat, two-arm dumbbell press	8 x 70	8 x 70	8 x 70	
S) Alternating leg extension	20 x 65	20 x 65		
S) Slideboard (w/ 15 lb vest)	3 x 30 crosses			
S) One-leg curl	10 x 60	10 x 60	10 x 60	
Cylinder Circuit #4	30 x __			

Thursday:
Lift/Run

Exercise		
O) Flat dumbbell press	12 x 75	12 x 75
RUN >>>>>>>>>>>>>>>>>	2 x 8 court crosses	
O) High lat rear	12 x 75	12 x 75
RUN >>>>>>>>>>>>>>>>>	2 x 12 Sideline crosses	
O) Ham decline	12 x 75	12 x 75
RUN >>>>>>>>>>>>>>>>>	2 x 4 court crosses	
O) Dumbbell hang clean	8 x 75	8 x 75
Step slide >>>	Length of basketball court down and back	
O) Side dumbbell raise, lunge	8 x 75	8 x 75
3 SIDE SQ. >>>>>>>>	30 sec	30 sec
O) Alternating dumbbell curl	8 x 75	8 x 75
Jump Ups (onto 4-ft box)	8 x __	8 x __
O) Reverse dip	10 x __	10 x __
Dunk with medicine ball	10 x __	10 x __
Cylinder Circuit #5	30 x __	

	1&2	3&4	5	
	:44	:45	:46	(250 yds) x 2
	:43	:44	:45	(200 yds) x 2
	:22	:23	:24	(125 yds) x 2
				1150 yds

Application Training

Monday: (Official Test)
MAX vertical jump use vertical jump tester to test jumping height (before weights)

Vertical jump TEST
20 yd shuttle TEST
30-second step slide TEST

Conditioning Test:
2 x 32 Court Crosses
Rest 4:00 b/s

	1&2	3&4	5
	3:45	3:50	3:55

(1003 yds) x 2
2006 yds

ON YOUR OWN / AS A TEAM:

*ANY DAY OF THE WEEK THE TEAM CAN GET
TOGETHER AND PLAY THEY SHOULD*

BY POSITION:

Monday:			Thursday:		
1&2	-	Applied Skills #4	1&2	-	Shooting Game #1
3&4	-	Applied Skills #4	3&4	-	Shooting Game #1
5	-	Applied Skills #4	5	-	Shooting Game #1

Table 5.2. Phase 4 – Week #26

Name: ___   Week #26   2ND Week of September

Comment: 1:00 b/s B exercises, :45 sec b/s S exercises, :45 sec b/s O exercises, :55 b/ exercises

Resistance Training / Conditioning Training

Monday:
Lift/Run

	1&2	3&4	5	
O) Flat dumbbell press	12 x 75	12 x 75		
RUN >>>>>>	:58	:59	1:00	(250 yds) x 2
O) Ham decline	2 x 10	court crosses		
RUN >>>>>>	12 x 75	12 x 75		
O) Dumbbell snatch	2 x 8	court crosses		
RUN >>>>>>	:44	:45	:46	(250 yds) x 2
	8 x 70	8 x 70		
O) Dumbbell push press	2 x 6	court crosses		
30-second step slide >>>>>>	8 x 80	8 x 80		
	:22	:33	:34	(188 yds) x 2
O) Side dumbbell raise	30 sec	30 sec		
3 SIDE SQ. >>>>>>>	8 x 75	8 x 75		1376 yds
O) Triceps push-down	30 sec	30 sec		
Jump Ups (onto 4 ft box)	8 x 80	8 x 80		
Cylinder Circuit #3	8 x ___	8 x ___		
	30 x ___			

Tuesday:

S) High lat front	10 x 70	8 x 70	8 x 75	
S) Close low lat	10 x 70	8 x 70	8 x 75	
S) Leg dragging	2 x baseline to half court			
S) Rear deltoid swim	20 x ___	20 x ___		
B) Squat	10 x 60	8 x 70	8 x 70	8 x 75
B) Baby squat	1.5 minute	1.5 minute	1.5 minute	
S) Alternating leg extension	20 x 65	20 x 65		
S) One-leg curl	10 x 60	10 x 60	10 x 60	
Cylinder Circuit #4	30 x ___			

Thursday:
Lift/Run

	1&2	3&4	5	
O) Incline bench press	8 x 80	8 x 80	8 x 80	
2 x Movement Course # 2 >>>>>				
O) Pull-up	max reps	max reps		
2 x Movement Course #2 >>>>>				
O) Medicine ball, push-up	10 x ___	10 x ___		
RUN >>>>>	:58	:59	1:00	(250 yds)
	2 x 10	court crosses		
O) Clean and jerk	8 x 75	8 x 75		
Step slide >>>>>	3 x length of basketball court			250 yds
O) Side dumbbell raise, lunge	8 x 75	8 x 75		
2 x 100 truns of Jump Rope >>>>>	(30 jumps off each leg; 40 jumps off both)			
O) Alternating dumbbell curl	8 x 75	8 x 75		
Dunk with medicine ball	8 x ___	8 x ___		
Medicine ball underhand backward throw	15 x ___	15 x ___		
Cylinder Circuit #5	30 x ___	10 x ___	10 x ___	

Application Training

ON YOUR OWN / AS A TEAM:

Tuesday:
CONSTRUCTIVE TEAM PLAY
Friday:

BY POSITION:

Monday:

1&2 - Applied Skills #5

3&4 - Applied Skills #5

5 - Applied Skills #5

Thursday:

1&2 - Shooting Game #2

3&4 - Shooting Game #2

5 - Shooting Game #2

Table 5.3. Phase 4 – Week #27

Name:	Week #27	3rd Week of September

Comment: 1:00 b/s B exercises, :45 sec b/s S exercises, :45 sec b/s O exercises, :55 b/ exercises

Resistance Training / Conditioning Training

Monday:
Lift/Run

	1&2	3&4	5	
O) Flat dumbbell press	12 x 75	12 x 75	court crosses	
RUN >>>>>>>>>>>				
O) Dips (w/ 5 lb vest)	2 x 10	court crosses		
RUN >>>>>>>	max reps	max reps		
O) Dumbbell snatch	2 x 8	court crosses		
RUN >>>>>>>>>>>	2 x 70	8 x 70		
O) Dumbbell push press	2 x 12	Sideline crosses		
30-second step slide >>>>	8 x 80	8 x 80		
	30 sec	30 sec		
O) Side dumbbell raise	8 x 75	8 x 75		
Any Agility Ladder Drill	2 x 4 drills, 5 times through each drill			
O) Triceps push-down	8 x 80	8 x 80		
Jump Ups (w/ 5 lb vest)	8 x __	8 x __	(choose height of box 3ft or up)	
Cylinder Circuit #4	30 x __			

	1&2	3&4	5	
	:58	:59	1:00	(250 yds)
	:44	:45	:46	(250 yds)
	:43	:44	:45	(200 yds)
				700 yds

Tuesday:

S) High lat front.	10 x 70	8 x 70	8 x 75	
S) Dumbbell stroll (w/ 50 lb DB's)	100 yds			
S) Leg dragging	2 x baseline to half court			
S) Rear deltoid swim	20 x __	20 x __		
B) Squat	8 x 60	6 x 70	6 x 80	6 x 85
B) Free-weight upright row	8 x 75	8 x 75		
S) Alternating leg extension	20 x 65	20 x 65		
S) One-leg curl	10 x 60	10 x 60	10 x 60	
Cylinder Circuit #4	30 x __			

Thursday:
Lift/Run

O) Incline bench press	8 x 80	8 x 80	8 x 80
2 x Movement Course # 3 >>>>>			
O) Pull-up	max reps	max reps	
2 x Movement Course #3 >>>>>			
O) Medicine ball, balance ball push-up	10 x __	10 x __	
RUN >>>>>>>>>>>	2 x 4 laps around basketball court		
O) Dumbbell pull press	8 x 80	8 x 80	
Step slide >>>>	3 x length of basketball court		
O) Dumbbell upright row, lunge	8 x 75	8 x 75	
2 x 100 truns of Jump Rope >>>>	30 jumps off each leg; 40 jumps off both legs		
O) Hammer curl	8 x 75	8 x 75	
Dunk with medicine ball	8 x __	8 x __	
O) Shooters french press	8 x 75	8 x 75	
Medicine ball underhand backward throw	10 x __	10 x __	
Cylinder Circuit #5	30 x __		

Application Training

ON YOUR OWN / AS A TEAM:

Tuesday:
CONSTRUCTIVE TEAM PLAY
Friday:

BY POSITION:

Monday:

1&2	-	Applied Skills #6
3&4	-	Applied Skills #6
5	-	Applied Skills #6

Thursday:

1&2	-	Shooting Game #3
3&4	-	Shooting Game #3
5	-	Shooting Game #3

Table 5.4. Phase 4 – Week #28

Name: _____

Week #28   4th Week of September

Comment: 1:00 b/s B exercises, :45 sec b/s S exercises, :45 sec b/s O exercises, :55 b/ exercises

Resistance Training / Conditioning Training

Monday:
Lift/Run

O) Flat dumbbell press	12 x 75	12 x 75	1&2	3&4	5
RUN >>>>>>>>>>	2 x Double court ladder		1:04	1:06	1:08 (313 yds)
O) Dips	max reps	max reps			
RUN >>>>>>>>	2 x 10 court crosses		:58	:59	1:00 (313 yds)
O) Dumbbell snatch	8 x 75	8 x 75			
RUN >>>>>>>>	2 x 12 sideline crosses		:43	:44	:45 (200 yds)
O) Dumbbell push press	8 x 80	8 x 80			826 yds
30-second step slide >>>>>	30 sec	30 sec			
O) Side dumbbell raise	8 x 75	8 x 75			
Any Agility Ladder Drill	2 x 4 drills, 5 times through each drill				
O) Triceps push-down	8 x 80	8 x 80			
Jump Ups (w/ 5 lb vest)	8 x ___	8 x ___			
Cylinder Circuit #3	30 x ___				

Tuesday:

S) High lat front.	10 x ___ 70 8 x 70 8 x 75
S) Close low lat	10 x ___ 70 8 x 70 8 x 75
S) Leg dragging	2 x baseline to half court
S) Rear deltoid swim	20 x ___ 20 x ___
B) Squat	8 x 60 6 x 70 6 x 80 6 x 85
B) Backward lunge, dumbbell upright row	8 x 75 8 x 75
S) Step-up, shoulder fly	8 x 70 8 x 70
S) Musketeer lunge	10 x ___ 10 x ___ 10 x ___
Cylinder Circuit #4	30 x ___

Thursday:
Lift w/ Run

O) Incline bench press	8 x 80 8 x 80
O) Pull-up	max reps max reps
2 x Movement Course #1 >>>>>>>	
O) Medicine ball, balance ball push-up	10 x ___ 10 x ___
RUN >>>>>>>>>	2 x 4 laps around basketball court
O) Dumbbell pull press	8 x 80 8 x 80
O) Backward lunge, dumbbell upright row	8 x 75 8 x 75
2 x 100 truns of Jump Rope >>>>>	30 jumps off each leg; 40 jumps off both legs
Dunk with medicine ball	8 x 75 8 x 75
O) Hammer curl	8 x ___ 8 x ___
S) Shooters french press	8 x 75 8 x 75
S) Crabbing	The length of the basketball court
Cylinder Circuit #5	30 x ___

Application Training

ON YOUR OWN / AS A TEAM:

Tuesday:
CONSTRUCTIVE TEAM PLAY
Friday:

BY POSITION:

Monday:

1&2	-	Applied Skills #2
3&4	-	Applied Skills #2
5	-	Applied Skills #2

Thursday:

1&2	-	Shooting Game #4
3&4	-	Shooting Game #4
5	-	Shooting Game #4

Table 5.5. Phase 4 – Week #29

Name:

Comment: 1:00 b/s B exercises, :45 sec b/s S exercises, :45 sec b/s O exercises, 1:30 b/ exercises

Week #29 — 1st Week of October

Resistance Training

Monday:

B) Flat dumbbell press	8 x 70	8x 70	8 x 70
S) Moon push-up	8 x __	8 x __	
B) Military press	8 x 70	8x 70	8 x 70
B) Shoulder fly	8 x 70	8x 70	8 x 70
S) Crabbing	The length of the basketball court		
S) Hands on balance ball push-up	10 x __	10 x __	
Cylinder Circuit #3 30 x __	3) 2 x 2, 50-yard crosses :15		

Tuesday:

B) Pull-up	max reps	max reps	max reps
B) Free-weight upright row	8 x 70	8 x 75	6 x 75
B) Squat	6 x 65	6 x 70	6 x 75
S) One-leg extension	20 x 65	20 x 65	
S) Step-up	15 x __	15 x __	
S) Musketeer lunge	10 x __	10 x __	10 x __
Cylinder Circuit #4	30 x __		

Thursday:

B) Incline dumbbell press	6 x 80	6 x 85
S) High lat rear	8 x 75	8 x 75
B) Dumbbell pull press	8 x 70	8 x 70
S) Split dumbbell pullover	10 x 70	10 x 70
S) Squat-press	8 x 70	8 x 70
S) Step-up, shoulder fly	8 x 70	8 x 70
S) Slideboard	2 x 30 crosses	
Cylinder Circuit #5	30 x __	

Conditioning Training

Monday:
Dynamic Warm-up

	1&2	3&4	5	
1) 2 x 10 court crosses	:58	:59	1:00	(313 yds) x 2
Rest 1:55 b/s				
2) 2 x 12 Sideline crosses	:43	:44	:45	(200 yds) x 2
Rest: 1:25 b/s				
		:16	:17	(100 yds) x 2
Rest: :30 b/s				1226 yds

Thursday:
Dynamic Warm-up

	1&2	3&4	5	
1) 4 x 1/4 mile	1:32	1:34	1:30	(440 yds)
Rest 3:00 b/s				440 yds

Application Training

ON YOUR OWN:

Tuesday: CONSTRUCTIVE TEAM PLAY
Friday:

BY POSITION:

Tuesday:
1&2 -
3&4 -
5

Table 5.6. Phase 4 – Week #30

Name:

Comment: 1:00 b/s B exercises, :45 sec b/s S exercises, :45 sec b/s O exercises, 1:30 b/ exercises

Week #30 — 2nd Week of October

Resistance Training	Conditioning Training	Application Training

Resistance Training

*LIFTING IS OPTIONAL THIS WEEK

Monday:
- B) Flat dumbbell press — 8 x 70   8x 70   8 x 70
- S) Moon push-up — 8 x —   8 x —   8 x —
- B) Military press — 8 x 70   8x 70   8 x 70
- S) Shoulder fly — 8 x 70   8x 70   8 x 70
- S) Crabbing — The length of the basketball court
- S) Hands on balance ball push-up
- Cylinder Circuit #3   30 x —   10 x —   10 x —

Tuesday:
- | | max reps | max reps | max reps |
- B) Pull-up — max reps   max reps   max reps
- B) Free-weight upright row — 8 x 70   8 x 75   6 x 75
- B) Squat — 6 x 65   6 x 70   6 x 75
- S) One-leg extension — 20 x 65   20 x 65
- S) Step-up — 15 x —   15 x —
- S) Musketeer lunge — 10 x —   10 x —   10 x —
- Cylinder Circuit #4 — 30 x —

Thursday:
- B) Incline dumbbell press — 6 x 85   6 x 90
- S) High lat rear — 8 x 70   8 x 70
- B) Dumbbell pull press — 8 x 70   8 x 70
- S) Split dumbbell pullover — 10 x 70   10 x 70   70
- S) Squat-press — 8 x 70   8 x 70
- S) Step-up, side dumbbell raise — 8 x 70   8 x 70
- Cylinder Circuit #5 — 30 x —

Conditioning Training

Monday:
Dynamic warm-up

	1&2	3&4	5	
1) 2 x double court ladder	1:04	1:06	1:08	(313 yds) x 2
Rest: **2:05 b/s**				
1) 2 x 12 sideline crosses	:43	:44	:45	(200 yds) x 2
Rest: **1:25 b/s**				
3) 2 x 2, 50-yard crosses	:15	:16	:17	(100 yds) x 2
Rest **:30 b/s**				1226 yds

Thursday:
Dynamic warm-up

	1&2	3&4	5	
1) 2 x 1/2 mile	2:30	2:33	2:36	(880 yds) x 2
Rest 5:00 b/s				1760 yds

Application Training

ON YOUR OWN:

Tuesday:
CONSTRUCTIVE TEAM PLAY
Friday:

Thursday:

BY POSITION:

Tuesday:
1&2 -
3&4 -
5

CHAPTER 6

PHASE 5
(In-Season Workouts)

PHASE 5 ANALYSIS

Resistance Training

Phase 5 begins at the start of fall team practice and the new basketball season. This workout plan progresses from week 31 through the end of the training year (week 52). Week 52 carries a team into the fourth week of March and the Final Four. This phase becomes a period of maintenance. It is important for the athlete to continue resistance training during the season to avoid a loss of muscle mass. While some muscle loss will occur regardless of the training, due to the stress and duration of the long season ahead, the loss can be minimized with a maintenance resistance program.

One special factor should be considered with regard to leg training during the basketball season. You will notice a large drop off during this phase in both the volume and number of exercises performed for legs. The basketball playing surface is hard, and the season is long. Even though leg work is planned, it may not be advisable. Continually ask your players how their legs feel. If they complain of weakness in their legs, then prescribe rest first. If rest does not help them feel stronger, then opt to weight train the legs. Fatigue may be the problem, not muscle loss. This phase is designed around a typical college basketball schedule. Each week's exercise prescription is slightly different to accommodate for the games being played.

Purpose: The purpose of this phase is to maintain the levels of power and endurance gained by the athlete during the preceding phases.

Goal of the workout: In this phase, the primary objective is to work as hard as possible, helping the athlete to slowly increase the amount of resistance lifted on the core exercises each week, whenever possible, and to induce MMF on the last set of all supporting exercises.

Exercises: The exercises during this phase consist of core lifts, and supporting and assisting exercises.

Exercise order: The order of the exercises is traditional in that it addresses the larger muscle groups first in the workout and the smaller muscle groups later.

Rest between sets (b/s on comment): The amount of rest between the sets of an exercise is :55 between the sets of B exercises and :45 is allowed between sets of S exercises. NO TIME is allowed between exercises in the C circuit routines. The rest periods during the workout can be adjusted if needed. Remember that during the in-season portion of training, the athletes face an on-going battle for time between study, sport/conditioning, and personal time. Burnout is most apt to happen during this phase, so keep the workout short, but challenging.

These workouts can be completed in 15 to 20 minutes.

Rest between exercises (b/e on comment): The amount of rest between exercises remains at 1:00.

Number of sets and repetitions: The number of sets and repetitions in phase-5 workouts vary. Core lifts are performed with lower repetitions and sets, while supporting exercises are conducted with higher repetitions and sets. Pushing exercises are done with around six repetitions on the average. Pulling exercises, on the other hand, are performed with an average of 8 repetitions. Variations in the number of repetitions required are somewhat flexible, but the general idea is to provide both load-related stressors and endurance-related stressors on the working muscles.

Special sets or repetitions: Other than performing circuits, no other special sets or repetition formats are included in this phase. On week 37 of this phase, three games are played. A warm-up set is performed, followed by a heavy set. The last set is reduced to provide an endurance stress (eg. 10 x 70, 5 x 85, 12 x 70). The sets are performed this way to provide a variety of stimulus for the muscle.

Repetition style and speed: During this phase, the style of repetition is less strict on the core lifts, but more strict on the supporting lifts. This combination of repetition style will insure that both power and endurance needs are maintained.

Tempo or cadence of movement (repetitions): The repetitions in this phase should be executed with a pausing tempo on the core lifts, and a more constant tempo on the supporting lifts. This combination of movement tempo will ensure that both power and endurance needs are maintained.

Running and Conditioning

The majority of conditioning training during this phase is incorporated into basketball practice, drills, and on-the-court play. However, some post-practice conditioning may be desired in the early days of practice to add the final touches to the athlete's conditioning regimen. If post-practice conditioning is not part of the practice plan, some players will undoubtedly be placed at a disadvantage. Because of their playing status, their physical conditioning may suffer. For this reason, all the athletes are encouraged to run on their own. If certain athletes are having problems, then special times can be assigned for them to come by and perform assigned running, treadmill, stair climber, or bike work. This suggestion also holds true for any injured athlete. If the injured athlete is not needed at practice, then practice time could be reserved for the athlete to engage in conditioning and weight training.

Table 6.1. Phase 5 – Week #31

Name: _____   Week #31   3rd Week of October

Comment: :55 b/s B exercises, :45 sec b/s S exercises, NO TIME b/s C exercises, 1:00 b/ exercises

Resistance Training

Monday:

B) Flat dumbbell press	6 x 80	6 x 80
B) Close-grip lat	8 x 75	8 x 75
B) Dumbbell pull press	8 x 75	8 x 75
S) Split dumbbell pullover	10 x 70	10 x 70
S) Hamstring on balance ball	15 x —	15 x —
S) Power Skip	10 x —	10 x —
S) Donkey kicks	20 x —	20 x —
Dunk with medicine ball	8 x —	8 x —
Cylinder Circuit #3	30 x —	—

Wednesday:

B) Incline dumbbell press	8 x 75	8 x 75
S) High lat rear	8 x 70	8 x 70
B) Medicine ball underhand backward throw	10 x —	10 x —
S) Roll-out	10 x —	10 x —
S) Squat-press	8 x 70	8 x 70
S) Step-up, side dumbbell raise	8 x 70	8 x 70
S) Hamstring on balance ball	12 x —	12 x —
Cylinder Circuit #5	30 x —	—

Friday:

Circuit All   1 x

C) Ham decline	10 x 70
C) High lat rear	10 x 70
C) Dumbbell snatch	10 x 70
C) One-arm dumbbell row	10 x 70
C) Shoulder fly	10 x 70
C) Free-weight upright row	10 x 70
C) Two-arm dumbbell press (seated)	10 x 70
C) Rear deltoid swim	20 x —
C) One-leg press	15 x 60
C) Backward lunge	20 x —
Cylinder Circuit #6	30 x —

Conditioning Training

Monday: (POST PRACTICE)

1) 2 x Double court ladder
Rest 2:05 b/s

1&2	3&4	5	
1:04	1:06	1:08	(313 yds)
			626 yds.

Wednesday: (POST PRACTICE)

1) 2 x 10 court crosses
Rest 1:55 b/s

:58	:59	1:00	
			(313 yds)
			626 yds.

Table 6.2. Phase 5 – Week #32

Week #32   4th Week of October

Comment: 55 b/s B exercises, :45 sec b/s S exercises, NO TIME b/s C exercises, 1:00 b/ exercises

Resistance Training

Monday:

B) Flat dumbbell press	6 x 80	6 x 80
B) Close-grip lat	8 x 75	8 x 75
B) Dumbbell pull press	8 x 75	8 x 75
S) Split dumbbell pullover	10 x 70	10 x 70
S) Hip flex	15 x __	15 x __
S) Power Skip	10 x __	10 x __
S) Donkey kicks	20 x __	20 x __
Dunk with medicine ball	8 x __	8 x __
Cylinder Circuit #3	30 x __	

Wednesday:

B) Incline dumbbell press	8 x 75	8 x 75
S) High lat rear	8 x 70	8 x 70
B) Medicine ball underhand backward throw	10 x __	10 x __
S) Roll-out	10 x __	10 x __
S) Squat-press	8 x 70	8 x 70
S) Step-up, side dumbbell raise	8 x 70	8 x 70
S) Hamstring on balance ball	12 x __	12 x __
Cylinder Circuit #5	30 x __	

Friday:

Circuit All,	1 x
C) Ham decline	10 x 70
C) High lat rear	10 x 70
C) Dumbbell snatch	10 x 70
C) One-arm dumbbell row	10 x 70
C) Shoulder fly	10 x 70
C) Free-weight upright row	10 x 70
C) Two-arm dumbbell press (seated)	10 x 70
C) Rear deltoid swim	20 x __
C) One-leg press	15 x 60
C) Two-leg curl	15 x 60
Cylinder Circuit #6	30 x __

Conditioning Training

Monday: (POST PRACTICE)

1) 3 x 12 Sideline crosses   :43   :44   :45   (200 yds)
Rest: 1:25 b/s   612 yds.

Wednesday: (POST PRACTICE)

1) 4 Section Fartlek   10:00

* Every Day (PRE PRACTICE)
Perform a pre-practice, static stretch warm-up routine. Also include some dynamic stretches to prepare for the dynamic activity of practice.

Table 6.3. Phase 5 – Week #33

Week #33

Week #33

1st Week of November

Name:

Comment: :55 b/s B exercises, :45 sec b/s S exercises, 1:00 b/ exercises

Resistance Training

Monday:
B) Bench press	6 x 80	6 x 80
B) Pull-up (w/ 10 lb vest)	max reps	max reps
B) Dumbbell hang clean	8 x 70	8 x 70
S) Straight dumbbell pullover	10 x 70	10 x 70
B) Squat	12 x 65	12 x 65
B) Side dumbbell raise, lunge	10 x 65	10 x 65
S) Two-leg curl	12 x 65	12 x 65
Drop Jumps	8 x ___	8 x ___
Cylinder Circuit #3	30 x ___	

Thursday:
B) Close incline press	8 x 70	8 x 75
S) Close low lat	8 x 70	8 x 75
B) Two-arm dumbbell press (seated)	8 x 70	8 x 75
B) Free-weight upright row	8 x 70	8 x 75
S) Roll-out	10 x ___	10 x ___
B) Squat-press	8 x 70	8 x 70
S) Alternating leg lunge	10 x ___	10 x ___
Jump Rope	200 turns	
Cylinder Circuit #4	30 x ___	

Saturday: Game #1

Conditioning Training

Monday: (POST PRACTICE)

1) 2 x 10 court crosses	:58	:59	(313 yds)
Rest 1:55 b/s		1:00	
2) 1 x 2 court crosses	:09	:09	(62 yds)
Rest :25b/s		:10	
			682 yds.

Table 6.4. Phase 5 – Week #34

Name:

Week #34

2nd Week of November

Comment: .55 b/s B exercises, :45 sec b/s S exercises, NO TIME b/s C exercises, 1:00 b/ exercises

Resistance Training			Conditioning Training			

Conditioning Training

Monday: (POST PRACTICE)

	1&2	3&4	5
1) 2 x 6, 50 yard crosses	:56	:57	:58	(300 yds)
Rest: 1:55 b/s			
2) 1 x 4, 50 yard crosses	:35	:36	:37	(200 yds)
Rest 1:00 b/s			
				800 yds.

Resistance Training

Monday:

B) Bench press	6 x 80	6 x 80
B) Pull-up (w/ 10 lb vest)	max reps	max reps
B) Dumbbell hang clean	8 x 70	8 x 75
S) Straight dumbbell pullover	10 x 70	10 x 70
B) Squat	12 x 65	12 x 65
B) Side dumbbell raise, lunge	10 x 65	10 x 65
S) Two-leg curl	12 x 65	12 x 65
Drop Jumps	8 x ___	8 x ___
Cylinder Circuit #3	30 x ___	

Thursday: Game #2

Friday:

Circuit All,	
C) Incline bench press	1 x
C) Two-arm dumbbell row	10 x 70
C) Dips	10 x 70
C) Military press	max reps
C) Split dumbbell pullover	10 x 70
C) Cable upright row	10 x 70
C) Two-arm dumbbell press (seated)	10 x 70
C) Rear deltoid swim	20 x ___
C) Preacher curl	10 x 70
C) Reverse dip	10 x 70
C) Two-leg press	10 x 80
S) Single leg hops	30 x ___
Cylinder Circuit #4	30 x ___

Table 6.5. Phase 5 – Week #35

Name: _____   Week #35   3rd Week of November

Comment: :55 b/s B exercises, :45 sec b/s S exercises, NO TIME b/s C exercises, 1:00 b/ exercises

Resistance Training

Monday: (POST PRACTICE)

B) Bench press	6 x 80	6 x 80
B) Close-grip lat	8 x 70	8 x 75
B) Dumbbell push press	6 x 75	6 x 80
B) Free-weight upright row	8 x 70	8 x 75
S) Alternating dumbbell curl	8 x 70	8 x 75
S) Triceps push-down	8 x 70	8 x 75
Jump Rope	200 turns	
Jump Ups	8 x ___	8 x ___
B) Squat	10 x 70	10 x 70
Cylinder Circuit #5	30 x ___	

Wednesday:

Circuit All	1 x
C) Incline bench press	10 x 70
C) Two-arm dumbbell row	10 x 70
C) Dips	max reps
C) Military press	10 x 70
C) Split dumbbell pullover	10 x 70
C) Cable upright row	10 x 70
C) Two-arm dumbbell press (seated)	10 x 70
C) Manual rear deltoid	10 x ___
C) Preacher curl	10 x 70
C) Reverse dip	10 x 70
C) Two-leg press	10 x 80
S) Single leg hops	30 x ___
Cylinder Circuit #6	30 x ___

Saturday: Game #3

Conditioning Training

	1&2	3&4	5	
1) 2 x 6 court crosses	:32	:33	:34	(186 yds)
Rest 1:00 b/s				
2) 2 x 4 court crosses	:22	:23	:24	(124 yds)
Rest :40 b/s				
3) 3 x 2 court crosses	:08	:08	:09	(62 yds)
Rest :25 b/s				806 yds.

Table 6.6. Phase 5 – Week #36

Name: Week #36   4th Week of November

Comment: :55 b/s B exercises, :45 sec b/s S exercises, NO TIME b/s C exercises, 1:00 b/ exercises

Resistance Training			
Monday:			
B) Bench press	6 x 80	6 x 80	
B) Close-grip lat	8 x 70	8 x 75	
B) Dumbbell push press	6 x 75	6 x 80	
B) Free-weight upright row	8 x 70	8 x 75	
S) Manual shrug	20 x ___	20 x ___	
S) Alternating dumbbell curl	8 x 70	8 x 75	
S) Triceps push-down	8 x 70	8 x 75	
Jump Rope	200 turns		
Jump Ups	8 x ___	8 x ___	
B) Squat	10 x 70	10 x 70	
Cylinder Circuit #5	30 x ___		

Thursday:	
Circuit All	1 x
C) Push-up	15 x ___
C) High lat rear	10 x 70
C) Zigzag push-up	10 x 70
C) One-arm dumbbell row	10 x 70
C) Medicine ball circuit	10 x each exercise
C) Bar Shrug	20 x 65
C) Two-arm dumbbell press (seated)	10 x 70
C) Manual rear deltoid	10 x ___
C) One-leg press	15 x 60
C) Backward lunge	20 x ___
Cylinder Circuit #6	30 x ___

Saturday: Game #4

Conditioning Training

Monday: (POST PRACTICE)

1) 3 x 6, 50 yard crosses	1&2	3&4	5	(300 yds)
Rest **1:55 b/s**	:56	:57	:58	900 yds.

Table 6.7. Phase 5 – Week #37

Week #37

1st Week of December

Name:

Comment: :55 b/s B exercises, :45 sec b/s S exercises, NO TIME b/s C exercises, 1:00 b/ exercises

Resistance Training

Conditioning Training

Tuesday: Game #5

Thursday:
B) Bench press	10 x 70	5 x 85	12 x 70
B) Close-grip lat	10 x 70	5 x 85	12 x 70
B) Behind neck press	10 x 70	5 x 85	12 x 70
S) Manual shrug	20 x ___	20 x ___	70
B) Dumbbell squat	10 x 70	10 x 70	
S) Straight dumbbell pullover	10 x 70	10 x 70	
S) One-leg extension	10 x 70	10 x 70	
S) Two-leg curl	10 x 70	10 x 70	
Cylinder Circuit #3	30 x ___		

Friday: Game #6

Saturday: Game #7

Monday: (POST PRACTICE)

	1&2	3&4	5
1) 20 x 2 court crosses	:09	:09	:10
Rest :20 b/s			(62 yds)
			1240 yds.

Table 6.8. Phase 5 – Week #38

Name:

Week #38

2 nd Week of December

2nd Week of December

Comment: :55 b/s B exercises, :45 sec b/s S exercises, NO TIME b/s C exercises, 1:00 b/ exercises

Resistance Training	Conditioning Training

Monday:
B) Incline bench press	6 x 80 6 x 80
B) Close-grip lat	8 x 70 8 x 75
B) Clean and jerk (light)	8 x 70 8 x 70
S) Side lunge, shoulder fly	10 x 65 10 x 65
S) EZ-bar curl	8 x 70 8 x 75
B) Dumbbell french press	8 x 70 8 x 75
B) Squat	8 x 70 8 x 75
S) One stiff leg dead	10 x __ 10 x __
S) Donkey kicks	20 x __ 20 x __
Cylinder Circuit #3	30 x __

Tuesday:
Circuit All	1 x
C) Dips	max reps
C) High lat front	10 x 70
C) Ham 10 chest	10 x 70
C) Close low lat	10 x 70
C) Smith Military	10 x 70
C) Backward lunge, dumbbell upright row 10 x 70	
C) Two-arm dumbbell press (seated)	10 x 70
S) Manual shrug	20 x __
C) Roll-out	10 x __
C) Baby squat	1.5 minutes
C) Two-leg curl	15 x 60
Cylinder Circuit #4	30 x __

Thursday:

Game #8

Friday:
Circuit All	1 x
C) Push-up	15 x __
C) High lat rear	10 x 70
C) Zigzag push-up	10 x __
C) One-arm dumbbell row	10 x 70
C) Medicine ball circuit	10 x each exercise
C) Bar Shrug	20 x 65
C) Two-arm dumbbell press (seated)	10 x 70
C) Rear deltoid swim	20 x __
C) One-leg press	15 x 60
O) Backward lunge	20 x __
Cylinder Circuit #5	30 x __

Table 6.9. Phase 5 – Week #39

Name: _____   Week #39   3rd Week of December

Comment: :55 b/s B exercises, :45 sec b/s S exercises, NO TIME b/s C exercises, 1:00 b/ exercises

Resistance Training	Conditioning Training

Monday:
B) Flat dumbbell press	6 x 80	6 x 80
B) Close-grip lat	8 x 75	8 x 75
B) Dumbbell pull press	8 x 75	8 x 75
S) Split dumbbell pullover	10 x 70	10 x 70
S) Hip flex	15 x ___	15 x ___
S) Power Skip	10 x ___	10 x ___
S) Donkey kicks	20 x ___	20 x ___
B) Dunk with medicine ball	10 x ___	10 x ___
Cylinder Circuit #3	30 x ___	

Tuesday:
B) Incline dumbbell press	8 x 75	8 x 75
S) High lat rear	8 x 70	8 x 70
B) Dumbbell pull press	8 x 70	8 x 70
S) Roll-out	10 x ___	10 x ___
S) Box squat	15 x ___	15 x ___
S) Slideboard	2 x 30 crosses	
Cylinder Circuit #4	30 x ___	

Thursday:
Circuit All	
C) Ham decline	1 x
C) High lat rear	10 x 70
C) Moon push-up	10 x 70
C) Close high lat	15 x ___
C) Shoulder fly	10 x 70
C) Free-weight upright row	10 x 70
C) Two-arm dumbbell press (seated)	10 x 70
C) Rear deltoid swim	10 x 70
C) One-leg press	20 x ___
C) One-leg curl	15 x 60
Cylinder Circuit #5	15 x 60
	30 x ___

Saturday: Game #9

Table 6.10. Phase 5 – Week #40

Name: Week #40 4th Week of December

Comment: :55 b/s B exercises, :45 sec b/s S exercises, NO TIME b/s C exercises, 1:00 b/ exercises

Resistance Training	Conditioning Training

Monday:
B) Incline bench press 6 x 80 6 x 80
B) Close-grip lat 8 x 70 8 x 75
B) Clean and jerk (light) 8 x 70 8 x 70
S) Side lunge, shoulder fly 10 x 65 10 x 65
S) EZ-bar curl 8 x 70 8 x 75
B) Dumbbell french press 8 x 70 8 x 75
B) Squat 8 x 70 8 x 75
S) One stiff leg dead 10 x __ 10 x __
S) Donkey kicks 20 x __ 20 x __
Cylinder Circuit #4 30 x __

Tuesday:
Circuit All 1 x
C) Dips max reps
C) High lat front 10 x 70
C) Ham 10 chest 10 x 70
C) Close low lat 10 x 70
C) Smith Military 10 x 70
C) Backward lunge, dumbbell upright row 10 x 70 10 x 70
C) Two-arm dumbbell press (seated) 10 x __
C) Roll-out 1.5 minutes
C) Baby squat 15 x 60
C) One-leg curl 30 x __
Cylinder Circuit #5

Thursday: Game #10

Friday:
Circuit All 1 x
C) Smith incline press 10 x 70
C) High lat rear 10 x 70
C) Zigzag push-up 10 x __
C) Close high lat 10 x 70
C) Medicine ball circuit 10 x each exercise
C) Bar Shrug 20 x 65
C) Two-arm dumbbell press (seated) 10 x 70
C) Manual rear deltoid 10 x __
C) One-leg press 15 x 60
C) Side lunge 15 x 60
Cylinder Circuit #6 30 x __

Table 6.11. Phase 5 – Week #41

Name: Week #41   1st Week of January

Comment: :55 b/s B exercises, :45 sec b/s S exercises, NO TIME b/s C exercises, 1:00 b/ exercises

Resistance Training		Conditioning Training

Monday:
Circuit All
○ Dips   1 x
                                                                max reps
○ High lat front   10 x 70
○ Ham 10 chest   10 x 70
○ Close low lat   10 x 70
○ Smith military   10 x 70
○ Backward lunge, dumbbell upright row 10 x 70
○ Two-arm dumbbell press (seated)   10 x 70
○ Roll-out   10 x __
○ Baby squat   1.5 minutes
○ Hamstring on balance ball   10 x __
Cylinder Circuit #5   30 x __

Wednesday: Game #11

Thursday:
Circuit All
○ Ham decline   1 x
○ High lat rear   10 x 70
○ Moon push-up   10 x 70
○ Close high lat   15 x __
○ Shoulder fly   10 x 70
○ Free-weight upright row   10 x 70
○ Two-arm dumbbell press (seated)   10 x 70
○ Manual rear deltoid   10 x 70
○ One-leg press   10 x __
○ Two-leg curl   15 x 60
Cylinder Circuit #6   15 x 60
                                                                30 x __

Saturday: Game #12

Table 6.12. Phase 5 – Week #42

Name: Week #42   2nd Week of January

Comment: :55 b/s B exercises, :45 sec b/s S exercises, NO TIME b/s C exercises, 1:00 b/ exercises

Resistance Training	Conditioning Training

Monday:
Circuit All,
C) Smith incline press — 1 x
C) High lat rear — 10 x 70
C) Zigzag push-up — 10 x 70
C) Close high lat — 10 x —
C) Manual side raise — 10 x 70
C) Manual upright row — 10 x —
C) Two-arm dumbbell press (seated) — 10 x 70
C) Rear deltoid swim — 20 x 70
C) One-leg press — 15 x 60
C) Hamstring on balance ball — 10 x —
Cylinder Circuit #5 — 30 x —

Wednesday: Game #13

Thursday:
Circuit All
C) Incline dumbbell press — 1 x
C) Close high lat — 15 x 65
C) Incline dumbbell fly — 10 x 70
C) High lat front — 12 x 65
C) Behind neck press — 10 x 70
C) Cable upright row — 15 x 65
C) Alternating dumbbell press — 12 x 70
Dumbbell shrug — 10 x 70
C) Shoulder fly — 25 x 70
C) Rear deltoid swim — 10 x 70
C) Box squat — 20 x —
C) Donkey kicks — 15 x —
Cylinder Circuit #6 — 20 x —
— 30 x —

Saturday: Game #14

Table 6.13. Phase 5 – Week #43

Name: _____   Week #43   3rd Week of January

Comment: :55 b/s B exercises, :45 sec b/s S exercises, NO TIME b/s C exercises, 1:00 b/ exercises

Resistance Training	Conditioning Training

Monday:
B) Bench press — 10 x 70   6 x 80   5 x 90
B) Pull-up — max reps
B) Close-grip lat — 8 x 75   6 x 85
B) Dunk with medicine ball — 8 x ___   8 x ___
B) Medicine ball underhand backward throw — 10 x ___   10 x ___
S) Straight dumbbell pullover — 10 x 70   10 x 70
B) EZ-bar curl — 8 x 75   6 x 85
S) Close grip push-up — 15 x ___   15 x ___
S) Step-up, shoulder fly — 8 x 70   8 x 70
S) Slideboard — 2 x 30 crosses
Cylinder Circuit #5 — 30 x ___

Wednesday: Game #15

Thursday:
Circuit All
C) Incline dumbbell press — 1 x
C) Close high lat — 15 x 65
C) Incline dumbbell fly — 10 x 70
C) High lat front — 12 x 65
C) Behind neck press — 10 x 70
C) Cable upright row — 15 x 65
C) Alternating dumbbell press — 12 x 70
                                 10 x 70
C) Dumbbell shrug — 25 x 70
C) Shoulder fly — 10 x 70
C) Rear deltoid swim — 20 x ___
C) Jump Rope — 200 turns
C) Jump Ups — 15 x ___
Cylinder Circuit #6 — 30 x ___

Saturday: Game #16

Table 6.14. Phase 5 – Week #44

Name: _____

Week #44   4th Week of January

Comment: :55 b/s B exercises, :45 sec b/s S exercises, NO TIME b/s C exercises, 1:00 b/ exercises

Resistance Training   Conditioning Training

Monday:
B) Bench press   10 x 70   6 x 80   5 x 90
B) Pull-up   max reps
B) Close-grip lat   8 x 75   6 x 85
B) Dunk with medicine ball   8 x __   8 x __
B) Medicine ball underhand backward throw   10 x __   10 x __
S) Straight dumbbell pullover   10 x 70   10 x 70
B) EZ-bar curl   8 x 75   6 x 85
S) Two-arm dumbbell triceps extension   8 x 75   8 x 75
B) Two-leg press   10 x 70   6 x 80   5 x 90
S) Slideboard   2 x 30 crosses
Cylinder Circuit #4   30 x __

Wednesday: Game #17

Thursday:
Circuit All   1 x
C) Incline dumbbell press   15 x 65
C) Close high lat   10 x 70
C) Incline dumbbell fly   12 x 65
C) High lat front   10 x 70
C) Behind neck press   15 x 65
C) Cable upright row   12 x 70
C) Alternating dumbbell press   10 x 70
C) Dumbbell shrug   25 x 70
C) Shoulder fly   10 x 70
C) Rear deltoid swim   20 x __
C) Jump Rope   200 turns
S) Dumbbell stroll (w/ 50 lb DB's)   50 yds
Cylinder Circuit #5   30 x __

Saturday: Game #18

Table 6.15. Phase 5 – Week #45

Name:

Week #45

1st Week of February

Comment: :55 b/s B exercises, :45 sec b/s S exercises, NO TIME b/s C exercises, 1:00 b/ exercises

Resistance Training		Conditioning Training

Monday:
Circuit All,   1 x
C) Push-up   15 x __
C) High lat rear   10 x 70
C) Zigzag push-up   10 x 70
C) Close low lat   10 x 70
C) Manual side raise   10 x __
C) Manual upright row   10 x 70
C) Two-arm dumbbell press (seated)   20 x 60
C) Rear deltoid swim   15 x 60
C) One-leg extension   15 x 60
C) Two-leg curl   30 x __
Cylinder Circuit #4

Wednesday:
Circuit All   1 x
C) Ham decline   8 x 75
C) Close-grip lat   8 x 75
C) Hands on balance ball push-up   15 x __
C) Close high lat   10 x 70
C) Shoulder fly   10 x 70
C) Free-weight upright row   10 x 70
C) Dumbbell push press   8 x 75
C) Rear deltoid swim   20 x __
C) One-leg press   15 x 60
C) Two-leg curl   15 x 60
Cylinder Circuit #5   30 x __

Thursday: Game #19

Saturday: Game #20

Table 6.16. Phase 5 – Week #46

Name: _____

Week #46

2nd Week of February

Comment: :55 b/s B exercises, :45 sec b/s S exercises, NO TIME b/s C exercises, 1:00 b/ exercises

Resistance Training	Conditioning Training

Tuesday:

Game #2 1

Wednesday:

B) Flat dumbbell press	6 x 80	6 x 80
B) Close-grip lat	8 x 75	8 x 75
B) Dumbbell pull press	8 x 75	8 x 75
S) Split dumbbell pullover	10 x 70	10 x 70
S) Hip flex	15 x ___	15 x ___
S) Power Skip	10 x ___	10 x ___
S) Donkey kicks	20 x ___	20 x ___
B) Dunk with medicine ball	10 x ___	10 x ___
Cylinder Circuit #4	30 x ___	

Friday:

Circuit All	
C) Incline dumbbell press	1 x ___
C) Close high lat	15 x 65
C) Incline dumbbell fly	10 x 70
C) High lat front	12 x 65
C) Behind neck press	10 x 70
C) Cable upright row	15 x 65
C) Alternating dumbbell press	12 x 70
C) Dumbbell shrug	10 x 70
C) Shoulder fly	25 x 70
C) Rear deltoid swim	10 x 70
C) Jump Rope	20 x ___
S) Dumbbell stroll (w/ 50 lb DB's)	200 turns
	50 yds
Cylinder Circuit #5	30 x ___

Table 6.17. Phase 5 – Week #47

Name: _____   Week #47   3rd Week of February

Comment: :55 b/s B exercises, :45 sec b/s S exercises, NO TIME b/s C exercises, 1:00 b/ exercises

Resistance Training	Conditioning Training

Sunday:

Game #2 2

Monday:

B) Incline bench press	6 x 80	6 x 80
B) Close-grip lat	8 x 70	8 x 75
B) Clean and jerk (light)	8 x 70	8 x 70
S) Side dumbbell raise, lunge	10 x 65	10 x 65
S) EZ-bar curl	8 x 70	8 x 75
S) Shooters french press	8 x 70	8 x 75
S) Around the world legs	1 x around the basketball court	
S) Donkey kicks	20 x ___	20 x ___
Cylinder Circuit #5	30 x ___	

Thursday:

Game #2 3

Friday:

Circuit All	1 x
C) Feet on balance ball, push-up	15 x ___
C) High lat rear	10 x 70
C) Zigzag push-up	10 x ___
C) Close high lat	10 x 70
C) Bent dumbbell raise	10 x 65
C) Crabbing	The length of the basketball court
C) Two-arm dumbbell press (seated)	10 x 70
C) Rear deltoid swim	20 x ___
C) One-leg press	15 x 60
C) Two-leg curl	15 x 60
Cylinder Circuit #6	30 x ___

Table 6.18. Phase 5 – Week #48

Name:

Week #48   4th Week of February

Comment: :55 b/s B exercises, :45 sec b/s S exercises, NO TIME b/s C exercises, 1:00 b/ exercises

Resistance Training	Conditioning Training

Sunday:

Game #2 4

Monday:
B) Incline bench press	6 x 80 6 x 80
B) Close-grip lat	8 x 70 8 x 75
B) Clean and jerk (light)	8 x 70 8 x 70
S) Side dumbbell raise, lunge	10 x 65 10 x 65
S) EZ-bar curl	8 x 70 8 x 75
S) Two-arm dumbbell triceps extension	8 x 75 8 x 75
S) Around the world legs	1 x around the basketball court
S) Donkey kicks	20 x — 20 x —
Cylinder Circuit #3	30 x —

Thursday:
Circuit All	1 x
C) Smith close incline press	10 x 70
C) Pull-up	max reps
C) Flat dumbbell fly	10 x 75
C) Roll-out	15 x —
C) Bent dumbbell raise	10 x 65
C) Crabbing	The length of the basketball court
C) Dumbbell push press	10 x 70
C) Rear deltoid swim	20 x —
S) Single leg hops	40 x —
S) Two-leg curl	15 x 60
Cylinder Circuit #5	30 x —

Saturday:

Game #25

Table 6.19. Phase 5 – Week #49

Week #49

Name:

Comment: :55 b/s B exercises, :45 sec b/s S exercises, NO TIME b/s C exercises, 1:00 b/ exercises

Resistance Training		Conditioning Training	1st Week of March

Monday:
B) Bench press   10 x 70   6 x 80   5 x 90
B) Pull-up   max reps
B) Close-grip lat   8 x 75   6 x 85
B) Dunk with medicine ball   8 x __   8 x __
B) Medicine ball underhand backward throw   10 x __   10 x __
S) Straight dumbbell pullover   10 x 70 10 x 70
B) EZ-bar curl   8 x 75   6 x 85
S) Close grip push-up   15 x __   15 x __
B) Two-leg press   10 x 70 6 x 80   5 x 90
S) Slideboard   2 x 30 crosses
Cylinder Circuit #3   30 x __

Tuesday: Game #2 6

Thursday:
Circuit All   1 x
C) Smith close incline press   10 x 70
C) High lat rear   10 x __
C) Flat dumbbell fly   10 x 75
C) Roll-out   15 x __
C) Manual side raise   10 x __
B) Dumbbell squat, two-arm dumbbell press 10 x 70
C) Rear deltoid swim   20 x __
S) Single leg hops   40 x __
C) Two-leg curl   15 x 60
Cylinder Circuit #5   30 x __

Saturday: Game #2 7

Table 6.20. Phase 5 – Week #50

Name:

Week #50   2nd Week of March

Comment: :55 b/s B exercises, :45 sec b/s S exercises, NO TIME b/s C exercises, 1:00 b/ exercises

Resistance Training   **Conditioning Training**

Monday:
Circuit All   2 x
C) Ham decline   10 x 70   10 x 70
C) High lat rear   10 x 70   10 x 70
C) Hands on balance ball push-up   15 x __   15 x __
C) Close high lat   10 x 70   10 x 70
C) Shoulder fly   10 x 70   10 x 70
C) Free-weight upright row   10 x 70   10 x 70
C) Two-arm dumbbell press (seated)   10 x 70   10 x 70
C) Rear deltoid swim   20 x __   20 x __
C) One-leg press   12 x 60   12 x 60
C) Two-leg curl   12 x 60   12 x 60
Cylinder Circuit #5   30 x __   __

Friday: Game #2 8

Saturday: Game #2 9

Table 6.21. Phase 5 – Week #51

Name:

Comment: :55 b/s B exercises, :45 sec b/s S exercises, NO TIME b/s C exercises, 1:00 b/ exercises

	Week #51	3rd Week of March
Resistance Training	Conditioning Training	

Sunday:

Game #30

Monday:

B) Incline bench press	6 x 80	6 x 80
B) Close-grip lat	8 x 70	8 x 75
B) Dumbbell upright row	8 x 70	8 x 70
S) Side dumbbell raise	10 x 65	10 x 65
S) EZ-bar curl	8 x 70	8 x 75
S) Shooters french press	8 x 70	8 x 75
B) Two-leg extension	15 x 70	
S) Side lunge	10 x —	
S) Donkey kicks	20 x —	
Cylinder Circuit #3	30 x —	

Thursday:

Circuit All	1 x
C) Feet on balance ball, push-up	15 x __
C) High lat rear	10 x 70
C) Zigzag push-up	10 x __
C) Close high lat	10 x 70
C) Manual side rais e	10 x __
B) Dumbbell squat, two-arm dumbbell press	10 x 70
C) Alternating dumbbell press (seated)	10 x 70
C) Rear deltoid swim	20 x __
C) One-leg press	12 x 60
C) Two-leg curl	12 x 60
Cylinder Circuit #4	30 x __

Saturday:

Game #31

Table 6.22. Phase 5 – Week #52

Name:

Week #52   4th Week of March

Comment: :55 b/s B exercises, :45 sec b/s S exercises, NO TIME b/s C exercises, 1:00 b/ exercises

Resistance Training	Conditioning Training

Sunday: Game #32

Monday:
B) Incline bench press   6 x 80   6 x 80
B) Close-grip lat   8 x 70   8 x 75
B) Dumbbell upright row   8 x 70   8 x 70
S) Side dumbbell raise   10 x 65 10 x 65
S) EZ-bar curl   8 x 70   8 x 75
S) Shooters french press   8 x 70   8 x 75
B) Two-leg extension   15 x 70
S) Side lunge   10 x —
S) Donkey kicks   20 x —
Cylinder Circuit #5   30 x —

Thursday:
Circuit All   1 x
C) Push-up   15 x 70
C) High lat rear   10 x 70
C) Zigzag push-up   10 x 70
C) Close high lat   10 x 70
C) Manual side raise   10 x 70
B) Dumbbell squat, two-arm dumbbell press   10 x 70
C) Alternating dumbbell press (seated)   10 x 70
C) Rear deltoid swim   20 x 60
C) One-leg press   12 x 60
C) Two-leg curl   12 x 60
Cylinder Circuit #6   30 x —

Saturday: Game #33

Conditioning Exercises and Drills

The exercises and drills contained within the 52-week basketball training program presented in Part 2 were selected to enable individuals to increase their muscular strength, cardiorespiratory conditioning, and functional ability as it pertains to playing basketball. The resistance exercises were chosen to provide these athletes with increases in strength and power, as well as sensible increases in muscle size. No muscle group is left out. The highest integrity of strength between muscle groups is obtained, thus lowering the potential for injury. By combining variations in repetitions, sets, and intensities, resistance exercises ensure that the entire spectrum of muscle fiber types is addressed.

The conditioning exercises that are recommended in this Part of the text are designed to help players achieve a strong foundation of cardiorespiratory fitness. The conditioning exercises included in the year-round, 52-week basketball training program attempt, as often as possible, to simulate physical demands and motor skills involved in a typical basketball game. Composed of anaerobic and aerobic exercises, the conditioning program assists individuals in bridging the gap between times when bursts of explosive speed are required, and other times when play might continue up and down the court for many transitions.

The incorporation of power, functional, and agility exercises round off the entire exercise selection. These exercises are designed to assist the athlete in moving from having a basic level of strength and conditioning to a point where he is prepared and able to use his physical ability to play basketball at his fullest potential.

Flexibility Exercises

Flexibility training is often the most overlooked and underemphasized component of a physical conditioning program. Many athletes are aware of the need for having an improved level of flexibility, but have a difficult time making time for flexibility training in their fitness programs. Flexibility training is often underapplied because of the difficulties athletes and coaches have in setting flexibility-related goals, and measuring any newly acquired increases in range of motion.

Flexibility is critical in all sports activities. Often, athletes can find themselves in unsafe positions during the course of competition. If the athletes' muscles and connective tissues lack pliability, they are more likely to be injured. Preventing injury should be the primary objective of any coach or athlete involved in a sport. Therefore, flexibility training must be considered a primary part of the conditioning program, rather than an occasional activity that is just undertaken before practice.

In order to understand the importance of a regular flexibility program, consider how having a lack of flexibility can negatively affect the act of performing a vertical jump. As a basketball player, you are probably highly concerned with improving your vertical jumping ability. In order to improve this skill, it is very important to have good muscular strength and flexibility in all your muscles, particularly those in your hips and legs.

Consider then the primary muscle group that helps you create lift from the ground when jumping – the quadriceps. The four muscles of the quadriceps are responsible for extending your leg to a full and straight position. The quadriceps group is the large muscular area that extends from just above your knee to your hip in the front portion of your leg. The faster and more forceful your quadriceps can straighten your leg during a jumping motion, the higher you will go. However, the hamstring group, located on the rear of your upper leg, can interfere with the speed of contraction of the quadriceps. The primary action of the hamstring group is to bend the knee by pulling the heel toward the buttocks. If your hamstrings are inflexible, then they will slow the speed of your jumping movement by inadvertently trying to keep your knee in a somewhat bent position, thus minimizing your jumping ability. In other words, the strength in one muscle group can depend on how flexible you are in another.

Figure 7.1.
The faster and more force-
fully your quadriceps can
straighten your leg during a
jumping motion, the higher
you will go.

Factors That Limit Flexibility

Range of motion can be limited by several psychological, as well as physiological, factors. The psychological issues that threaten your flexibility are far more difficult to isolate and discuss within the scope of this text. However, your ability to control the levels of stress in your lives can play a large role in how successful your flexibility training will be. Whether your stress is physical, environmental, emotional, or mental, ultimately it will affect your ability to relax your muscles and therefore, receive the full benefit from your flexibility training.

Physically, your connective tissue is the primary structure that limits your range of motion. Fascia, ligaments, joint capsules, and tendons are the most inflexible of the tissues targeted during flexibility training. The connective tissues are composed of a dense network of semi-rigid fibers composed primarily of collagen. The connective tissues are structured, as such, to protect your joints from dislocating and preventing your muscles from being disconnected from your bones.

Even though they are more pliable than your connective tissues, your muscles also limit your range of motion. Your muscles continually battle the forces of gravity. In trying to stand up to gravity, your muscles perform only as they know how (i.e., to continually contract and to make major and minor adjustments in your posture and balance). These efforts often leave your muscles fatigued, injured, and most certainly shortened.

Each of these tissues can be successfully lengthened to some degree. Muscle of course can be lengthened much more than connective tissues. However, if a flexibility routine is performed consistently and sensibly over an extended period of time, even the connective tissue can undergo a mild remodeling.

Physical and Psychological Dimensions of Pain

Pain is always lurking on the fringes of your physical efforts. If you go too far, it rushes up to remind you to stay back. Although seemingly of a pure physical origin, pain can be psychologically intensified, making it all the more unbearable. Pain is a definite deterrent keeping you from performing physical exercise that challenges you to exceed your limits. No marathoner has ever trained for a race without having to run with pain. No weight lifter has set a new personal best with out having to face and deal with pain.

One of the largest drawbacks in performing flexibility training is the pain involved. Your muscles have gone through a lifetime of hardening and shortening. You cannot expect to create a change in your muscle's current state without feeling some discomfort. Despite the pain, however, there are rewards for your sometimes painful efforts to improve your level of flexibility. As with any physical exercise, what is important in dealing with pain while stretching is to know your body and to recognize which pain is destructive to your personal health.

Previously, stress was discussed as a limiting factor in muscle relaxation. As a point of fact, feeling pain is a stressful occurrence. As such, it is likely that if you feel discomfort, you are going to tense your muscles. In turn, tense muscles do not stretch as well as relaxed muscles. Therefore, when performing flexibility training, you need to find a way to minimize your pain as much as possible in order to relax and promote a more permanent state of flexibility.

The key to stretching successfully is to avoid pain. To ensure your safety, it is essential to never stretch through pain, but rather to stretch around it. For this reason, during the stretching session, it is important that you incorporate and utilize a variety of releasing methods.

Releasing Methods

Several techniques can be applied to help release yourself from whatever pain barriers you may encounter while stretching. Being able to relax your muscles is the key to reducing the pain of a stretching session. In this regard, your pain-releasing methods must begin with a warm-up.

Warming Up

Warming up is an essential part of any sound exercise format. In flexibility training, the warm-up is critical in increasing the extensibility of the muscles and connective tissues. It also results in an increase in the temperature of your muscles, which can have a positive impact on your stretching session. Because stretching is physically less demanding than an activity such as running, it may be best to choose some type of passive, warm-up method, rather than an active one.

Active warm-ups typically involve activities like jogging, skipping, or some type of callisthenic activity. Active warm-ups are good at warming up your body's muscles and connective tissues, but they are more critical in increasing your body's chemical and physiological functions, like heart rate, respiratory rate, and oxygen exchange. The major drawback of performing muscular action to warm the body up is that blood and other fluids move into the muscle, making the muscle more rigid. Also, the muscles become highly charged with nerve information, which can make them less likely to fully relax when stretched.

Passive warm-ups consist of activities that do not involve muscular effort to increase the body's temperature. Sitting in a hot tub of water or standing under a hot shower are examples of passive warm ups that are very effective. Placing warming pads on the areas to be stretched can also help to passively warm up the body. However, because the pads are localized, only selected sections of muscle can be heated at one time. Once you have gotten thoroughly warm, it is important to stay warm. Therefore, it is best to wear some type of loose-fitting, warm-up apparel, which does not bind as you stretch.

Proprioceptive Neuromuscular Facilitation

Another way to minimize pain while still increasing range of motion is through the application of proprioceptive neuromuscular facilitation (PNF). The PNF technique was originally developed by Herman Kabat, M.D. and his associates as a treatment for the pain and muscle shortening associated with neuromuscular ailments. The primary purpose of this technique is to help the muscle understand that it is safe to lengthen further when being stretched.

The muscles contain receptors called muscle spindles and Golgi tendon organelles (GTO). During stretching, the muscle's spindles communicate to the brain that the muscle is being lengthened, while the GTO senses tension at the musculotendon junction. The spindles react to being lengthened by sending a quick impulse to the spine, which in turn sends a message back to the muscles, causing them to contract. The GTO senses the tension caused by the stretch on the tendon and may call for additional muscle fiber contraction to avoid overstretching the tendon. This "knee jerk" reaction is called the stretch reflex.

Pain receptors also become involved at this point to prevent you from wanting to stretch further. Once the information from these stretch receptors reaches the brain, the brain examines the safety and condition of the muscle, and sends a return message that either allows the muscle to relax or keeps the muscle tight as a means of protection. PNF techniques attempt to override the hesitancy of the muscle spindles and Golgi organelles. PNF techniques communicate to the brain that the muscles are safe, and that the brain should send relaxation messages to the muscle rather than a contract message.

The PNF communications are performed by having the athlete either to contract his muscles before he attempts to stretch them or to contract an opposing muscle group. In other words, if you contract your hamstrings muscles, located on the back of your upper leg, then you can more easily stretch your hamstrings. This phenomenon is called irradiation. Also, the hamstrings stretch more easily, if prior to the stretch, you contract the quadriceps muscles, located in the front upper leg. This phenomenon is called Sherrington's Law of Reciprocal Enervation. These pre-stretch contractions send messages to the brain that compete with the information arriving from the muscle spindles and Golgi organelles. Therefore, the communications from the stretch receptors are somewhat inhibited, and the muscles are allowed to stretch even further.

PNF Relaxation Techniques

Contract–relax: This technique involves the stretched muscle being moved to a point of slight discomfort. The arm or leg can be moved into place by the athlete himself or by a partner. The athlete should then contract the opposing or antagonist muscle group for 10 seconds, then relax for 5 seconds. The athlete can then move the originally stretched muscle back into a stretch position and hold the stretch for 15 seconds. This exercise can be repeated two to three times on each selected muscle group.

Hold–relax: The hold-relax technique involves the stretched muscle being moved to a point of slight discomfort, similar to the contract-relax method. The arm or leg can be moved into place by the athlete or a partner, as before. The difference between this and the contract-relax method is that after the muscle is stretched, the athlete is instructed to isometrically contract the stretched muscle against an object or his partner. The athlete then holds that contraction for 10 seconds, then relaxes for 5 seconds. The athlete or partner can then move the muscle back into a stretched position and hold the stretch for 15 seconds. This exercise can be repeated two to three times on each selected muscle group.

Rocking During the Stretch

Another excellent method to release pain during the stretch is the use of subtle rocking motions. Rocking is a method every mother uses to ease her baby's discomfort and pain. If you have ever seen anyone in great pain, they often hug and rock themselves in order to reduce their discomfort. The motion of rocking creates a subtle contacting and relaxing of the muscle fibers. This contracting and relaxing mimics the action of the PNF technique, only the muscle contractions are less deliberate. Because motion is incorporated during this releasing technique, you might consider this to be dynamic, or ballistic stretching. These terms, however, are often attached to stretching movements with wider ranges of forceful motion, and undertaken by a more athletic population. Rocking is soft and subtle by comparison, and is, therefore, more usable by everyone who would like to incorporate some movement into their stretching routine.

Often, an athlete experiences muscle tightness and an early onset of pain at the beginning of a new stretching session. This muscle tightness and pain is disheartening to the athlete. Many athletes complain at the beginning of a stretching session that they are as tight as they were the last session. Often, the nervous system is reluctant to release its initial protective hold on the muscle tissue. The athlete can advance through the tightness pain more easily by subtly rocking through the stretching position. By placing the muscle in a pain-free position and then slowly introducing it to greater levels of tension, the muscle can better reach its fullest stretching potential for that stretching session.

An example of a stretch where rocking can be applied is during forward flexion exercises, where the athlete is sitting with his legs extended in front of him. The athlete leans forward from the waist, with his back completely straight through the spinal column. He then begins to gently rock from his left to right buttocks. If the athlete can lean forward enough to grab the back of his calves, he can then use the backs of his wrists or even his elbows as bumpers, rocking from buttock to buttock, allowing his elbows to touch the floor on either side of his outstretched legs. With each rocking motion, the athlete allows his legs to extend toward their full and locked-out position. The objective of this stretch is to stretch the hamstrings and lower back. This exercise, even though excellent for flexibility, should be approached with caution due to the high stress forward flexion places on the lower lumbar spine. Almost every stretching exercise can be rocked into with subtle movement of the hip, or by flexing and contracting opposing muscle groups.

Sensory Contrasting

Another technique to make your stretching easier is to send other sensory information to the brain that can compete with information arriving from the pain receptors. PNF techniques do this to some degree by sending information to the brain from the mechanical receptors and sensory receptors. This rush of competing information causes the clarity of the pain information to be dissolved. As a result, the pain is lessened. This situation is like having many crossed radio signals arriving to your radio at the same time, and you being unable to receive a clear sound.

While stretching, try rubbing your clothing against your skin or try rubbing your hands up and down the area being stretched. For example, if you are stretching your hamstrings by positioning your leg on an elevated bar or other stationary object, then try rubbing your hands lightly up and down your leg. If your pant legs are loose, you may just slide your pants back and forth across your skin. This light abrasion against your skin will send sensory information to compete with the pain information, and thus lessen your discomfort.

Some Practical Techniques to Avoid Painful Stretching

- Stretch one limb at a time: Any time you can stretch one leg or arm by itself, you will experience less pain. At the beginning of an exercise, this will help you to relax. If one hamstring is being stretched, some discomfort may occur. But if both hamstrings are being stretched you are going to experience the same discomfort, multiplied by two.

- Don't hold your breath: When you weight train, you may occasionally hold your breath to create stability. The stability is caused by the breath's tightening effect on your muscles. When stretching, you do not want to be tight. If you are tight, you are going to have pain. So to avoid pain, you must breath out as you move into the stretched position.

- Stay loose at the ends: Being relaxed is the biggest secret to pain-free stretching. As you stretch, be aware of your body. You may think you are relaxed, but if you really study yourself, you may find that you are tense in some place. Even now, as you sit reading this paragraph, some part of your body may not be relaxed. A method to help you relax is to always be able to wiggle your fingers and toes during the stretch. If you are tense, you will clinch your fingers and toes, and this tension will likely extend upward into your legs and arms.

- Start soft: When you first initiate your stretching routine, perform as many exercises as possible on a more forgiving surface. A thick gymnastics mat is a good place to start. After you become more flexible, you will want to move to progressively harder surfaces, and ultimately on to the surface on which you perform your sport. This progression is like that of resistance training. An analogy can be drawn between the hardest surfaces used when stretching and the heaviest weights used during resistance training. Your muscles will tense the most when you use a very heavy weight. Your muscle will also tense more when you are sitting on a hard surface. The surface you sit upon attempts to match the force pressing down upon it. A softer surface absorbs part of that force and allows your muscles to partially relax. The objective when stretching is to remain loose and relaxed. This is something you have to teach your body how to do, just like teaching your body to handle a heavier and heavier resistance. This step takes time. A soft-to-hard surface progression will help you to build flexibility.

- Stretch later in the day: As you move and work, you shift fluids in and out of the muscles and connective tissues. As the day nears its end, you have shifted a lot of your body fluids out and away from various intracellular structures. This shift in fluid occurs as a result of gravitational forces pulling the fluid out of the cells and natural losses of water through breathing and perspiring. This reduction in fluid in the cell spaces reduces tension in the body's tissues, thus making stretching easier. This factor is another reason passive warm-ups prove more beneficial when stretching. During muscular activity, blood rushes into the muscle. But as the blood enters, it makes the muscle tissues swell. This swelling makes the muscle fibers press against capillaries and arterioles that are responsible for removing the blood. Therefore, the blood cannot leave as fast as it enters. Athletes sometime refer to this phenomena as the pump. If a muscle is filled with fluid, it is harder to stretch. This pump can also occur if your stretching session lasts for too long.

- Stay hydrated. This may seem contradictory to what was just discussed, but to maximize your level of success in stretching, you must stay properly hydrated. Therefore, you must drink a lot of fluid and eat foods with natural juices. The muscles and their individual fibers have many layers of connective tissue between them. These tissues are not only responsible for keeping the muscles in their correct locations, but they also keep the muscles and fibers separated from one another. These connective tissues act as waterslides, upon which the fibers can surf cleanly back and forth without sticking. The fluid in the tissues helps to separate the fibers. If you are dehydrated, a greater chance exists for the muscle fiber to bind and stick. While, to a point, fluid around the cells makes stretching more difficult, you need fluid in the connective tissues. In reality, you are performing a balancing act. As such, you need to choose the best time of the day to exercise that insures you are getting the best of both situations. The critical aspect is where the fluid is located during the stretching session. Having the fluid slightly outside the cell, in the connective tissues, is better than having the inside of the cell filled with fluid.

- Apply mild traction: Traction is performed by pulling the arms or legs slightly away from the body. For example, mild traction is applied during stretching involving a bar. Dancers and gymnast use bars placed along the wall at different heights. When you stretch your hamstrings by using a bar, your leg is elevated off the ground. This positioning places your leg out and away from your body, while still allowing you to lean forward at the waist and stretch the hamstrings in the conventional manner. Another exercise where traction can be applied is during passive-partner stretching for the hamstring. In this exercise, your partner lies on his back on the floor, with one leg up to be stretched and with his other leg lying on the floor. You stand above him, grasping his ankle with both hands. You begin the exercise by pulling his leg straight upward, as if to put his foot flat on the ceiling above you. Then, begin pushing the leg toward your partner's face. You are essentially pulling the muscle in two directions at once. This action not only seems to reduce your level of pain, but also remarkably increases your range of motion. This phenomena probably occurs because the sensory, mechanical, and pain receptors are being asked to interpret the two actions taking place rather than one, thereby diffusing the intensity of both sets of information. There are also some structural deformations that are probably occurring in the muscle fibers and connective tissues that allow for greater mobility and relaxation.

How to Become More Flexible

Two types of tissue elongation or remodeling can occur as a result of flexibility training. Plastic elongation is the more permanent lengthening of tissue, while elastic elongation is the less permanent. For range of motion increases, it is best to promote plastic elongation by holding the stretch for longer periods and repeating the stretch more often during the stretching session. Many athletes have experienced an inability to maintain their range of motion. If they have mastered the aforementioned releasing techniques, and are still not experiencing increases in their ranges of motion, then it is most likely because they are not holding the stretch long enough to promote a plastic elongation of the muscle and connective tissue. Like overloading the body to increase strength and power during resistance training, overstretching must be included during flexibility training to make the body permanently more flexible. By holding the stretch a little longer, or by stretching a little farther each time, you will create a state of overstretching.

Plastic Elongation

Stretching techniques that promote plastic elongation are impractical as prepractice stretch routines because of the time required to make the stretching session effective. These methods of stretching, however, are a useful addition to an individual's stretching program if the athlete is having difficulty in improving his flexibility. This type of stretching, termed static because of the "stop-and-hold" style of the stretch, is particularly effective for muscle groups that are highly inflexible.

Stretching to promote plastic elongation is a relatively straightforward task. First, thoroughly warm up the muscle with about five minutes or so of gentle calisthenics or preferably 10 to 15 minutes of submersion in a hot bath. Choose two or three different exercises or postures that compliment one another by stretching the same body areas. The combination of exercises will create a series or a combined set of movements. Then to facilitate plastic elongation, choose an appropriate exercise and perform the stretch to a point of mild discomfort. Once you feel discomfort, you can choose to apply one or all of the releasing methods previously discussed. You can also choose to stop and then release the stretch. Repeat the stretch with your releasing methods of choice or total release about four times and move to another of your chosen exercises in the series. Repeat the process again for each of the next exercises.

This combining of exercises will help you address a wide range of muscle fibers in this targeted area. One exercise will usually address certain muscle fibers, but leave out others. Using one stretching exercise can facilitate the performance of another. You are, in a way, massaging and kneading the muscles and their individual fibers by placing them in a variety of slightly different positions. For this reason, performing exercises back and forth, in pairs, or in circuits, will aid in your ability to stretch effectively.

Continue through the series as many times as necessary until you feel you have reached a predetermined position in each stretch that has been established as your short-term goal for the session. Once you reach your goal and feel basically pain free, or at least very little discomfort, then breathe out and try holding the stretch for a count of 10 and then relax. Repeat the stretch again, and then breathe out and hold for 12 seconds. As you learn to relax in the held position, you can hold your breath longer. How long you should hold the stretched position is debatable. Eventually, these exercises could be held for minutes at a time, as long as you feel comfortable, and pain is at a minimum.

Some studies have suggested that performing four repetitions of an exercise held for 30 seconds will produce results that are just as good as performing more repetitions held for a longer time. However, these studies failed to address the question of whether these times and repetitions were best for establishing new flexibility goals or maintaining a range of motion already achieved. You will have to decide the times and repetitions that seem to provide you with the desired results. You can choose to repeat the process of stretching and holding at least four times, holding a little longer each time. If you begin to feel tightness when returning to the muscle's stretched position while exercising, or if the muscle begins to tremble while you are in a relaxed position, then end the stretching session and proceed to the your cool down routine. In this situation, cool the muscle with ice, or preferably sit in a cool tub of water for about 15 minutes to avoid excessive muscle soreness and to promote muscle repair.

At each added new level of the stretch, you will find yourself naturally tensing the muscle to protect it from any discomfort. When first trying to increase your level of flexibility, take 20 to 30 minutes to work through the series of stretches, teach your body to relax, and reduce your tendency to tense the muscle while stretching. Because of the time involved in this type of stretching, you may only be able to target one muscular area, like the hamstrings, lower back, or groin. However, remember that this is your problem area of the body and the purpose of this technique is to minimize your problems.

As you become more experienced and more easily relaxed, you may rely less on the releasing techniques and may be able to move more quickly to the stretch and holding portion of the stretching session. Because plastic elongation techniques are pushing into wider ranges of motion, and overstretching is occurring, you must allow sufficient time of recovery between plastic elongation sessions. As such, allow at least three to four days between sessions. When you first begin, you may only want to stretch using plastic elongation techniques once per week. As you become stronger and more resilient, you can reduce the time between the sessions. Any time you feel sore or uncomfortable, elect not to perform the more strenuous plastic elongation practices. Instead, skip the flexibility training for that day, or perform a less-demanding, elastic-elongation routine.

Elastic Elongation

Like the aforementioned technique, static stretching requires a "stop-and-hold" style of stretch. However, this type of stretch requires less time to perform, making the results of the exercises less permanent. The techniques and durations involved in plastic elongation stretching can create temporary muscle laxity and possible joint instability. Therefore, the less-demanding elastic stretch is better for prepractice warm-up routines, or anytime the athlete needs a quick warm-up stretch. Having the muscles become too loose as a result of the style of stretch may be dangerous during activities requiring quick changes of direction. The primary purpose of this type of stretch should be to serve as a maintenance technique, a means of reminding the muscle how far it can stretch as a result of performing the more permanent style of stretching.

Performing plastic-elongation stretches involves several steps. First, thoroughly warm up the muscle with about 5 to 10 minutes or so of gentle calisthenics or light activity, or until a light sweat begins to occur. Calisthenics are a better choice of warm-up of movement activities in this case, because you are most likely about to engage in some type of physical exercise after the stretching session, such as basketball practice. Choose one or two stretching exercises or postures for each major area of the body. This selection of exercises will help to loosen the body in preparation for more strenuous exercise. Choose one of the exercises and perform the stretch to a point of mild discomfort. Once you feel discomfort, then you can choose to apply one or more of the releasing methods previously discussed. You can also choose to stop and then release the stretch. Repeat the stretches with your chosen releasing methods or total release about two times. Then move to another of your chosen exercises in the series.

This style of stretching is also a static stretch. As a result, once you have completed the releasing methods and moved toward a suitable goal position for the exercise, you should hold the position for 6 to 10 seconds. Stretching to the point of discomfort can be your goal. Once you reach the point of discomfort, back off just slightly to relieve the tension in the muscle, breath out, and relax into the stretch. Stop, and then repeat the stretch again by attempting to stretch the muscle slightly further to the next point of discomfort, backing off slightly, and then again relaxing and holding for 15 to 20 seconds. Then, move to the next stretching exercise. These stretches can be held for longer periods. How long you hold the stretch depends on how much time you have for stretching. These stretches are elastic, because the overall stretching session is short in duration, and no emphasis is placed on any one area of the body. The entire stretching session may only last 10 to 15 minutes.

Partner Stretching

Plastic and elastic elongation techniques can also be performed with a partner. Partner stretching is often termed as passive stretching, because the athlete being stretched has his arm or leg moved through the stretch without having to engage his own muscles to move the limb himself. Having the athlete stretch with a partner can serve several purposes:

- Motivation: One or both of the athletes in the pair exercising together may need a partner to insure they show up for the workout and perform all the exercises properly.

- To push past equipment: Some sports, like football, involve bulky equipment that may hinder the athlete from stretching through his full range of motion. In such a case, a partner may be helpful.

- Relaxation: If the athletes trust one another, then each athlete can relax his own muscles completely, while his partner is stretching him. It is important that each partner communicates with the other during the entire range of motion. The athlete being stretched should dictate as to how far the stretch should proceed. The athlete moving the arm or leg into the stretched position, should never take it upon himself to set new goals for the athlete being stretched. Cooperation is the key to establishing trust while partner stretching. The largest drawback to stretching with a partner is that the partner does not know when you are in pain. As a result, you are more likely to stay a little tense, just in case your partner pushes you too far. You may not even realize that you are tense. Your anxiety may be more on a subconscious level. For this reason, partner stretching should be reserved for efforts involving elastic elongation of your muscles. On the other hand, it is better to stretch by yourself in order to improve your plastic elongation of your muscle. Keep in mind that total relaxation in the stretched position is the key to a more permanent improvement in range of motion.

Dynamic Stretch

Dynamic flexibility refers to the ability of a joint to move through its range of motion during actual physical activity. This type of flexibility is a critical part of any type of movement, especially sports-related movement. The less hindered the movement by inflexible muscles or joints, the more efficient that movement will be. You often see dancers and gymnasts warming up by swinging their legs and arms up and down and back and forth. Such a swinging motion is a dynamic stretch because it causes the muscle to stretch through an exaggerated range of motion. In such an exercise, the rapid swinging of the leg creates momentum that causes the leg to be stretched further than it normally would during other stretching techniques. Sports movements require the legs and arms to move rapidly. If a muscle is not prepared to reach the particular length that might result from momentum, then an injury may occur. Use dynamic stretching anytime, but especially during the in-season phases of training. These stretches can be added where they are needed to the warm-up stretch routine provided ahead in the chapter. These stretching techniques should be used only after a thorough warm-up, and with caution. The likelihood of an injury occurring is higher when the athlete is moving at a higher rate of speed, and his muscles are rapidly being lengthened to their limit.

Dynamic Stretches

■ LOWER BODY STRETCHES

● Mid-range and High Swings (Hamstrings and glutes)

While standing and holding a support, think of the leg as a pendulum. Keeping the kicking leg and the supporting leg straight, swing the leg forward and upward to about waist level. After each upward swing, reset the leg by briefly stopping on the floor behind you. To perform the high swing, establish your body position as you did in the mid-range swing, except now you are attempting to swing the leg higher than waist level. (Figures 7.2a to 7.2c)

Figure 7.2a   **Figure 7.2b**   **Figure 7.2c**

● Lateral Swings (Inner thigh and groin)

The leg once again acts as a pendulum, this time swinging out to the side to a comfortable height. Upon resetting the kicking leg, allow it to swing in front of the support leg. (Figures 7.3a and 7.3b)

Figure 7.3a   **Figure 7.3b**

● Rotational Swings (Hips)
Basically, this exercise involves you swinging your legs from back to front in a circular path. An inside swing makes a clockwise circle in front of your body, while an outside swing makes a counter clockwise circle. Rotational swings help release resistance within the full range of the hip. Both swings originate from behind the body and move across the center line in front of your body. The kick begins below waist level, and as it continues, it rises above waist level and makes a circular arch. The swing is completed when it moves back behind the body, where it originally began. (Figure 7.4)

Figure 7.4

■ UPPER BODY STRETCHES

● Midline Swings (Chest, back, and shoulders)
This stretch involves dynamically opening and closing your arms. As you cross your hands over your body, you can end their arch by slapping your shoulder blades. This step will provide you with kinesthetic feedback as to the depth of your stretch. (Figure 7.5)

Figure 7.5

● Windmills (Shoulder girdle)
Rotate your arms both forward and backward. This dynamic rotation of the shoulder assists in reducing resistance throughout the entire shoulder girdle. Perform the windmills in a variety of directions and planes. (Figure 7.6)

Figure 7.6

Type of stretch:	When to stretch:
• *Plastic elongation*	• Any time the athlete can.
• *Elastic elongation*	• In-season pre-practice, and days between plastic elongation.
• *Releasing techniques*	• Applied during any stretching session.
• *Dynamic stretching*	• In-season pre-practice, and pre-game.

Table 7.1. Types of stretches and guidelines for when to perform.

Application and Order of Stretching Techniques

It is best to follow a specific order when performing stretching exercises (refer to Table 7.1). Certain strengths and initial ranges of motion should be established before certain exercise techniques are attempted (refer to Table 7.2). Simple static stretching, using the elastic elongation techniques, should be attempted first when beginning a stretching program. Because these static stretch techniques are the safest, they are best for beginners. After you stop experiencing post-exercise muscle soreness and discomfort, you can begin to add some of the releasing techniques. It may take two or more weeks to establish enough muscle conditioning and strength to avoid experiencing delayed muscle soreness. By incorporating releasing techniques, you will be able to establish new ranges of motion. As a result, the delayed muscle soreness is likely to return. Begin with only the sensory contrasting method.

Later, you can incorporate rocking into your program. Once you have conditioned yourself and are experiencing little to no discomfort using rocking and sensory contrasting, you can begin to involve PNF techniques. By contracting and relaxing your muscles yourself during self-administered PNF, you are more in control of your own discomfort. It is important to wait before applying PNF techniques, because if your muscles have not been strengthened in a lengthened position, you can strain the muscle tissue when you try to engage a muscle contraction in a stretched position. At this point, static stretching, using the plastic elongation techniques, can be added to your flexibility training on a two-days-per-week basis, with about four days between each session. You should begin applying your releasing techniques during plastic elongation stretching as well. As your season approaches, you should now be performing all the techniques with little discomfort. Dynamic stretching can now be added to your elastic stretching routine to enhance the functionality level of your stretching efforts as they relate to playing basketball.

Technique order:

- Elastic elongation static stretching

- Sensory contrast

- Rocking

- PNF

- Plastic elongation static stretching

- Dynamic

Table 7.2. Recommended order for performing stretching techniques

Basic Stretching Exercises

The following exercises can be used during any stretching session. These exercises can be used during a prepractice warm-up, or during an off-season routine to create more permanent flexibility in muscles in which you are experiencing trouble. The outcome of your stretching routine will be determined by which protocol you follow. For a quick warm-up before a practice or a game to address a problem area, you would follow the elastic-elongation protocol. The following exercises are only suggestions. Many different stretching exercises and postures other than these exist. If you have a favorite, or know of other exercises that work well for your particular body type, then feel free to include them into your stretching routine.

Figure 7.7

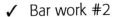 LOWER BODY EXERCISES

- Hamstring Stretches:
  - ✓ Bar work #1

    With one leg extended to the bar, stretch the hamstring and lower back by pointing the toe high, keeping the knee straight and then leaning forward (Figure 7.7).

  - ✓ Bar work #2

    Rotate the leg inward on the bar, sliding the emphasis to the groin (Figure 7.8).

Figure 7.8

✓ Bar work #3

Lean forward toward the outside of the leg on the bar (Figure 7.9).

Figure 7.9

✓ Bar work #4

Lean forward to the inside of the leg on the bar (Figure 7.10).

Figure 7.10

✓ Feet-together hamstring stretch

Bend your left leg, while keeping your right leg straight, and attempt to place your chest on your knee. Switch legs. Next, attempt to keep both legs straight, while placing your chest to your knees. This stretch can be facilitated by gently rocking from elbow to elbow, while leaning forward (Figure 7.11).

Figure 7.11

✓ Legs apart

To stretch the hamstrings and groin, keep your knees locked and attempt to place your head on your right knee; then switch to the left, and then to the middle. Reach as far back through your legs as possible (Figure 7.12).

Figure 7.12

✓ Partner stretch #1:

Lying flat on your back, place your arms straight out to your sides and keep your legs straight. Have your partner raise and push one leg up toward your chest, while holding the other leg flat to the floor. You can easily apply PNF techniques to this stretch (Figure 7.13).

Figure 7.13

✓ Partner stretch #2:

This stretch position is the same as the previous stretch, but requires the stretching leg to bend. You must hold your upper leg tightly to your chest, while your partner attempts to push your foot toward your face. Again, the hamstrings are the primary focus of the stretch. PNF techniques can be applied in this instance as well (Figure 7.14).

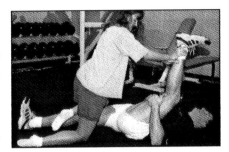

Figure 7.14

● Lower Back Stretches:

✓ Cannon ball

Perform this stretch by lying on your back and creating a ball with your body, thereby stretching your lower back muscles (Figure 7.15).

Figure 7.15

✓ Chair sitting

On a chair, lean forward between your legs and gently stretch the lower back (Figure 7.16).

Figure 7.16

✓ Knees-bent, pulling forward

A variation of the chair stretch, this and other slight variations of this stretch can help some individuals who have tightness or discomfort find a more relaxed stretching posture (Figure 7.17).

Figure 7.17

✓ Partner cannonball

This stretch is similar to the cannonball. Be careful to avoid overstretching. This version of the cannonball is excellent for individuals who have bigger thighs or torsos who cannot achieve a normal range of motion without assistance (Figure 7.18).

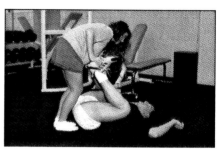

Figure 7.18

✓ Dog stretch

From a kneeling position, attempt to place your buttocks on your heels. Place your forehead on the floor and extend you arms at their full length in front of you, while allowing your hands to remain on the floor. This stretch is also good for stretching the chest, ankles, and quadriceps (Figure 7.19).

Figure 7.19

● Gluteal and High Hamstring Stretches:

✓ Cross legs – ankle to face

Lying on your back, cross your legs so that the ankle of your top leg rests on the knee of your lower leg. Stretch your top leg by bringing your top knee to the pit of your arm and your top ankle toward your face (Figure 7.20).

Figure 7.20

✓ Standing face to foot

From a standing position, place the foot of one leg on a support that is a little greater than hip height, bending the knee of the supported leg to the side. With the upper leg supported, lean forward. Move your chest toward your calf (Figure 7.21).

Figure 7.21

● Gluteal, Hip, and Lower Back Stretches:

✓ Lying twist

Lying on your back with your legs extended, cross one knee over your body to the floor. Keep your elbows, head, and shoulders flat on the floor and stretched in the opposite direction (Figure 7.22).

Figure 7.22

✓ Reverse twist

Sitting on the floor, with your legs straight in front of you, bend your right leg and cross it over your left leg. Place your left elbow on the outside of your right knee and twist your torso to the right. Repeat on the other side. This exercise rotates the spine, stretching the muscles of the lower back, hips, and torso (Figure 7.23).

Figure 7.23

● Groin Stretches:

✓ Butterfly

Perform this traditional groin stretch by sitting, bending the knees, and placing the soles of your feet together. Use your elbows to push down on your knees promoting the stretch to new depths (Figure 7.24).

Figure 7.24

✓ Side lunges

This is a great stretch for the groin, but it can also stretch the Achilles tendon and quadriceps of the bent leg. Lunge to the side while balancing yourself on the toe of your bent leg (Figure 7.25).

Figure 7.25

✓ Reverse butterfly

The objective of this relatively difficult to perform stretch is to lower your pelvis all the way to the floor, while keeping your feet in contact with the floor. Wedging your feet against a wall and placing your knees on a cushion or stretching mat will reduce your level of discomfort and enhance your ability to relax. PNF tech-

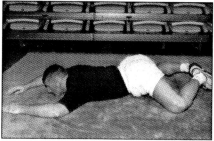

Figure 7.26

niques can be used in this instance by lightly pressing the knees into the floor, followed by complete relaxation, while lowering your pelvis and inner thigh to the floor (Figure 7.26).

✓ Split with slow rotations

Use caution with this stretch because it places heavy demand on the inner knee. Stand in a straddle position, with your feet more than shoulder-width apart. Then rotate, first facing to the left and then facing to the right. Allow your hips to turn in the direction you are facing. The rotations stretch all the muscles of the groin (Figure 7.27).

Figure 7.27

● Quadriceps and Hip Flexor Stretches:

✓ Lying quad stretch

This exercise is a traditional quadriceps stretch that is done lying on your side. To maintain balance, lean on your out-stretched arm, while pulling your foot to your buttocks (Figure 7.28).

Figure 7.28

✓ Chair to chair lunge

This stretch is excellent for the hip flexors, as well as the quadriceps. Kneel on one knee between two chairs. Place your hands on the chair in front of you, with your foot of the kneeling leg on the seat of the chair behind you. Push your hip forward to promote the stretch (Figure 7.29).

Figure 7.29

✓ Lunge stretch

Lunge forward with your right leg in front. Place your hands on your hips and push your hips forward. You'll feel this stretch in the upper hip area of the left leg. After sufficiently stretching the muscle, rock back, extending your right leg in front. Lean forward and move your chest to your thigh. You'll feel the stretch in the hamstring of the right leg. Repeat with the left leg in front (Figure 7.30).

Figure 7.30

● Calf Stretches:

✓ Runner's stretch

Using a chair or other support, stretch your calf by driving the heel into the ground, while maintaining a straight leg (Figure 7.31).

Figure 7.31

✓ Hanging calf stretch

In this stretch, use your body weight to press your heel to the floor. Standing on a ledge or a step with your heel hanging over the edge, be sure the ball of your foot is placed firmly on the step, and slowly drop your heels as far below the step as possible (Figure 7.32).

Figure 7.32

■ UPPER BODY STRETCHES

● Shoulder and Chest Stretches:

✓ Front shoulder and chest

Gripping a stationary object with your hand, twist your body away from your outstretched arm (Figure 7.33)

Figure 7.33

✓ Rear shoulder

Pull your arm across your neck, and turn your head away from the shoulder being stretched (Figure 7.34).

Figure 7.34

✓ Front and rear shoulder and chest with rope

Holding a stick or rope at arms length above the head, arch your back and push the rope behind you. Place the rope behind your back and then lean forward, pulling the rope up toward your head (Figure 7.35).

Figure 7.35

✓ Table top

Sit on the floor with your knees bent and feet flat on the floor. Place your arms behind with your palms also flat to the floor. Push your hips up until your stomach is flat and parallel to the floor. You should look like a table, with your body completely flat from your knee to your shoulders.

✓ Right and left upper back

Grasp a stationary object and cross your arm across your body. Bend your knees slightly, and twist your body away from the outstretched, anchored hand (Figure 7.36).

Figure 7.36

✓ Trunk stretch

Stretch by leaning at the waist in all directions, front, back, and to the sides. Then, rotate gently in large circles.

✓ Cat stretch

This stretch for the upper back is performed in a kneeling position, with your hands placed flat on the floor in front of you. Push your hands against the floor away from your knees. Do not allow your hands to slide. Roll your upper back up and away from the floor, like a cat (Figure 7.37).

Figure 7.37

✓ Lower back bridge

Lie face down on the floor. Using your arms, push yourself upward, until your chest and stomach have cleared the floor. Allow your hip and legs to remain in contact with the floor. If you cannot extend your arms to full length, then push up and lean on your elbows instead (Figure 7.38).

Figure 7.38

● Arm Stretches:

  ✓ Triceps

    Using one arm to pull the other. Grab the elbow behind your head and pull (Figure 7.39).

Figure 7.39

  ✓ Biceps

    Use a rope (or a weight plate) to stretch the biceps. Extend your arm out straight to your side, and point your wrist downward while keeping the crook of the outstretched arm facing upward (Figure 7.40).

Figure 7.40

A Recommended Warm-Up Routine

The following series of exercises can be performed prior to practice or a game to prepare the body for more intense activity. Before you begin stretching, make sure to thoroughly warm up, using calisthenics or some other light activity. Then, utilizing the exercises previously discussed, consider this series of stretches:

* Windmills — 10 with each arm, forward and back.

* Midline swings — 10 times.

* Triceps — Hold 15 seconds; relax; hold 15 seconds.

* Biceps — Hold 15 seconds; relax; hold 15 seconds.

* Split with rotations — 6 rotations (move your feet further apart with each rotation).

* Side lunge groin into toe up (each side) — Hold 15 seconds; relax; hold 15 seconds.

* Hamstrings with feet together — Hold 15 seconds; relax; hold 15 seconds.

- Upper hamstring — Hold 15 seconds; relax; hold 15 seconds.
- Cannon ball — Hold 15 seconds; relax; hold 15 seconds.
- Lying twist — Hold 15 seconds; relax; hold 15 seconds.
- Lying quad stretch — Hold 15 seconds; relax; hold 15 seconds.
- Butterfly — Hold 15 seconds; relax; hold 15 seconds.
- Legs apart hamstrings and groin — Hold 15 seconds; relax; hold 15 seconds.
- Lower back bridge — Hold 15 seconds; relax; hold 15 seconds.
- Dog stretch — Hold 15 seconds.
- Cat stretch — Hold 15 seconds.
- Runner's stretch — Hold 15 seconds; relax; hold 15 seconds (each leg).

Summary

Regardless of which stretching method you choose, keep in mind that it is very important to incorporate flexibility into any training program you adopt in order to achieve better and safer performances on the court. The first concern of any strength coach or athlete should be to minimize injury. Flexibility is the key to an athlete's longevity in a sport. If you are injury free, you can spend more time on the court, and therefore, be better able to assist your team. The need to engage in a sound stretching routine on a regular basis cannot be overestimated.

CHAPTER 8

Strength and Power Exercises

If you are seeking to constructively increase your body size or increase your level of raw muscular power and strength, you must incorporate resistance training into your workout program. Resistance can be applied in a variety of different ways. Regardless of the type of resistance you use, it should provide an overload to your muscles.

When you overload a muscle, it becomes stressed. In turn, the muscle takes actions to fortify itself against this stress by storing more of your body's energy substrates (food) and by creating more structural components to better utilize these substrates. This step is done to protect the muscle against the potential stress of future overloads. As the number of workouts increase through out the training year, the number of potential overloads increase as well. This continues the muscle's protective processes. This is how the muscle increases it's strength and becomes larger over a period of time. Resistance training fools the body into storing more of what you eat as muscle.

Fatigue of the muscle is the ultimate indicator that an overload is being applied correctly. This indicator is called *momentary muscular failure* (MMF). MMF occurs when you have worked to the point where your arm or leg will no longer move. It is not important that MMF be achieved during every exercise and exercise session. Even though momentary muscular failure (MMF) is a primary method of indicating whether the muscle is being adequately overloaded, MMF can be overused. Overuse of MMF can result in the loss of strength and muscular size. This is because MMF is the most intense indicator of muscular work, and unless adequate recovery is allowed between workouts involving MMF, the athlete can become overworked. This overwork can result in an inability of the athlete's body to readily repair itself.

When engaged in resistance training, a moment of rest following MMF will rapidly restore muscle movement. Resting allows the circulatory system to remove fatigue-producing waste products. Shorter rest periods remove fewer waste products, resulting in an inability of the muscle to perform as well on the next set of the exercise.

MMF and overload can be achieved in resistance training in a variety of different ways, including the following:

- Increase the repetitions of an exercise.

- Increase the resistance of an exercise.

- Taker shorter rest periods between exercises and exercise sets.

- Increase the cadence or tempo of the exercise movement.

- Increase the length of the workout session.

- Take fewer days of rest between performing a particular exercise.

- Perform longer exercise sessions.

How much muscular overload you require depends on how much muscle you need to do your job. As a basketball player, you do not need as much muscle as a bodybuilder or wrestler. On the other hand, if you play in the post positions, you are probably going to need some added muscle to help you do your job better. This is not to say that other positions in basketball need less muscle than a post player. All basketball players essentially perform the same movements when they play. Each athlete requires an optimal level of muscle. What that optimal level is for you depends on how you feel while you are playing. If you feel weak, you most likely need more muscle. If you are already very muscular, but you feel slow or lack mobility, you may have exceeded your optimal level of muscle and may benefit from reducing your level of overload during your resistance training.

Figure 8.1. Each athlete requires an optimal level of muscle.

Repetitions

Any exercise movement can be repeated once or many times, including resistance exercises. When a movement is repeated, it is called performing repetitions or reps. During the workouts included in this book, you are presented with a variety of different repetition patterns. The basic reason for the diversity in recommended repetition patterns is because your body is capable of doing a variety of different kinds of work. By overloading you with both high and low repetition patterns, the workouts try to address all of your body's strength requirements. The exact number of repetitions performed during the sets of a particular exercise is not overly important for a basketball player. If you were an athlete in a more specialized, physically focused activity, like the mile run, then the majority of your workouts might concentrate on a higher-repetition pattern. These higher repetitions would provide the miler with the strength he required, while still addressing his muscular endurance requirements. The reverse would be practiced for a shot putter. The majority of the thrower's workouts would center on low-repetition patterns. The physical requirements of basketball players, on the other hand, demand both endurance and power. Therefore, your workout repetitions will vary throughout the training year.

Your repetition pattern must be considered over an extended period (i.e., several weeks). In this book, you'll notice the repetitions on most of the core exercises start high on week one, and around week twelve, they have gotten progressively lower. This subtle reduction in repetitions is used to slowly increase improvements in muscular power. In the early weeks of training, higher repetitions are used to fully fatigue the muscle, thus increasing the potential for added muscular size and endurance. This increase in muscular size, provides you with a strong muscular base upon which you can begin increasing muscular power. This slow reduction in repetitions over time is called *periodization*. Periodization is a model of training that helps provide training overloads in a subtle and progressive manner. Periodization helps you to slowly adapt to the stresses of training, preventing any overloads from causing excess fatigue or overtraining.

Sets

Fatigue may occur while performing repetitions. When you reach the point of fatigue, a brief rest period may be taken until your body has temporarily recovered. This rest will allow additional repetitions to be completed. These groups of repetitions are called sets. The rest periods between the sets can last as long as needed. A longer rest period will result in a greater recovery, and should be used when the resistance or intensity of exercise is high. The shorter rest period will result in less recovery and should be used when the resistance or intensity of exercise is relatively low.

The purpose of performing sets in the workout is to allow for the completion of more total repetitions in a given workout period. As a result, a greater amount of work is accomplished, and therefore, more overload is placed on the muscle. This process is beneficial for both power and endurance athletes. A power athlete's work should be based on the amount of weight moved with each repetition, while an endurance athlete's work should be based on the number of repetitions performed, as well as the time required to perform the repetitions. Because the basketball player fits into both categories, the workouts in the book present a variety of workouts that require both types of work to be performed.

An athlete's need for endurance versus power will determine how many sets he should perform during a workout. If the desired result is power, then fewer sets and repetitions will be called for, but an increase in intensity will be needed. This added intensity will require the athlete to take longer rest periods between sets of the exercise. If the desired result of the workout is endurance, then the repetitions and sets are increased with a reduction in intensity. With less emphasis being placed on intensity, the athlete can thereby take shorter rest periods between sets of the exercise.

Frequency (How Long Should You Rest Between Exercise Sessions)

The amount of rest you should allow between exercise sessions varies between 24 to 72 hours, and will depend on how severely you worked a particular muscle or muscle group during the exercise session. You may be able to wait just 24 hours before working a muscle group again, if you did not experience MMF during your workout, and the number of sets and repetitions you performed were low. At the other extreme, if you experienced MMF more than once on any exercise and the sets and repetitions were high, 72 hours might be needed for you to adequately recover. This type of overload is most often seen in a bodybuilding program, and, only on occasion, would this type or workout apply to other athletes. If you experienced MMF once on each exercise, and the sets and repetitions during the workout were moderate, you might consider 48 hours before working the muscle group again as sufficient time for adequate recovery.

Forty-eight hours is the most common time for recovery between exercise sessions. It is possible to structure workouts nearly every day of the week. However, in doing so, it is essential that the body be divided into separate areas of work. In this way, various parts of the body can be rested while other body parts are being worked (refer to Table 8.1).

Monday	Tuesday	Wednesday	Thursday	Friday
• chest	• back	• off	• chest	• back
• shoulders	• legs		• shoulders	• legs

Table 8.1. A sample split-routine workout

It has been suggested that an athlete can work-out as often as is physically possible. To a point, this may be true, as long as fatigue and overtraining symptoms do not arise. Such overtraining or burnout can be avoided by varying the intensity (the amount of weight lifted) and volume (number of sets and repetitions) of your weekly workouts. The size of the muscle being worked can dictate the length of time allowed for recovery. The larger the muscle group, the longer the recovery period should be. Because a larger muscle will have more depleted and damaged tissue, it will require more time to heal and replenish. Because of the smaller size of its muscles, the upper body requires less time for recovery than the lower body, and therefore, can be worked more often.

Athletes who are just initiating their resistance training program should be allowed more time for recovery over that of more experienced athletes. An individual must be gradually introduced to the demands placed on his body by resistance training to avoid injury and overwork syndrome.

Duration (How Long a Workout Should Last)

It is essential that each muscle group is worked efficiently during the course of a week. As was previously mentioned, it is possible to divide the body's muscles into work groups, working different groups on different days. Studies have shown that the body can respond most effectively to a resistance workout if the workout is performed within a forty-five minute to one-hour time period. This limit in the amount of time working out insures that the level of fatigue experienced is not doing more harm than good. Therefore, it is the responsibility of the athlete or the conditioning coach to design a workout that can be completed in the recommended time frame. Of course, all factors considered, it will not harm your muscular system if your workout were to last longer than an hour. However, it is easier to create muscular fatigue levels if a limit is placed on workout duration. For example, let's say you worked out for two hours in the weight room, and during that two hours, you performed only forty-five minutes of actual work. In other words, you rested for an hour and fifteen minutes between exercises and exercise sets. Your teammate, on the other hand, worked out for an hour, but he worked for forty-five minutes, and allowed himself only fifteen minutes of rest. In fact, your friend is getting more of a workout.

At times, when the weight of the object that is being moved is extremely heavy, more rest must be allowed between sets of the exercise. The added rest allows for additional recovery to insure the completion of the next set. In a case where more rest is required, then less sets and repetitions should be included in the workout. The reduction in sets and repetitions will allow the workout to fit into the one-hour limit. The reduction of sets and repetitions is customary when muscular power is the objective of the workout. In this case, the weight or resistance, rather than the number of sets and repetitions, dictates the intensity of the workout. At other times, performing an increased number of sets and repetitions will be the primary objective of the workout. It will then be necessary to reduce the rest time between the sets of the exercises in order to accomplish more sets and repetitions in the same forty-five minute to one-hour time period.

Intensity (How Difficult the Exercise or Workout Should Be)

The intensity of a resistance exercise program can be controlled by varying the amount of weight lifted, the time of recovery between sets, the total volume of work (i.e., the number of sets and repetitions in a workout), and the tempo or cadence of the movement. Intensity is the key to maximizing the potential for improvement. By creating an appropriate overload and conquering the overload, the body will respond by strengthening itself to meet the physical challenge imposed upon it.

• *Weight.* The weight of the object being moved is often considered the foremost measure of intensity. If the weight increases, so does the intensity level of the workout. For example, it's obviously more difficult to move 100 pounds than 50 pounds.

• *Time.* Intensity can be increased or decreased by altering the amount of time allowed for the athlete to rest. This resting time can be between sets, workouts, exercises, or even repetitions. If less time is allowed for rest between sets, then the intensity of the exercise increases in relation to time. If more time is allowed for rest between sets, then the intensity of the exercise decreases in relation to time. For example, it will be more difficult to move 200 pounds on the bench press for an additional set of 10 repetitions if you wait only thirty seconds compared to if you wait two minutes.

• *Volume of work.* The total number of sets and repetitions in a given workout can also dictate the level of intensity. If you are accustomed to doing three sets of the bench press for eight repetitions, you can increase the intensity by adding another set of eight repetitions to that exercise. This additional set results in the total volume of work increasing from twenty-four repetitions to thirty-two repetitions for that exercise.

• *Tempo or cadence of movement patterns.* While performing an exercise, it is possible to increase or decrease the intensity of a set of repetitions by altering the tempo or cadence of the movement. If a set of 10 repetitions is started at a regular tempo or cadence and is continued at that same regular pace, then muscular fatigue will be higher than if temporary pauses are included at various repetitions in the exercise. This factor is seen commonly when athletes perform the bench press. For example, a set of eight repetitions may be assigned, with the first five repetitions completed at a regular cadence. But as the point of fatigue nears, the athlete will typically extend his arms to the fully locked-out position. This locked-out position enables the athlete to pause for a few seconds. During these few seconds, the muscle is allowed to recuperate slightly, therefore reducing the level of intensity. Pauses like these may be beneficial in an instance where power is the objective. When developing power, the amount of weight being moved is the primary objective of the workout, and these pauses will allow that weight to be moved for the designated number of repetitions.

In cases where endurance and/or muscular hypertrophy is the main goal of the training session, a steady movement cadence can be more beneficial to the athlete. This movement cadence is recommended, because in order to produce hypertrophy or muscular endurance, the muscle must be pushed to greater and greater levels of fatigue. Just as it would not benefit you to put your hands on your knees at half court during a game because you felt fatigued, it is essential for you to be capable of working through increasing levels of fatigue. This can be accomplished by performing continuous movements, using a constant cadence.

Recovery

The most essential aspect of the overload principle is not the workout itself, but your recovery from the workout. The purpose of a workout is to stress the body, or to break it down. All factors considered, a workout designed to help a basketball player to be better able to meet the physical challenges and demands imposed by a basketball game should place a higher degree of stress on the individual than that of the game itself.

Proper recuperation consists of sleep and proper nutrition. The combination of these two elements promotes a level of physical replacement that restores the body back to its original state, plus adds a little extra to help it to perform better the next time such a workout is performed. How much recuperation an athlete needs depends on how severe his overload was. If the workout was extremely hard, then more recovery will be needed. This balance of rest versus work is managed by considering the training principles of frequency, duration and intensity of exercise.

Complete rest may not always be necessary to promote recovery. This factor is why most contemporary exercise programs involve alternating intensities between training sessions. Gains made during the training cycle depend on the intensity of the workouts. You may want to make your workouts difficult in order to challenge your body to respond. However, this step will cause your level of fatigue to increase as the training week progresses. This fatigue will lower your ability to be intense. For instance, if you used the same workload at the end of the week that you did at the first of the week, the workload used at the first part of the week may be too much for you at your current level of fatigue. However, if the workload was reduced a small amount toward the end of the week, then your intensity level would be nearly as high at the end of the week as it was at the first. This is because your level of fatigue would make the lighter workout seem relatively more difficult. In this way, your workout would not be so difficult that you might develop overwork or fatigue-related problems.

Resistance Training Techniques

Many different resistance training techniques exist. Essentially, each technique manipulates the repetitions, sets, and rest times to create a training effect. While each of these techniques can be useful to athletes, it is often difficult to determine if the technique is best used for enhancing muscular size, endurance, or power. The following sections are intended to clarify any confusion surrounding these techniques.

Resistance Training for Muscular Size

Muscles increase in size in the body's attempt to protect itself from the stresses placed upon it by resistance training. Often, a higher level of lean muscle mass can be beneficial for athletes who play basketball. For example, an increase in muscle size is viewed in a negative light for baseball players. Increase in muscle size can help you stabilize and protect the joint, increase your joint leverage, allow you to better move resistance, and improve your body composition. While basketball players do not need the muscle mass of a bodybuilder, optimal levels of muscle size can have a positive impact.

Increasing muscle size requires manipulating the intensity, duration, frequency, volume and cadence of your workouts. Primarily, the training volume must be increased, which will also have a positive effect on your level of muscular endurance. Note that hypertrophy-type workouts will not directly enhance muscular power. In fact, during a hypertrophy phase of training, your power will most likely decrease due to the stresses placed on the muscle. Periodic hypertrophy training will, however, provide an increased potential for power because of gains in joint leverage that result from an increased level of muscle mass.

It is best to perform muscle-size or *hypertrophy*-type workouts during the first two to four weeks of the post-season phase of training. These workouts are designed to reawaken less active muscle fibers and to establish a muscular base upon which you will later build your power. Hypertrophy workouts can also be included at the beginning of new phases of training to shock sluggish muscle fibers back into action.

Each of your muscles, even though appearing solid, are constructed of layer upon layer of microscopic fibers. These fibers are the cells of the muscle and vary in type (refer to Table 8.2). Some fibers are designed for endurance-type work, and are called Type I or *slow oxidative* (SO). Type IIb or *fast glycolitic* (FG) fibers are designed for short, powerful activities. The third most notable type of muscle fiber, called a *fast glycolitic oxidative* (FOG) or Type IIa, can perform both endurance and power-type work. Several other muscle fiber types exist that assist the three main types of fiber.

Some muscles may have more SO muscle fibers than FG fibers, but mostly, a muscle is a mixture of all the different types of muscle fibers. Which muscle fibers are used in a particular instance depends on the intensity (resistance level) and duration of the activity.

Fast Twitch (FG) **Type IIa**	Used during all out efforts, or changes in intensity. Used during heavy resistance training, sprinting, or throwing. These fibers fatigue easily, but can produce extreme power outputs.
Fast Oxidative **Glyocolotic** **(Fog)** **Type IIb**	Used as an intermediate fiber to assist both the FG and SO muscle fingers. FOG fiver have both the capacity for endurance and power, but not as much as the SO or FG fibers.
Slow Oxidative (SO) **Type I**	Used during endurance exercises. These fibers do not fatigue easily and contribute little to power.

Table 8.2. The three primary types of muscle fiber.

For the most part, muscle fibers are recruited from smallest to largest. This factor can be utilized to develop a resistance training program that will enhance muscular size. Your body is designed to recruit the smallest, SO fibers first, with the FOG and FG fibers following in that order. The FG fibers are the largest (refer to Figure 8.2).

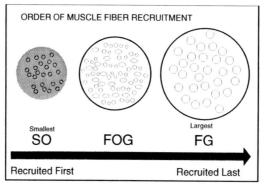

Figure 8.2. Order of muscle fiber recruitment.

During hypertrophy-type training, MMF must be experienced often during the workout. In order to produce the highest level of muscle fatigue possible, you must maintain strict exercise form, and the *tempo of movement must be constant*. Performing your exercises in this manner will work each of the muscle's fiber types to complete exhaustion, and help each fiber to grow larger and perform better. It is important to have a higher number of sets and repetitions during this style of training, because the early repetitions in a hypertrophy set give the SO fibers an opportunity to become fatigued. If the resistance of the exercise is too high, then the FG fibers will contribute their efforts too soon, thus cheating the SO's of their chance to work. Therefore, the weight used during hypertrophy training should be moderate to light.

A drawback of muscle hypertrophy training is that it is very intense, and if it is performed for too long during the training cycle, this type of training can result in reduced muscular improvement. Therefore, hypertrophy training should be undertaken sparingly. Moreover, no single style of training is essentially better, especially highly intense work such as hypertrophy training.

Because you are adding more volume to every workout in hypertrophy training, you will not have time to effectively work the entire body during a single workout. Remember, you want to limit your workout time to 45 minutes to an hour. Therefore, you must split your workouts by working different body parts on different days. By spacing your workouts over four days or even six days, you can concentrate a larger amount of work on one or two areas of your body and achieve better results for your efforts (refer to Tables 8.3 and 8.4).

Monday	Tuesday	Wednesday	Thursday
• chest	• back	•off	• overall body movements
• shoulders	• upper shoulders		• biceps
• triceps	• abdominals		• legs

Table 8.3. A sample three-day, split-routine workout program.

Monday	Tuesday	Wednesday	Thursday	Friday
• chest	• back	•off	• chest	• back
• shoulders	• upper shoulders		• shoulders	• upper shoulders
• biceps	• triceps		• biceps	• triceps
• abdominals	• legs		•abdominals	• legs

Table 8.4. A sample four-day, split-routine workout program.

Repetition Styles for Muscular Size

During hypertrophy training, you are trying to do everything possible to increase the potential for exhaustion during the exercise set. By trying to perform one extra repetition or squeeze in one more set before your workout time expires, you may thoroughly work all your current active muscle fibers and bring a few more inactive fibers into action. How you perform each repetition can enable you to achieve a greater level of muscular involvement and fatigue.

Because the number of repetitions during exercise sets can vary greatly, it is recommended that you perform a relatively high number of repetitions in order to insure adequate fatigue levels among the different muscle fiber types. The number of repetitions you should perform per exercise can range from 8 to 15 on core and supporting exercises, and 25 or higher for exercises involving the abdominals, lower back, neck, and calves. Regardless of the number of repetitions you perform, the resistance used must still be high enough to induce MMF. Each of the following repetition styles can be performed together or separately.

• *Peaking repetitions (voluntary muscle contractions)* This repetition style involves a voluntarily and forceful contraction of the muscle that is engaged while performing an exercise. By concentrating on the movement of the resistance, and by forcefully contracting the muscle at the same time, an even greater number of muscle fibers can be incorporated into action. Make the muscle as hard as you can. If you are using a weighted barbell, an easy method to insure that you are performing the repetition correctly is to isometrically force your hands toward one another during the concentric (i.e., raising) phase of the lift. You can then isometrically force your hands apart from one another as the bar begins the eccentric (i.e., lowering) phase of the lift. In either case, your hands will not slide along the bar. The added stress, however, will force additional muscle fibers into action. You might complain that the isometric actions prevent you from using heavier weights. Keep in mind that lifting heavy weight during this particular stage of training is not the primary objective of your workout. The objective, however, is reaching a point of fatigue.

• *Forced repetitions.* Forced repetitions occur when a workout partner or *spotter* helps you accomplish one or two extra repetitions after you have reached MMF. Since fatigue is the basic goal of the hypertrophy stage, forcing extra repetitions will promote further fatigue on the muscle. Only one or two extra forced repetitions are suggested per set. Remember that recuperation is the key to building muscle. If too much stress is placed on the muscle, then the recuperative processes may be hindered.

Figure 8.3

• *Rest or pause repetitions.* Rest repetitions are similar to forced repetitions. This style of repetition should be performed if the resistance becomes very unmanageable, even with a spotter present. Rest repetitions are performed by stopping the exercise and placing the weight back on its supports or floor when you feel the next repetition cannot be performed. After a few seconds, the athlete can resume the exercise. Resting 3 to 5 seconds for each repetition you plan to perform will allow you to just complete the extra repetitions before MMF occurs.

Pause repetitions are similar to rest repetitions. In pause repetitions, however, the resistance is not returned to a complete resting position. Instead, the lifter just temporarily pauses in a *locked-out* position. On the bench press, for example, the pause would occur when the lifter's arms are fully extended from his chest. This style of repetition is more difficult because the resistance never leaves the athlete's possession. Remember that during a hypertrophy stage of the workout plan, the resistance should be moved at a constant tempo until momentary muscular failure occurs. As a result, at the point where the athlete feels that another repetition is impossible, a brief pause is normally a welcome occurrence. Regardless of the repetition style you employ, always use a spotter in lifts that extend the weights over your body or your head.

Types of Sets for Muscular Size

The number of sets and repetitions you perform in your resistance program can be varied to produce certain training effects. The possible arrangement styles of sets and repetitions are endless. Regardless of which arrangements you choose, always remember what your primary objective is for your training phase.

• *Straight sets.* Traditionally, sets are performed in a straightforward manner. If three sets of a certain exercise are prescribed, then each of the three sets is performed in its entirety before moving on to the next exercise (refer to Table 8.5). This method works well during a hypertrophy stage of training. When using straight sets, attention must be directed toward the style of repetition the athlete is performing. Make sure the tempo of movement is constant, and the athlete is "peaking" or voluntarily contracting the muscle. The use of "rest", "pause" and "forced" repetitions can also be applied. The resistance used during a straight-set approach can remain the same from set to set, if so desired. In this case, the weight should be sufficiently heavy to challenge the lifter on each set to insure he reaches proper fatigue levels. Concentration on the style of repetition is the key in this instance.

SET #1	SET #2	SET #3
10 reps	10 reps	10 reps

Table 8.5. An example of a 3-set, straight-set resistance training prescription.

• *Pre-exhaustion sets.* Pre-exhaustion sets are an excellent method of inducing fatigue during a hypertrophy stage of training. This type of set involves combining two exercises, with no rest taken between the exercises (refer to Table 8.6). The first exercise is a supporting exercise, while the second is a core exercise. This technique condenses workout time and induces a higher level of fatigue. By performing the supporting exercise to exhaustion, the isolated muscle is thoroughly fatigued. Then, move directly to the core exercise. The core exercise involves working less fatigued muscles to further exhaust the previously isolated muscle. In this text, the pre-exhausting combination of exercises is termed a *super-set.*

	SET #1	SET #2	SET #3
• Dumbbell flies	12 reps	12 reps	12 reps
• Bench press	8 reps	8 reps	8 reps

Table 8.6. An example of a three-set, next 2 pre-exhaustion set.

• *Super-sets.* Super-sets are another type of combination set. A super-set consists of two to four exercises that target the same body part. These combined exercises are performed one after another with little to no rest between each exercise. The high volume of work done during this type of set assures fatigue. This technique enables more work to be jammed into the 45-minute to one-hour time frame.

	SET #1	SET #2	SET #3
Bench press	8 reps	8 reps	8 reps
Dumbbell fly	12 reps	12 reps	12 reps
Dips	15 reps	15 reps	15 reps

Table 8.7. An example of a three-set, next 3 super-set.

• *Push-pull super sets.* Push-pulls are a type of super-set that allows the athlete to combine exercises that work opposing muscle groups. Usually, the athlete will initially begin working the predominantly large muscle groups. After all the sets of the two opposing exercises are performed, you can move on to other push-pull combinations. The entire body can be worked in this fashion.

	SET #1	SET #2	SET #3
• Bench press	8 reps	8 reps	8 reps
• Pull-up	10 reps	10 reps	10 reps
• Military press	8 reps	8 reps	8 reps
• Upright row	8 reps	8 reps	8 reps
• Biceps curl	10 reps	10 reps	10 reps
• Triceps extensions	10 reps	10 reps	10 reps
• Squats	8 reps	8 reps	8 reps
• Leg curls	10 reps	10 reps	10 reps

Table 8.8. An example of a push-pull routine.

• *Drop sets.* Drop sets are performed by reducing either the amount of resistance used during an exercise or the rest allowed between sets of the exercise. Some methods of decreasing the weight during an exercise have little direction. Randomly stripping resistance off might allow you to prolong the set, but this style of dropping can be easily misused. Make sure that your drops follow some structure that can be documented. By documenting each workout, you can compare your efforts against future workouts. As for structure, consider the following method of decreasing the resistance during an exercise. For example, if you had planned to perform three sets of ten repetitions (30 repetitions) with an increasing level of resistance on each set, but time for your workout is short, then completely warm up and start at a weight near to what you would have used on your the last set of the exercise. This way you are assured that you will work with your heaviest possible weight even during this workout, and as a result, also gain some strength and power benefits. When failure occurs, have your spotter assist in performing one forced repetition. Then, strip the weight off to a degree that will allow you to achieve four to five additional repetitions before MMF occurs a second time. Force one repetition, and resume the process until all 30 repetitions that you originally designated for yourself are completed. This type of set is highly intense.

Drop sets can also be performed by dropping the rest time allowed between the sets of an exercise. During this type of drop set, you will most likely choose to keep the same amount of resistance for each set. Start by allowing around 45 seconds of rest between the first and second set. Then, drop 10 seconds off your rest time for each set that follows.

Drop sets should not be performed unless you are well trained, because of the potential for stress-related injuries. Make sure you have very good spotters, and make sure you communicate your levels of fatigue to them (refer to Figure 8.4). The amount of rest you take following your drop-set workouts will need to be longer to allow for adequate recuperation of the muscle. Drop sets can best fit into a workout plan prior to a weekend rest period.

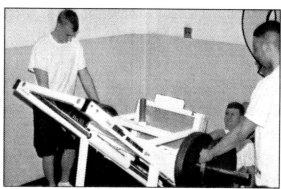

Figure 8.4

• *Reverse pyramid sets*. Reverse pyramid sets are like drop sets, only in reverse (refer to Table 8-9). The resistance will remain the same for each set. However, with each set, you continue to add repetitions. You can keep the rest time between the sets a constant, or if MMF is your ultimate goal, the rest time between sets can be decreased to ensure that full exhaustion is accomplished.

	SET #1	SET #2	SET #3
• Bench press	10 reps	12 reps	14 reps

Table 8.9. An example of a reverse pyramid set.

How Many Sets for Muscular Size

When designing a workout for a student athlete, many constraints exist that affect workout time. During the hypertrophy stage, you should attempt to perform as many sets as possible to insure complete muscle fatigue. The available time, however, may not allow you to perform 16 to 20 sets for your chest, 12 to 16 sets for your shoulders, 10 to 15 sets for your triceps, 10 sets for your abdominals and finally 8 sets for your calves, like the workout of a bodybuilder. Even if you could perform such a workout, it would be ill-advised because of the energy expended during the effort. Some energy might need to be saved for practicing basketball skills. During a hypertrophy workout, you should perform 30 to 60 sets (all exercises) that collectively require about 40 minutes to complete (refer to Table 8.10).

30 sets	x 20	seconds per set =	10 minutes
30 sets	x 1	minute per set =	30 minutes
			40 minutes (give or take)

Table 8.10. An example of a hypertrophy workout.

This workout is possible because you can super-set some exercises and some can be performed using a pre-exhaustive type of set, both of which save time during the workout, while insuring the volume of work remains the same. Also, the resistance is far less (55 to 70 % of one-repetition max) than that used during the power-building stages of the workout plan, a level which allows for less rest to be taken between exercises and exercise sets. The level of resistance cannot be high because of the fatigue that results from the increased training volume, repetition, and set styles, and the increased tempo of the movement. Ultimately, however, you would benefit by using more resistance during hypertrophy training. Since the hypertrophy stage may only last for two to four weeks, large increases in resistance will be impossible. Hopefully, however, if you keep good records, more resistance can be used to begin your next hypertrophy stage.

Movement Speeds for Increasing Muscular Size

The actual speed that an exercise should be performed during hypertrophy phases should be slower. Even though slow movement speeds will reduce the amount of resistance that can be used, keep in mind that moving resistance during this phase is not your primary objective. Slower movements reduce momentum and inertia. Momentum and inertia are great for quickly telling your muscles to rely primarily on FG muscle fibers. You want to make sure, however, that every muscle fiber receives its share of work. Slower movement speeds are, therefore, better for hypertrophy phases.

Resistance Training for Muscular Power

All factors considered, the faster you can move a heavy resistance, the more powerful you are. By the same token, the faster you can move your body against a resistance, or against gravity, the more powerful you are. If you run faster, jump higher, or throw further, you are displaying improvements in power. The element of speed is a result of increased power. Power is not the result of speed. Some strength coaches feel that it is necessary to perform resistance workouts with very low resistance at relatively high speeds in order to optimize speed or power output. Other strength coaches feel that the moving a heavy resistance will produce better results. In fact, both philosophies have merit and should be applied during your training.

Even though most traditional weight training exercises are performed with heavy resistance and result in externally slow movement speeds, the external speed of the arm or leg is independent of what is occurring inside the muscle. The contractile units (actin and myosin myofilaments) are still working rapidly. It is this work that generates the muscle's force. Some athletes may seem to move very slowly, but if they are moving as fast as possible, the muscular force is still very high. The external speed of an athlete's arm or leg may, therefore, be hindered by a lack of coordination of the muscles involved. This loss of control can result from the weight or girth of the limb being greater than the supporting muscle groups can manage. This factor is sometimes seen in the athlete who concentrates on working his large muscle groups (prime movers) and disregards his supporting muscles. The ability to manage the weight of the body segment is referred to as *strength-to-body-weight ratio.*

A loss of coordination most often results in losses of power output. Increasing your strength-to-body-weight ratio, and understanding how your body moves during an exercise will benefit your power out. Being more aware of body positions can help you to direct all your efforts in one direction, rather than wasting energy on misdirected movement patterns. During resistance training, your energy is wasted in subtle ways, like having the resistance move slightly off the correct path or improperly positioning our knees, elbows, or other body segments.

The primary objective during resistance training for *power* is not to achieve muscle fatigue, or momentary muscular failure (MMF), as was the case in *hypertrophy*-type resistance training. In fact, muscular exhaustion may reduce power output. The fundamental objective during the power phase is to produce a forceful repetition. In order to produce a powerful repetition, movement strategies that enhance inertia or momentum are brought into play. Reactive techniques should also be applied.

Reactive techniques require a rapid transition from a stretch into a full muscle contraction. These techniques are applied because power is produced via the nervous system. Proper power training can result in improvements in motor unit recruitment, an increased firing rate of the motor units, enhanced synchronization of the motor units, and clearer, faster nerve information arriving to the muscle (disinhibition). In short, due to power training, the nervous system can become stronger, sending a fast and clear signal that calls more muscle fibers into play, thereby producing more powerful movements.

The volume of work during power training should become lower and lower as the weeks of training go by. As such, the repetitions, sets, and exercise in a workout should all be lower than those employed in the hypertrophy stage of the training cycle. This lowering of the volume insures that each repetition is a quality power repetition. Since the amount of work is lower, the level of necessary training can be condensed into a period of three days per week (refer to Table 8.11). It can also remain at four days per week, if you so desire (refer to Table 8.12).

Monday	Tuesday	Wed.	Thursday
• chest	• back	• off	• overall body movements
• shoulders	• upper shoulders		• biceps
• triceps	• abdominals		• legs

Table 8.11. An example of a three-days-per-week power-training program.

Monday	Tuesday	Wed.	Thursday	Friday
• chest	• back	• off	• chest	• back
• shoulders	• upper shoulders		• shoulders	• upper shoulders
• biceps	• triceps		• biceps	• triceps
• abdominals	• legs		• abdominals	• legs

Table 8.12. An example of a four-days-per-week power-training program.

During a three-day, power-training program, it is possible to isolate body segments on the Monday and Tuesday parts of the routine. Each repetition should be performed quickly against heavy resistance, with more rest allowed between exercise sets. The exercises on Thursday can involve the overall body, which will distribute workloads over many body segments. This distribution can result in less resistance for each body segment, allowing for a type of active recovery.

The distribution of body segments during a four-day, power training program is similar to that of the four-day hypertrophy program. However, the power-training workout concentrates on speed and resistance, rather than the volume and style of work. Because fewer sets and repetitions are performed, the workout can still be accomplished in 45 minutes to an hour, as the following example illustrates:

20 sets X 20	seconds per set	=	7 minutes
20 sets X 2	minute rest per set	=	40 minutes
			47 minutes (give or take)

The Power-Producing Repetition

In order to get the most power from conventional resistance training, the speed of the repetition should increase as the resistance increases. You should not attempt to move a light resistance as fast as possible during conventional resistance training exercises, since moving at high speeds can produce injuries. The increased exposure to injuries occurs because the athlete must remain attached to the resistance he is moving. When the resistance stops, the momentum of the resistance continues tearing and pulling at the athlete's joints. Far better methods of incorporating external limb speed for power exist besides conventional resistance training. Such high-speed methods involve resistances that can be released, as well as jumping drills. These high-speed activities are discussed in Chapter 9.

Performing a repetition for power should be highly reactive. Think of clapping your hands together very hard without making any sound. In order to do this, you have to decelerate your hands just as they are about to make contact. This is a reactive movement. At a certain point, you must react and change the speed of your hands to prevent contact.

A power-producing repetition must be performed in the same way. For example, on the bench press exercise, the bar descends from arms length toward your chest, picking up speed as it travels. You must attempt to decelerate the movement about two inches from your chest. The bar's only contact with your body should be a slight brush against your T-shirt. This transition from eccentric muscle contraction to concentric muscle contraction is called the *amoritization phase* The faster the bar descends, the faster the amoritization phase must be to prevent the bar from bouncing off your chest.

Decelerating the bar is a learned skill. The bar can pick up more speed on the descent, but only when you are conditioned for it (refer to Figure 8.5). This heightened level of reactivity is the sole objective during power type training. With this in mind, certain types of repetition styles and techniques can be applied, including rest, pause, and cheat repetitions.

Figure 8.5

• *Rest or pause repetitions.* Rest and pause repetitions have been previously discussed as a visible means of improving the hypertrophy of muscle. Resting and pausing can also aid in increasing power. Brief pauses in a locked-out or supported position after a repetition can insure the quality of the next repetition. Briefly locking out allows some of the lactic acid produced during the movement to be removed from the muscle. An accumulation of lactic acid can result in momentary muscular failure (MMF). MMF is desirable during hypertrophy training, but during power training, MMF should occur rarely, if ever. If MMF occurs on a regular basis, then the nervous system will be unable to fully recuperate. This inability to properly recover from your workouts can eventually force you to reduce the amount of resistance used during your training, subsequently reducing your gains in power.

A pause can be incorporated into each repetition during power type training. During the first sets and repetitions of the exercise, the pause should be brief, lasting only a half second. However, as fatigue is felt and the weight becomes increasingly heavy, the pause can last from two to three seconds. The recovery provided from this style of movement will allow each repetition to maximize its fullest potential for reactivity and intensity.

• *Cheat repetitions.* Cheating occurs naturally as you become fatigued. Your body will subtly readjust its mechanics to help you achieve a stressful repetition. Therefore, always be aware of your posture while performing a lift. During hypertrophy training, minimizing your body's natural tendency to cheat can help you fatigue and strengthen certain muscle fibers. During power training, you still need to minimize your natural tendency to cheat. However, as you approach the final repetitions of an exercise and your performance goal is threatened by fatigue, a small cheat can relieve some highly fatigued muscle fibers and bring fresh fibers into action. These fresh muscle fibers may not have been innervated without the applied "cheat." Accordingly, you can justify the allowance of your body's natural tendency.

Most of theses cheating moves are initiated from the hips, and produce small, but forcefully reactive movements that create momentum. The production of momentum changes the body's mechanics, giving the athlete a better advantage over the weight being lifted. The successful performances of super core lifts, such as the power clean or snatch, rely heavily on momentum and reactive movements. As was previously discussed, these reactive movements are beneficial during power training. Cheating must only involve subtle variations of the strictest form of an exercise. Excessive swinging, jerking, bouncing, or arching of the body can result in injuries.

Types of Sets for Muscular Power

• *Straight sets.* Straight sets were previously discussed in the earlier section on hypertrophy training. However, the straight set is a corner stone of power training. During power training, less than eight repetitions per set are suggested. While the number of sets vary during power training, the recommended number of sets should be relatively low to allow for the use of more resistance. In addition, if the number of repetitions you perform are also relatively low, you are more likely to focus all your efforts to insure that each repetition is highly reactive. How you choose to arrange the pattern of repetitions in a given set should be based on your power requirements. During particular phases in this text, the suggested workouts take you through a regular decent in the number of repetitions you perform. This prescription is recommended to slowly introduce you to heavier resistances that will progressively increase your power output. This style of workout structure also introduces you to a variety of different types of work patterns. Using straight repetition sets, these increases in resistance and decreases in repetitions can be approached more systematically (refer to Table 8.13).

SET #1	SET #2	SET #3
• 6 reps	• 6 reps	• 6 reps

Table 8.13. An example of a straight-set routine for muscular power.

• *Pyramid sets.* Because a pyramid workout contains sets with both high and low repetitions, it is best used during a transition phase of training. The pyramid can be performed for a couple of weeks between hypertrophy training and the beginning of the power training phases. Using the pyramid, you can keep the resistance the same and achieve MMF on each set for hypertrophy benefits, or you can progressively increase the resistance with each set and focus on producing power on the last set of the pyramid (refer to Table 8.14).

SET #1	SET #2	SET #3
• 12 reps	• 10 reps	• 8 reps

Table 8.14. An example of a pyramid-set routine for muscular power.

TRAINING VARIABLES AND RESULTS

	MUSCLE HYPERTROPHY	MUSCLE ENDURANCE	MUSCLE POWER
General Intensity:	High	Low	High
• Resistance levels	High	Low	High
• Number of repetitions	High (8 reps. +)	High (8 reps +)	Low (-8 reps)
• Number of sets per exercise	High (4 sets +)	Low (-4 sets)	Low (-4 sets)
• Tempo or cadence of exercise	Continuous	Continuous	Discontinuous
Duration of Exercise Session	Longer (45 min. +)	Longer (45 min +)	Shorter (/= 45 min.)
Frequency of Exercise Session	*Based on fatigue	*Based on fatigue	*Based on fatigue
Number of Weekly Training Days	High (4 days +)	Medium (3 days)	Medium/high (+ or - 4 days)
Type of Resistance Reps Used	Forced reps. **Pause reps. Rest reps.	Normal exercise movement (Avoid excess MMF to reduce hypertrophy) Better to use less isolated exercises	Cheat reps Pause reps Rest reps
Speed of Repetitions	Slow	Normal	Fast (resistance must be heavy or releasable, i.e., plyometric)
Type of Sets Used	Straight sets Super sets variations Combination sets Pre-exhaustion sets Reverse pyramid sets Drop sets Pyramid sets	Straight sets Super sets variations Combination sets Pre-exhaustion sets Push-pull sets Drop sets Pyramid Sets	Pyramid sets Straight sets

* The more often you experience MMF during a workout, the more rest you will need before that body part should be worked again. For example, failure on all sets = 72 hours required rest. Failure on the last set only = 48 hours required rest. General fatigue on any sets = 24 hours required rest.

** Even through a pause rep is a power-producing repetition style, it can be used near the end of the set to enable extra repetitions to be performed.

Table 8.15. An overview of the variables involved in the three basic types of goal-related training.

Muscular Strength

To this point in the chapter, the focus has been on how to develop muscular hypertrophy, muscular endurance, and muscular power. The question arises: What about muscular strength? You may have seen a rhythmic gymnastic competition and heard an athlete referred to as "looking strong," while the same may have been said of an Olympic weight lifter. These are surely two different types of athletes. How can they both be strong? Radically simplified, strength is a relative property of athletics and is based on many things: coordination of movement, body type, flexibility, cardiorespiratory ability, etc.. In order to optimize your strengths, it is critical to recognize the physical requirements of your sport or position. Once you understand the physical requirements of your sport, you can then begin improving on your strengths and working on any areas that need addressing by constructing your training program to meet those requirements. In this way, you can become an exceptionally strong basketball player.

THE EXERCISES

In this section, the various resistance exercises that should be incorporated during your 52-week training program are detailed. Your selection of resistance exercises and the level of specificity of your workout should be based on the equipment available and the general layout of your workout facility. As detailed in chapters 1 through 6, the exercises you should select should also be determined by which training phase you are in.

The exercises have been grouped into four main categories: supercore, core, supporting, or assisting (Table 8.10). To a great extent, these categories refer to the number of muscle and joint segments involved during the performance of an exercise, rather than the fact that one group of exercises is better than the next. Because the body's musculoskeletal structure is a system by which the actions of one movement affect the actions of another, each exercise plays an important role in the strengthening of your body.

Supercore Exercises

Supercore exercises are complex exercises that involve the use of many joints and muscle groups. The level of resistance used with these exercises is usually high. If you cannot perform these exercises properly, or are unable to display functional flexibility in the various supercore positions, then you may suffer negative physical consequences if you attempt them. In fact, as a result of individual body mechanics, some athletes should probably never attempt the supercore exercises. Instead, such athletes should use the core exercises to achieve the power improvements they are seeking.

Supercore:
(Multiple muscle; unisolated)

- Push press
- Dumbbell push press
- Dumbbell snatch
- Dumbbell pull press
- Hang clean
- Dumbbell hang clean
- Clean and jerk
- Power row

Combo/Supercore:
(Combined supercore exercises)

- Side dumbbell raise lunge
- Dumbbell lunge/dumbbell upright row
- Dumbbell snatch/dumbbell push press
- Step up/shoulder fly
- Backward lunge/dumbbell upright row
- Step up/side dumbbell raise
- Side lunge/shoulder fly
- Squat press
- Dumbbell squat/two-arm dumbbell press

Core:
(Multiple muscle; semi-isolated)

- Bench press
- Incline bench press
- Smith incline press
- Flat dumbbell press
- Incline dumbbell press
- Ham decline
- Close incline press
- Close-grip lat
- Two-arm dumbbell row
- One-arm dumbbell row
- Military press

Core *(Continued)*

- Behind neck press
- Smith military press
- Smith behind neck
- Alternate dumbbell press
- Two-arm dumbbell press
- Free-weight upright row
- Straight bar curl
- EZ-bar curl
- Close-grip bench
- Squat
- One- or two-leg press
- Dead lift
- Dumbbell squat
- Dumbbell dead lift

Supporting:
(Single muscle; isolated)

- Smith close incline press
- Ham 10 chest
- Flat dumbbell fly
- Incline dumbbell fly
- Middle chest flex
- Lower chest flex
- High lat front
- High lat rear
- Close high lat
- Close low lat
- Straight dumbbell pullover
- Split dumbbell pullover
- Side dumbbell raise
- Front dumbbell raise
- Shoulder fly
- Manual side raise
- Cable upright row
- Manual upright row
- Dumbbell upright row
- Bent dumbbell raise
- Manual rear deltoid
- Preacher curl (cable)
- Alternating dumbbell curl

Supporting *(Continued)*

- Incline curl
- Concentration curl
- Shooters french press
- Two-arm dumbbell triceps extension
- Dumbbell french press
- Triceps push down
- Kickback
- One- or two-leg extension
- One- or two-leg curl

Assisting:
(Support and balance; isolated)

- Bar shrug
- Cable shrug
- Dumbbell shrug
- Manual shrug
- Dumbbell stroll
- Hammer curl
- Sit-up
- Quarter sit-up
- Ball throw
- Hanging abs
- Hyperextension
- Fluttering
- Scissoring
- Alternating superman
- Quarter elbow tuck-in
- Butt row
- Reverse sit-up
- Hip-up
- Side push-up
- Elbow hip dip
- Clock work
- Reverse hyperextension
- Skydiver
- Hi ya
- Bye ya
- Superman
- Standing calf raise

Assisting *(Continued)*

- Calf raise leg press
- BW one-leg calf

Additional Exercises:
(Functional exercises; support and balance)

- Dip
- Medicine ball/Ball ball push-up
- Hands on balance ball push-up
- Feet on balance ball push-up
- Medicine ball push-up
- Zigzag push-up
- Moon push-up
- Pull-up
- Roll-out
- Medicine ball circuits
- Rear deltoid swim
- 21 blaster (bicep)
- Reverse dip
- Close grip push-up
- Around the world legs
- Box squat/baby squat
- Hip flex
- Lunge – 3 pumps
- Alternating leg lunge
- Backward lunge
- Musketeer lunge
- One stiff leg dead lift
- Side lunge
- Step-up
- Slideboard
- Donkey kicks
- Hamstring on balance ball
- Crabbing
- Leg dragging
- Wrist flex
- Jump rope

Table 8.16. A listing of the various types of resistance exercises by exercise classification.

Core Exercises

Core exercises involve several muscle groups and joint combinations working together to perform an exercise movement. In most instances, you will use a heavy level of resistance with these exercises. Proper coordination of the muscles and joint groups is the key to success when performing core lifts. Combining core exercises with supporting exercises will build muscular strength and size to optimal levels.

Supporting Exercises

As a rule, supporting exercises involve a single joint and the action of a single muscle or muscle group. This isolation stimulates a large number of muscle fibers because the work being performed is not distributed over as many muscles as it is in supercore and core exercises. Because you use fewer muscle groups during supporting exercises, you display less strength. As a result, lower levels of resistance must be used. Your objective when performing supporting exercises should be to move the resistance with perfect technique. The application of a deliberate flexion of the muscle during the performance of a supporting exercise can increase the muscle tension even further, and subsequently, promote greater muscle growth. Supporting exercises can help correct muscular imbalances, as well as indirectly improve your capability of performing super core and core lifts. Supporting exercises are also good for helping rehabilitate injuries, because they provide a more direct stimulation to the muscles surrounding a particular joint. This action, in turn, helps to stabilize the injured joint area.

Assisting Exercises

Assisting exercises increase the stability of the body by addressing the core muscles (the abdominal muscles and other muscles of the mid-section and lower back). Assistance exercises also address the calves, neck, and muscles of the forearms. These muscular areas assist the athlete with balance and support during movements. Including assistance exercises in your exercise routine can also help improve the neural pathways throughout your body.

Functional Exercises

Functional exercises, like supercore exercises, are complex combinations of movements. Even though the exercises involve many joint and muscle groups, the level of resistance used is usually low. Typically, you employ your own body weight as the resistance. In turn, you are required to balance and support your own body weight or the weight of a highly moveable object. As such, these exercises require you to have better control of your body and body segments.

■ CHEST EXERCISES

● Bench Press
(Core)
Lying on your back, plant your feet firmly on the floor. Grip the bar with your hands at shoulder-width apart and support the bar at arms length. Lower the bar to your chest with your elbows out, then press the bar up by extending your arms.

Figure 8.6a

Figure 8.6b

● Incline Bench Press
(Core)

Lying on your back on an incline bench, plant your feet firmly on the floor. Grip the bar with your hands at shoulder-width apart and support the bar at arms length. Lower the bar to your upper chest, then press the bar upward by extending your arms.

Figure 8.7a

Figure 8.7b

- Smith Incline Press

(Core)

This exercise is performed just like the incline bench press previously described, but because the exercise is performed in a Smith machine which provides more stability, the muscles can be overloaded with more downward force.

Figure 8.8a   **Figure 8.8b**

- Dip

(Functional)

Support yourself with straight arms on dip bars. Leaning slightly forward as you descend, bend your elbows to lower your body until you feel a stretch in your shoulder muscles. Be sure your elbows are pointed in the same direction as the bar. Then, press upward, back to the starting position.

Figure 8.9a   **Figure 8.9b**

● Flat and Incline Dumbbell Press

(Core)

Lying on your back on a bench (or on an incline bench), plant your feet firmly on the floor. Grip a dumbbell in each hand and support each dumbbell at arms length at shoulder-width apart. Bend from the elbow to lower both dumbbells to your upper chest, and then press them up by extending your arms.

Figure 8.10a

Figure 8.10b

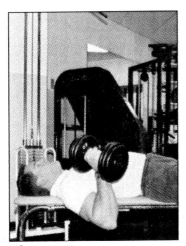

Figure 8.10c

Figure 8.10d

● Ham Decline

(Core)

With your back flat against the seat back, grasp the handles with each hand and extend both arms by pressing forward. Slowly bend your elbows to bring the handles back to your chest.

Figure 8.11a

Figure 8.11b

● Close Incline Press

(Core)

Lying back on an incline, plant your feet firmly on the floor. Grip the bar with your hands closer than shoulder-width apart and support the bar at arms length. Lower the bar to your upper chest, then press the bar upward by extending the arms. By moving the hands in closer, the mid-line of the upper chest is emphasized during this exercise.

Figure 8.12a

Figure 8.12b

● Smith Close Incline Press

(Supporting)

This exercise is a more stable version of the close incline press. Because it is more stable, you can concentrate more on flexing your hands together during the movement, thereby making the exercise more fatiguing on the muscles of the inner/upper chest.

Figure 8.13a

Figure 8.13b

● Ham 10 Chest

(Supporting)

Lying on your back, rest the pads of the machine on your upper arm. Raise your arms simultaneously in a semicircular movement until the pads touch over your chest. Return to the starting position.

Figure 8.14a

Figure 8.14b

● Flat and Incline Dumbbell Fly

(Supporting)

Lie on a flat bench (or on an incline bench) with your feet flat on the floor. Hold the dumbbells at arms length above your shoulders with your palms facing each other and the dumbbells nearly touching. Lower the dumbbells in a semicircular path to your chest level by bending your elbows. Return to the starting position following the same semicircular path.

Figure 8.15a

Figure 8.15b

Figure 8.15c

Figure 8.15d

● Middle and Lower Chest Flex

(Supporting)

Performed without weight, the primary purpose of this exercise is to provide muscle action awareness and control. The middle version of the chest flex is performed standing up with your upper body straight. Hold your arms at your sides at shoulder height. Bend your arms at the elbow so that your hands are pointing to the ceiling. Begin the exercise by slowly squeezing your elbows toward each other as if to force the air out of an imaginary beach ball. Your elbows will meet in front of your chest. Then, slowly return to the starting position.

The lower version of the chest flex involves the same principles of squeezing the chest muscles. Begin by standing up straight with your arms to your sides at shoulder height. This time, however, do not bend your arms. Begin the exercise by slowly squeezing your hands toward each other as if to force the air out of an imaginary beach ball. Your hands will meet in front of your legs at the waist. Then, slowly return to the starting position.

Figure 8.16a

Figure 8.16b

Figure 8.16c

Figure 8.16d

● Variations of the Push-up (Functional)

The push-up, a very traditional exercise, simply involves pushing your body from the floor or other objects by extending your arms. The most important factor to consider when performing any type of push-up is to contract your abdominal muscles. This abdominal involvement insures that your lower back remains as straight as possible during the movement. In this book, several challenging versions of the push-up are used to increase shoulder stability.

The medicine-ball push-up (Figure 8.17a) is performed by placing each of your hands on a fully inflated medicine ball or basketball and executing the push-up motion. Your objective is to maintain perfect push-up form while controlling the circular actions of the balls.

The feet-on-balance-ball push-up (Figure 8.17b) is performed by putting your feet on the balance ball and your hands on the floor. This positioning causes you to have to control your hips during the push-up action.

The hands-on-balance-ball push-up (Figure 8.17c) is performed by doing a push-up with your hands on a balance ball and your feet on the floor. Again, you must stabilize your shoulders to control the ball's circular actions.

The medicine-ball, balance-ball push-up (Figure 8.17d) is performed by placing your feet on a balance ball and each hand on a medicine ball or basketball. This exercise, of course, requires great body awareness and balance and is the most challenging version of the push-up.

Figure 8.17a

Figure 8.17b

Figure 8.17c

Figure 8.17d

● Zigzag Push-up (Functional)

This variation of the push-up is a precursor to a one-arm push up. Assume a push-up position with your hands wider than shoulder-width apart. Also, spread your legs about one-foot apart. Keeping both hands on the floor, lean your upper body toward your left hand and bend your left elbow until your chest is just above the floor. Your right arm should become straight as you move to the floor. Push yourself up by using primarily your left arm. Then, lean your body to the right and bend the elbow of your right arm to move again to the floor. Your left arm should become straight as you descend. You should appear as if you are moving from side to side as you perform this version of the push-up.

● Moon Push-up (Functional)

The Navy Seals' push-up of choice is the moon push-up (Figures 8.18a to 8.18c). To begin this exercise, assume a push-up position, with the exception that your body is bent at the waist with your buttocks angled high above your head. Begin bending your elbows while moving your head toward the floor, as if diving. Allow your face to move along the floor, while at the same time beginning to extend your arms toward full lock out. Once your arms are fully extended, you should have your shoulders and upper torso angled slightly in front of your hands. To return to the starting position, bend your elbows, lowering your body to the floor like a regular push-up. Allow your buttocks to move up and away from the floor toward their original starting position, while at the same time pushing your body back and up with your arms, until they are fully locked out once again.

Figure 8.18a

Figure 8.18b

Figure 8.18c

■ BACK EXERCISES

- Close-Grip Lat
  (Core)
  Kneeling with your legs secure, grasp the bar with both hands, using an under-hand grip. Keep your hands 6-to-10 inches apart. Use your back muscles by squeezing your shoulder blades together, while bending your elbows to enhance the contraction of your back muscles; pull the bar to your chest. Return to the starting position.

Figure 8.19

- Two-Arm Dumbbell Row
  (Core)

  Standing with your feet together and your knees bent, bend slightly at the waist. Hold a dumbbell in each hand. Use your back muscles by squeezing your shoulder blades together, while slowly pulling your elbows upward until your upper arm is parallel to the floor. Slowly return your arms to the starting position.

Figure 8.20a

Figure 8.20b

● One-Arm Dumbbell Row
(Core)

With the knee and arm of your non-lifting arm on a bench, bend slightly at the waist. Holding a dumbbell in the other hand, slowly pull your elbow upward until your upper arm is parallel to the floor. Return to the starting position. After completing the prescribed number of repetitions with one arm, switch arms.

Figure 8.21a

Figure 8.21b

● High Lat Front
(Supporting)

Kneeling with your legs secure, grasp the bar with both hands, using an overhand grip. Keep your hands 8-to-12 inches apart. Use your back muscles by squeezing your shoulder blades together. Arch your back as you bend your elbows and pull the bar to your chest. This action places greater emphasis on the contracting back muscles. Return to the starting position.

Figure 8.22a

Figure 8.22b

● Chin-Up
(Functional)

Grasp a pull-up bar with an underhanded grip. Cross your legs behind you and pull your body up until your chin reaches the bar. Return to the starting position.

Figure 8.23a

Figure 8.23b

● High Lat Rear
(Supporting)

Kneeling with your legs secure, grasp the bar with both hands, using an overhand grip. Keep hands 8-to-12 inches apart. Use your back muscles by squeezing your shoulder blades together. Arch your back as you bend your elbows and pull the bar behind your head to your shoulders. Return to the starting position.

Figure 8.24a

Figure 8.24b

● Close High Lat
(Supporting)

Kneeling with your legs secure, grasp a narrow handle V-shaped bar with both hands, with your palms facing one another. Use your back muscles by squeezing your shoulder blades together. Arch your back as you bend your elbows and pull the bar to your chest. Return to the starting position.

Figure 8.25a

Figure 8.25b

● Close Low Lat
(Supporting)

Sit with your back straight and your legs straight in front and your knees slightly bent. Grasp a narrow handle V-shaped bar with both hands. Use your back muscles by squeezing your shoulder blades together. Arch your back as you bend your elbows and pull the cable toward your stomach. Return to the starting position.

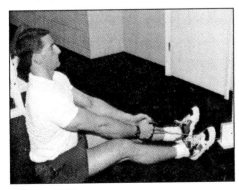

Figure 8.26a

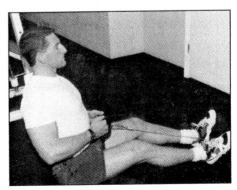

Figure 8.26b

● Straight Dumbbell Pullover
(Supporting)

Lie on your back on a bench with your feet flat on the ground. Hold a dumbbell with both hands above your chest. Use your back muscles to lower the dumbbell to a point above your head and parallel to the floor. Return to the starting position.

Figure 8.27a

Figure 8.27b

● Split Dumbbell Pullover
(Supporting)

Lie on your back on the floor with your legs straight and both arms at your side. Holding a dumbbell in each hand, raise one arm up and place it back behind the head (forming a 180 degree arc with your arm). At the same time, return that arm to the starting position and raise the other arm up and place it behind the head. Repeat, alternating arms.

Figure 8.28a

Figure 8.28b

● Roll-Out
(Functional)

Kneeling on a mat on the floor, grasp the bar with both hands at shoulder-width apart. Keeping your back straight, roll the bar forward until your arms are outstretched as far as they will go. Use your arms to press down onto the bar, while flexing the abdominals forward to roll back up to the starting position.

Figure 8.29a

Figure 8.29b

■ SHOULDER EXERCISES

● Military Press
(Core)

Sitting in an upright position with your back perfectly straight, plant your feet firmly on the floor. Grip the bar with your hands at shoulder-width apart and support the bar at arms length. Lower the bar to your upper chest, then press the bar up by extending your arms.

Figure 8.30a

Figure 8.30b

● Behind Neck Press
(Core)

Sitting in an upright position with your back perfectly straight, plant your feet firmly on the floor. Grip the bar with your hands at shoulder-width apart and support the bar at arms length. Lower the bar to a point behind your head at ear level, then press the bar up by extending your arms.

Figure 8.31a

Figure 8.31b

● Smith Behind Neck and Military Press
(Core)

Utilizing a Smith machine to increase linear overload, sit in an upright position with your back perfectly straight. Plant your feet firmly on the floor. Grip the bar with your hands at shoulder-width apart and support the bar at arm's length. Lower the bar to a point behind your head at ear level, and then press the bar up by extending your arms. When performing the military press, assume the same body position, but slide the bench back to allow the bar to move in front of your chin, just above your collarbone.

Figure 8.32a

Figure 8.32b

● Alternate Dumbbell Press (Easy and Hard)
(Core)

To perform the hard version of this exercise, start with both arms extended overhead. Alternate arms – lowering one arm to the shoulder, while keeping the other arm extended overhead. To perform the easy version, start with both dumbbells resting at shoulder level. Alternate arms – extending one dumbbell to arms length, while keeping other at shoulder level.

Figure 8.33a

Figure 8.33b

● Two-Arm Dumbbell Press
(Core)

This exercise is performed like the alternating dumbbell press. However, in this exercise, both dumbbells are extended upward at the same time. Attempt to push the chest forward as the dumbbells ascend in an arc that is just slightly above and behind the head.

Figure 8.34a

Figure 8.34b

● Dumbbell Push Press (Supercore)

Assume a standing position with the dumbbells resting at shoulder level. Keep your feet firmly planted at shoulder-width. Begin by quickly bending your knees about two to three inches. This movement allows the dumbbells to gain a downward momentum. Then, just as rapidly, extend your knees and, at the same time, press the dumbbells upward by extending your arms to a point directly over and just slightly behind your head. Then, lower the dumbbells under control to their starting position.

Figure 8.35a   **Figure 8.35b**

● Push Press (Supercore)

Assume a standing position with the barbell resting at shoulder level. Keep your feet firmly planted at shoulder-width. Begin by quickly bending your knees about two to three inches. This movement allows the barbell to gain a downward momentum. Then, just as rapidly, extend your knees and, at the same time, press the barbell upward by extending your arms to a point directly over and just slightly behind your head. Next, lower the barbell under control to the starting position.

Figure 8.36a   **Figure 8.36b**   **Figure 8.36c**

● Dumbbell Snatch
(Supercore)

Assume a squatting position with your back straight and your eyes up. To begin the exercise, rapidly pull the dumbbells from the floor by extending your knees and hips fully. It is critical to keep your back straight and your head and eyes angled slightly upward during the entire pull to avoid lower back stress. At the same time you are extending your legs, your arms should be pulling the dumbbells upward toward your forehead. Remember to keep your elbows higher than your wrist during the pull. When the dumbbells have reached their maximum height, flip your wrists under, securely catching the dumbbells, and extend your arms fully above the head. As the level of resistance used in the exercise increases, the height the dumbbells can be pulled will gradually become less and less. As a result, in order to safely finish the movement, you will have to squat lower and lower to secure the dumbbells at full-arm extension.

Figure 8.37a   **Figure 8.37b**

● Side Dumbbell Raise
(Supporting)

This exercise can be performed either standing or sitting. Sitting versions of any upper-body exercise allow for less lower-body involvement, resulting in greater upper-body exertion. Begin with the dumbbells at arms length in front of your lower torso if you're standing (Figure 8.38a and 8.38b). If you're sitting, the dumbbells should be straight down to the sides of the seat. Keep a very slight bend in your elbows throughout the movement to reduce stress on the elbow joint. Slowly raise the dumbbells upward and out to arms length at the sides of your body. Your palms should remain facing the floor throughout the movement. Once parallel to the floor, the dumbbells should be slightly in front of your body in a place where they can be seen in your peripheral vision. To finish the movement, slowly turn the dumbbells forward so that the thumb on each hand faces downward (as if pouring water from a pitcher). Slowly return the weights to their starting point.

Figure 8.38a

Figure 8.38b

● Front Dumbbell Raise
  (Supporting)

This exercise can be performed either standing or sitting. Begin with the dumbbells at arms length in front of the lower torso if you're standing. (If you're sitting, the dumbbells should be straight down to the sides of the seat.) Your palms should remain facing inward toward one another throughout the movement. Slowly raise the dumbbells upward and out to arms length in front of your body, parallel to the floor. A twist in the wrist can be added at the top of the movement, allowing your palm to face down toward the floor. This action will increase the level of muscle exertion. At this point, the dumbbells can be lowered to their starting position. This movement can be performed either in an alternating fashion, or with both dumbbells being moved simultaneously.

Figure 8.39a

Figure 8.39b

● Shoulder Fly
(Supporting)

This exercise is performed in a very similar fashion to that of the side dumbbell raise. The only difference is that instead of the dumbbells stopping at a point parallel to the floor, they are instead brought to a point all the way above the head, and then slowly returned to the starting point. This exercise is best utilized during a heavy stage of training. It can be performed standing with heavier resistance. The legs can be used in the same manner as the dumbbell push press to make the movement more complex.

Figure 8.40a

Figure 8.40b

● Manual Side Raise
(Supporting)

Using a partner to apply resistance, the worker sits in front of his partner (referred to as the "resistor"). The resistor sits behind. The worker begins by placing his arms to the side and slightly to the front of his body, with a slight bend in the elbows. The resistor begins the exercise by applying downward pressure on the worker's arms at points just below the elbows (Figure 8.41). The worker attempts to control the resistor's pressure by slowly allowing his arms to move down to his sides. Upon reaching the bottom of the movement, the worker begins to press his arms upward, along the path they have just traveled. At this point, the resistor attempts to apply enough downward pressure to the worker so that his arm movement is the same speed moving up as it was going down.

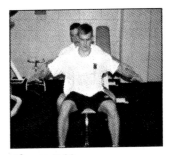

Figure 8.41

● Medicine-Ball Circuit
(Functional)

This exercise involves a series of movements with a medicine ball that are performed one after the other in a circuit fashion.

- The first maneuver is a wood-chopping movement (Figures 8.42a and 8.42b). Start with the ball extended above your head at arms length. The ball is then brought to a point between your legs just above the floor, using a squatting motion. Your back should remain straight, and your chin tilted slightly upward. Perform 10 to 15 repetitions.

- The second movement is a large circular rotation performed with the ball (figure 8.42c). Start with the ball extended above your head at arms length. The ball is then brought down and to your right in a clockwise motion. As the ball reaches your far right, you should begin to squat, carrying the ball just above the floor. Again, your back should remain straight, and your chin tilted slightly upward. The circle continues to your left as you move up and out of the squat. One repetition of the exercise is performed once your arms complete the circle and end at full extension above your head once more. Perform 10 to 15 repetitions both clockwise and counter clockwise.

- The third movement in the circuit is a sideways version of the wood chopper (Figures 8.42d and 8.42e). Begin the movement with the ball extended at arms length above and to the far left of your head. The ball is then brought to a point outside your right ankle just above the floor, using a squatting motion. Your back should again remain straight, and your chin tilted slightly upward. A repetition of the exercise is completed when the ball is moved up and back to its staring point. Perform 10 to 15 repetitions from upper left to lower right and from upper right to lower left.

This circuit is a great lower- and upper-body combination exercise, but will be felt most profoundly in the shoulder area.

Figure 8.42a

Figure 8.42b

Figure 8.42c

Figure 8.42d

Figure 8.42e

● Dumbbell Pull Press
   (Supercore)

Assume a squatting position with your back straight and your eyes up. To begin the exercise, rapidly pull the dumbbells from the floor by extending your knees and hips fully. It is critical to keep your back straight and your head and eyes angled slightly upward during the entire pull to avoid lower back stress. At the same time you are extending your legs, your arms should be pulling the dumbbells upward toward your forehead. Remember to keep your elbows higher than your wrists during the pull. When the dumbbells have reached their maximum height, flip the wrists under securely, catching the dumbbells at the level of the shoulders. Once the dumbbells are secure, complete the movement by performing a push-press movement to extend your arms fully above and slightly behind your head. As the level of resistance increases in this exercise, the height the dumbbells can be pulled toward your forehead will become less and less. As a result, in order to safely finish the movement, you will have to progressively squat lower and lower to catch the dumbbells at shoulder level.

Figure 8.43a

Figure 8.43b

Figure 8.43c

Figure 8.43d

Figure 8.43e

● Clean and Jerk
(Supercore)

This exercise is the same as the dumbbell pull press, except it is performed with a bar.

Figure 8.44a

Figure 8.44b

Figure 8.44c

■ TRAPEZIUS AND POSTERIOR SHOULDER EXERCISES

● Power Row
(Supercore)

This exercise is an exaggerated version of the upright row (free). Because the weight used in this exercise is about a fourth of that lifted in the power clean, the legs are used even more in this exercise than in the upright row. Start with a barbell at arms length

Figure 8.45a

Figure 8.45b

in front of your hips. Bend your knees two to three inches, allowing the bar to gain a downward momentum. Straighten your knees and, at the same time, begin pulling the bar upward with your arms. Allow your arms to bend at the elbow, while keeping your elbows always higher than your wrists. Allow the bar to reach chin level, and then slowly return the bar to the starting position. Since the weight is heavier, it is safer to allow your knees to bend slightly as the bar descends. The bar can then be caught on your upper thighs. This stop prevents the lower back from having to fully de-accelerate the weight. Stand straight up again and repeat the process.

● Hang Clean
(Supercore)

Hang cleans are performed exactly the same as the power row previously described. However, instead of the bar being pulled to the chin and returned to the start, the wrists are flipped under as they are during a power clean movement, and the bar is caught at chin level. To complete the movement, the bar is slowly returned to hip level.

Figure 8.46a

Figure 8.46b

● Dumbbell Hang Clean
(Supporting)

This exercise is just like the hang clean previously described, except for the fact that dumbbells are used instead. This version of the clean is relatively comfortable for a basketball player because his wrists are not forced back during the racking or chambering of the weight. Instead, the wrist can be rotated and allowed to remain straight. Working with dumbbells also requires more balance and concentration.

Figure 8.47a

Figure 8.47b

● Free-Weight Upright Row
  (Core)

Start with a barbell at arms length in front of your hips. Allow your arms to bend at the elbow. Always keep your elbows higher than your wrists. Allow the bar to reach chin level, and then slowly return the bar to the starting position.

Figure 8.48a

Figure 8.48b

● Cable Upright Row
  (Supporting)

Start with a bar and cable at arms length in front of your hips. Allow your arms to bend at the elbow. Always keep your elbows higher than your wrists. Allow the bar to reach chin level, and then slowly return the bar to the starting position.

Figure 8.49

- Dumbbell Upright Row
  (Supporting)

This exercise is performed like the other versions of the upright row, only it is performed with dumbbells. The use of dumbbells allows your wrist to be free to move during the exercise. This freedom is beneficial if you have shoulder discomfort during the other versions of the upright row. Also, balancing and controlling dumbbells can be difficult.

Figure 8.50a

Figure 8.50b

- Manual Upright Row
  (Supporting)

This exercise is a partner-assisted exercise with the same methods used to apply resistance in manual side raise applied here. The resistor sits facing the standing worker. Both participants grasp a towel, which is held at the hip level of the worker. The worker begins by pulling the towel upward toward his chin. The worker's elbows should be higher than his wrists. As the worker pulls up, the resistor applies force on the towel by steadily pulling downward. The speed of movement should remain the same in both directions.

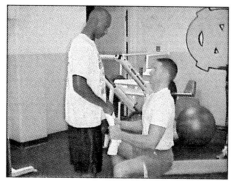

Figure 8.51a

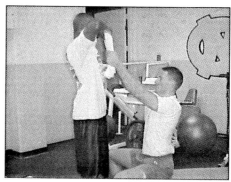

Figure 8.51b

● Bar or Cable Shrug
(Assisting)

Start with the bar at arms length in front of your hips. Keeping your arms perfectly straight, use your upper shoulder muscles to pull the weight upward as if to shrug. Make sure to keep your chin tucked down to your upper chest to allow your upper shoulder muscles to reach their maximum height. Then, slowly lower the bar downward to complete a full repetition of the exercise. The cable provides a more constant level of resistance than would a free-weight object.

Figure 8.52

● Dumbbell Shrug
(Assisting)

Start with a pair of dumbbells at arms length in front of your hips. Keeping your arms perfectly straight, use your upper shoulder muscles to pull the weight upward as if to shrug. Make sure to keep your chin tucked down to your upper chest to allow the upper shoulder muscles to reach their maximum height. Slowly lower the dumbbells downward to complete a full repetition of the exercise.

Figure 8.53a

Figure 8.53b

● Manual Shrug
(Assisting)

This version of the shrug requires a partner. Begin by sitting on a bench. Have your partner stand on the bench behind you and place his hands firmly on your shoulders. Your partner then applies downward pressure on your shoulders. Attempt to shrug upward against the pressure, and slowly return to the starting position. All manual exercises require complete cooperation. It is not a tug of war between you and your partner. All of the repetitions should be smooth and continuous.

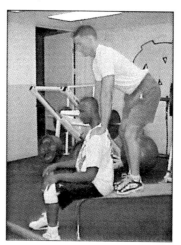
Figure 8.54a

Figure 8.54b

● Dumbbell Stroll
(Assisting)

This exercise is performed by carrying a dumbbell in each hand for a given distance while walking. The natural vertical rise and fall of the body while striding will create a small shrugging motion. This motion will effect the upper shoulders and trapezius muscle group. The gripping strength of the forearms and hands is also profoundly effected. This activity is a great exercise to measure the psychological willingness to complete the distance without stopping.

Figure 8.55

- Bent Dumbbell Raise
  (Supporting)

  Start with your feet and knees pressed firmly together. Bend your knees two to three inches. Both of these steps reduce pressure on your lower back. Bend at the waist until your upper back is parallel to the floor, and allow the dumbbells to hang freely and perpendicular to the floor. Arch your middle back just below the shoulder blades. Slowly pull the dumbbells upward and to the sides of your body, with your palms facing downward. The dumbbells should reach their end point when they are parallel to the floor, just slightly in front of your shoulders. You should see them in your peripheral vision.

Figure 8.56a   **Figure 8.56b**

- Manual Rear Deltoid
  (Supporting)

  A partner is used to apply resistance. The worker sits in front. The resistor sits behind. The worker begins by crossing his arms in front of his body, level with his the upper chest. The resistor begins by applying forward pressure on the worker's arms at the worker's elbows. While keeping his elbows high, the worker attempts to move his elbows back against the resistor's accommodating pressure. Upon reaching the furthermost point which the worker's elbows can travel, the worker begins to allow his arms to be pressed forward along the path they have just traveled. At this point, the resistor attempts to apply enough forward pressure to the worker so that his arm movement is the same speed moving forward as it was going back.

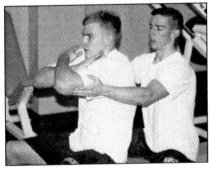

Figure 8.57a

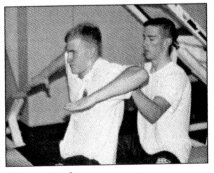

Figure 8.57b

- Rear Deltoid Swim
  (Functional)

This exercise can be performed with or without weights. Start by lying on your stomach, with your feet suspended two inches from the floor. Your hands are stretched out in front of your body, suspended two inches from the floor with your palms down. To begin the exercise, bring both hands in an arc along the sides of your body, being careful to never touch the floor. As your hands reach your buttocks, your hands are turned palm up. To complete the swimming motion, your hands are then returned to their starting position in front of your body.

Figure 8.58a

Figure 8.58b

■ ARM EXERCISES

- Straight-Bar Curl
  (Core)

Start with the bar at the upper-thigh level. Begin the exercise by pulling the bar toward your chin by flexing your arms at the elbows. Keep your elbows close to your sides, and slightly in the front of the body. Never lean back in order to lift the weight.

Figure 8.59a

Figure 8.59b

● Preacher Curl (Cable)
(Supporting)

Assume a sitting position on the preacher bench, with the back of your upper arms resting securely on the pad. Grasp the bar which is attached to a cable. This exercise can be performed with a free-weight bar as well. Begin the exercise by lifting the bar upward toward your chin by flexing your arms at the elbows. Return the bar slowly to the starting position to complete the repetition.

Figure 8.60

● Alternating Dumbbell Curl
(Supporting)

Assume a standing position. Grasp a dumbbell in each hand, and allow the dumbbells to hang freely at each side of your body. Begin the exercise by lifting one dumbbell upward toward your shoulder by flexing your arms at the elbows. Return the dumbbell slowly to the down position, before lifting the other dumbbell on the opposite side. Continue lifting the dumbbells in an alternating fashion.

Figure 8.61a   **Figure 8.61b**

- EZ-Bar Curl
  (Core)

  Start with the EZ bar held at upper-thigh level. Begin the exercise by pulling the bar toward your chin by flexing your arms at the elbows. Keep your elbows close to your sides, and slightly in the front of your body. Never lean back in order to lift the weight.

Figure 8.62a   **Figure 8.62b**

- Incline Curl
  (Supporting)

  Assume a sitting position on the incline bench with your back resting securely on the pad. Grasp a dumbbell in each hand, and allow the dumbbells to hang freely at each side of your body. Begin the exercise by lifting one dumbbell upward toward your shoulder by flexing your arms at the elbows. Return the dumbbell slowly to the down position, before lifting the other dumbbell on the opposite side. Continue lifting the dumbbells in an alternating fashion.

Figure 8.63

● Hammer Curl
(Assisting)

Assume a standing position. Grasp a dumbbell in each hand, and allow the dumbbells to hang freely at each side of your body. Begin the exercise by lifting one dumbbell, upward toward your shoulder by flexing your arms at the elbows. Your palms should always face inward as if you were holding a hammer during the entire movement. Return the dumbbell slowly to the down position, before lifting the other dumbbell on the opposite side. Continue lifting the dumbbells in an alternating fashion.

Figure 8.64

● Concentration Curl
(Supporting)

Assume a standing position and bend over at your waist and support yourself by spreading your legs wider than shoulder-width, with your knees bent slightly. Rest your non-working arm on your knee. Using only one dumbbell at a time, allow the

Figure 8.65a   **Figure 8.65b**

dumbbell to extend fully at arms length between your legs. Begin curling the dumbbell upward to the shoulder of your non-working arm by flexing your arm at the elbow. Turn your elbow out and away from your body as you curl the weight up to insure yourself the highest benefit from the exercise. This exercise is a very isolated exercise for the biceps and is usually reserved for hypertrophy-type training.

● Shooters French Press
(Supporting)

Standing up straight, grasp a straight barbell or EZ curl bar with a over-hand grip (palms toward you). The bar should be at arms length in front of you at your waist. Begin the movement by bending at the elbows and curling the bar upward to your chin. Then, press the bar above your head as if to perform a shoulder press. Allow the weight to come down behind your head, keeping your elbows as close to your head as possible. Using only your triceps, extend the bar back above your head at arms length. To complete the repetition, lower the bar back to your chin, and then reverse the curl downward to the starting position.

Figure 8.66a

Figure 8.66b

Figure 8.66c

Figure 8.66d

Figure 8.66e

● Two-Arm Dumbbell Triceps Extension
(Supporting)

Lying on a bench, grasp a dumbbell in each hand, and extend your arms fully above your upper chest. Begin the movement by bending at the elbows and allow both dumbbells to descend to a point beside your head. Your upper arms should remain perpendicular to the floor at all times and should remain stationary throughout the movement. To complete the repetition, extend your arms upward to their starting position.

Figure 8.67a

Figure 8.67b

● Dumbbell French Press
(Supporting)

Assume a sitting or standing position. Grasp one dumbbell by its head and extend it above your head at arms length. It is safer to used fixed dumbbells for this exercise. Removable collars may detach and cause injury. Lower the dumbbell until the lower head of the dumbbell is even with your ears, and then extend the dumbbell upward toward the starting position. Keep your elbows close to your head at all times.

Figure 8.68a

Figure 8.68b

● Triceps Push-Down
   (Supporting)

Using a close grip, grasp a bar attached to a high cable. Begin the exercise with your forearms parallel to the floor, making a ninety-degree angle between your upper arm and forearm. Keeping your elbows tucked tightly to your sides and just slightly in front of your body, extend your elbows downward to full extension. Complete the movement by allowing your arms to move upward, until once again your elbows form a ninety-degree angle.

Figure 8.69a   **Figure 8.69b**

● Kickback
   (Supporting)

Bend your knees two to three inches and then bend forward at the waist, as if you were skiing down hill. Grasp a dumbbell in each hand and tuck your upper arms up and to your sides. It is important for maximum effect that your upper arms remain parallel to **Figure 8.70a**   **Figure 8.70b** the floor at all times during the movement. To begin the exercise, extend the dumbbells to full arm extension, so that they match your upper arms' orientation with the floor. Various hand positions can be applied at this point in the movement. Your hands can end either with your palms facing inward toward your hips, up to the ceiling, or downward toward the floor. The variation in hand positions will affect which part of your triceps muscle is stressed by the exercise. To complete the movement, lower the dumbbells by bending only your elbows to their starting position.

● Reverse Dip
(Functional)

Begin with your back to a securely positioned bench. Place the heels of your palms on the edge of the bench closest to you, so your fingers extend over the edge. Your legs can be placed in various positions to provide greater difficulty during the exercise. The easiest version of the exercise is performed with your legs bent at the knees and your feet resting on the floor close to your body. Extending your legs straight, while still having your heels on the floor, adds additional exercise resistance. Even more resistance can be added by placing your feet and legs on top of another bench or a balance ball in front of you. Once you choose the body position, begin with your elbows fully extended. Slowly bend your arms at the elbows, lowering your body toward the floor. Complete the movement by extending your arms upward to a full and locked position. Additional emphasis can be applied to finish the movement by leaning slightly back once your arms are fully extended.

Figure 8.71a

Figure 8.71b

● Close Grip Push-up
(Functional)

This exercised is performed like a regular push up, with the exception that your hands are placed on the floor with your thumbs fully extended and touching. Be sure to keep your elbows close to your

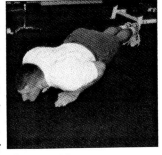

Figure 8.72a

Figure 8.72b

sides during this version of the push-up to insure that your triceps are emphasized, rather than your chest and shoulders.

● Close-Grip Bench
(Core)

This exercise is performed in the same position as the regular bench press, with the exception that your hands are moved in to a point about six-to-eight inches apart. The weight is lowered with your elbows tucked tightly to the sides of your body to a point just below the sweep of your chest. The movement is completed with your arms fully extended above your chest.

Figure 8.73a

Figure 8.73b

■ LEG EXERCISES

● Squat
(Core)

Assume a standing position inside a squat rack. Take the weight from the stands, and assume a shoulder-width stance with your toes turned slightly out. Look straight ahead at a point on the wall that you are facing. Begin the exercise by descending by flexing at

Figure 8.74a

Figure 8.74b

your knees. Keep your back completely straight so that your spine is in a natural alignment. Sit back as you descend so that your buttocks are moving to a point well behind your heels. This action will keep your shins in a position perpendicular to the floor, and prevent your knees from extending too far over your toes. Keep your knees in line with your second toes. Choose your depth. You can go to a point where your hamstrings are parallel to the floor, or you can go all the way down. Be sure not to bounce the bottom of the squat. To finish the movement, return upward to a standing position, bringing your hips slightly forward to place your back in perfect alignment.

● One or Two-Leg Press
  (Core)

This exercise can be performed with one or two legs. Some leg presses are made to provide iso-lateral motion, and are safer to use when performing one-leg version of leg presses. Solid platform leg press machines can be used, but you may choose not to turn the platform supports out of their locked position to prevent the platform from coming too far down and trapping your non-working leg. To perform the two-leg version of the press, place your feet flat and firmly in the middle of the platform. Turn your toes slightly outward. Push the weight to full-leg extension, and turn the platform supports to their unlocked position. Begin to lower the weight by flexing your knees to a point where the upper and lower parts of your leg form a right angle. To complete the movement, extend your knees to push the platform back to its starting position. For the one-leg version of the press, place your foot in the same position on the platform that it would be if you were doing a two-footed version of the press. Let the free leg occupy the space between the slides, or keep it tucked up and close to your abdominal to provide safety in case of the platform coming down too fast.

Figure 8.75a

Figure 8.75b

● One or Two-Leg Extension
(Supporting)

Either with one leg or two legs moving at the same time, extend your knee(s) to a full and locked position, using your upper thigh muscles (quadriceps). Pause briefly, and slowly lower the weight back to its starting point.

Figure 8.76a

Figure 8.76b

● One or Two-Leg Curl
(Supporting)

Flexing your knee, bring the heels of your leg toward your buttock. This exercise can be performed either in a lying or seated version of the leg curl machine. If in a lying position, attempt to keep your hips firmly against the bench to provide maximum muscle contraction in the hamstrings.

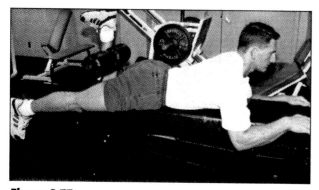

Figure 8.77a

Figure 8.77b

● Baby Squat
(Functional)

This exercise is basical-
ly a deep-knee bend.
You are performing a
squat movement with-
out resistance. If resistance is used, it can be
applied in the form of a
weighted vest. You are
usually assigned a time
within which to do this
exercise. Maintain a

Figure 8.78a

Figure 8.78b

constant tempo of movement throughout the time you are allotted to
perform the exercise. One repetition per second is the usual cadence for
this movement. Keep both feet flat on the floor, and hold your back as
straight as possible. Keep your knees aligned with your second toes, and
attempt to keep your shin straight up and down to the floor.

● Hip Flex
(Functional)

Begin by standing on
one foot. The non-sup-
port foot is the leg you
will be working. If you
need to hold on to
something for support,
you can. However,
learning to balance dur-
ing this exercise can
also benefit your efforts
to enhance your level

Figure 8.79a

Figure 8.79b

of muscular strength. Begin bringing the knee of your non-support leg up
to your chest by using the muscles of your hip. Lower your leg without
touching the floor. Keep a steady tempo while exercising to insure muscle fatigue.

- Alternating Leg Lunge
(Functional)

From a standing position, step with one leg out to the front of the body (Figures 8.80a and 8.80b). Allow your leg to bend at the knee, lowering your body toward the floor. Allow your back leg to bend when first learning the exercise. As you become more advanced at the exercise, keep your back leg straight, forcing your front leg to step out from the standing position even further. To finish, push back to a standing position off your front leg. Alternate legs throughout the exercise. This exercise can be done in a walking format from one point to another. In phase #1 of the workouts, a variation of the exercise is called "Lunge" (Three pumps). To perform this variation, as you step out from the standing position, keep your leg out front and then straighten it and bend it three times, before pushing yourself back to a standing position. This pumping of the leg will emphasize the level of muscle fatigue, which is the primary objective in phase #1.

Figure 8.80a

Figure 8.80b

- Lunge—Three Pumps
(Functional)

This exercise is performed like the alternating leg lunge, except when you lunge out, you do not subsequently return to a standing position. Instead, you remain in the extended position and straighten and bend the knee of your front leg three times. Remember to make sure your shin is straight up and down relative to the floor. During this exercise, your back leg may have to be slightly more bent to insure balance.

● Backward Lunge
  (Functional)

From a standing position, step back with one leg. This exercise involves a movement pattern that is the opposite of the alternating leg lunge. Allow your front leg to bend at the knee, thereby lowering your body toward the floor. Allow your back leg to bend when first learning the exercise. As you become more advanced at performing the exercise, keep your back leg straight, forcing yourself to step even further back from the standing position. This exercise can be done in a walking backward format from one point to another.

● Musketeer Lunge
  (Functional)

From a standing position, step with your right leg to a point behind your left leg, like performing a carioca or grapevine maneuver. As a result, the left leg is the supporting leg during the repetition. Allow your front leg (left leg) to bend at the knee, thereby lowering your body toward the floor. Keep your back leg as straight as possible. Push your left leg back up to a standing position, while at the same time, bringing your right leg beside your left leg to finish the repetition. Alternate the leg that steps behind during the exercise. This exercise can be done in a walking sideways format from one point to another. When doing this, the same leg always steps behind. Then, walk back, stepping behind with your opposite leg.

● One Stiff Leg Dead
  (Functional)

Standing on one leg, bend forward at the waist. As your upper body bends forward, keep your support leg straight. At the same time, allow your free leg to move behind your buttocks. Attempt to touch the floor or the shoe of your support leg with your fingertips. Return back up to the starting position. Once upright, allow the knee of your support leg to bend four to five inches, and then return that leg to full extension to complete the entire repetition. Repeat all the assigned repetitions on one support leg before switching to the opposite leg.

- Box Squat
  (Functional)

  Standing on one leg, perform a squat. In the learning stage of the exercise, you can hold on to a stable object for support, or have your free leg supported on a stable object. As you reach a more advanced stage, this exercise can be performed with no support. Your free leg and your arms are held straight in front of your body, while your support leg performs a squat until your buttock touches the heel of your support leg. The foot of your support leg should always remain flat on the floor. The knee on your support leg should always be kept behind the toe of that foot by pushing the buttocks back to a point well behind the heel of that foot.

Figure 8.81a

Figure 8.81b

- Donkey Kicks
  (Functional)

  Assume a kneeling position on all fours. Lean to your left and pick your right leg just slightly off the floor. Pull your right knee through your arms and attempt to touch your chin. Next, push your right leg back and up behind you and to the ceiling. Do not forcefully lock your knee out. Pull your knee back to the chin to repeat the first repetition. Do all the assigned repetitions with one leg before shifting to the opposite leg.

Figure 8.82a

Figure 8.82b

- Hamstring on Balance Ball
  (Functional)

Lay on your back on a large balance ball. Place your hands on your chest. Keep your hips high so that they are as high as your chest and parallel to the floor. Lift one leg off the floor and extend it fully straight so that it too is parallel to the floor and even with your hips and chest. The leg in contact with the floor should be at a ninety-degree angle at the knee. Slowly, while trying to remain on the ball and in balance, lower your buttocks to the floor, attempting to place them as close to the ball as possible. To complete the repetition, push your hip back upward until parallel with the floor again. Perform all the assigned repetitions with one leg, before moving on to the next leg.

Figure 8.83a

Figure 8.83b

- Dumbbell Squat
  (Core)

Grasp a dumbbell in each hand. Stand straight with your legs slightly less than shoulder width apart, with the toes turned lightly out. Lower the weight slowly to the floor by bending your knees. Use your legs to control the speed of decent. The dumbbells should be held outside your legs at arms length. Like in the squat exercise, your hamstrings should go to a point parallel to the floor, and your buttocks should be pushed back to a point well behind your heels. Your back should be straight, and your eyes should be fixed on a spot so that your chin is tilted slightly upward. The dumbbells should go to a point one or two inches from the floor. Extend your knees to return to the starting position. Allow your legs to do all the work.

Figure 8.84a

Figure 8.84b

- Dead Lift
  (Core)

Grasp a weighted barbell that is resting on the floor with an over-and-under grip (Figures 8.85a and 8.85b). Your strongest hand should be turned under so that the palm faces away from the shins, while your weaker hand should be turned toward the shins. The grip should be just outside your legs. Your legs should be positioned slightly less than shoulder width apart, with your toes turned lightly

Figure 8.85a

out. Your body should be positioned like the bottom position of a squat. Your hamstrings should be parallel to the floor, and the buttocks should be pushed back to a point well behind your heels. Your back should be straight, and your eyes should be fixed on a spot so that your chin is tilted slightly upward. With your arms perfectly straight, begin to extend your knees. Allow your legs to do all the work. Stand straight until the legs are fully extended. Once in a straight and standing position, lean slightly back. Lower the weight slowly back to the floor, using your legs to control the speed of decent. This movement completes the repetition.

Figure 8.85b

- Side Lunge
  (Functional)

From a standing position, step to the side with your right leg. Your left leg is the supporting leg during this repetition. Allow your right leg to bend at the knee, lowering your body toward the floor. Step far enough to the side so that your left leg is as straight as possible. Push your right leg back up to a standing position with both feet ending side by side to finish the repetition. Alternate the leg that steps to the side during the exercise.

- Slideboard
  (Functional)

  Assume a position on one side of the slide board. Pushing hard with one leg, propel yourself across the board to the other side. Once on the other side of the board, use the opposite leg to push yourself back.

Figure 8.86

- Step-up
  (Functional)

  Using a box or a secure bench, begin stepping onto and off of the box in an alternating-leg fashion. The best height for the box should allow the upper leg to be parallel to the floor when the foot of that leg is on the box. Be sure to lean forward to place all the stress on the leg on the box. Do not push off the floor with the down leg.

Figure 8.87a   **Figure 8.87b**

■ CYLINDER CIRCUIT EXERCISES

Cylinder circuit exercises are a series of circuit exercises for the torso (cylinder) of the body. The series involves several circuits that are mixed up across the weeks to provide variation and changes in intensity (Table 8.17). These exercises involve greater ranges of motion than those exercises typically found in more conventional sit-up routines. If you experience any pain or discomfort that goes beyond the normal muscle fatigue associated with exercising, then stop that particular exercise and choose another one from one of the other circuits. Among the exercises that can be incorporated into the cylinder circuits are the following:

● Sit-Up
(Assisting)

Place your hands over your ears. Anchor your feet under an object with your knees bent. This step will affect your hip flexor muscles, as well as your abdominals. Curl your upper body up, using the muscles of your stomach, until your elbows come past your knees. Lower your upper body downward, until the middle of your back touches the floor. This completes the repetition.

● Quarter Sit-Up
(Assisting)

Bend your legs slightly, while keeping your feet two inches off the ground. This step creates a natural arch in your lower back. Flatten the arch into the floor by lifting your hips up and contracting the abdominals.

● Ball Throw
(Assisting)

Perform sit-ups with a medicine ball. Release the ball as you come up. Use a partner or a wall to return the ball to you.

● Hanging Abs
(Assisting)

Hang from a chin-up bar. Pull your knees up. You can perform this exercise in a supported fashion with your feet touching the ground every time, or in a hanging position so that your feet do not touch, thus requiring more body control.

- Hyperextension
  (Assisting)

Using a glute/ham or hyperextension bench, secure your legs under the supports, and allow your body to bend forward from the waist toward the floor. Using your lower back to lift your body up, your legs remain straight during the entire movement. Your hands can be held over your ears.

- Butt Row
  (Assisting)

Using your hands for support, bring your knees to your chest. Then, push your legs away and lean back.

- Reverse Sit-Up
  (Assisting)

Using your arms for support, bring your knees to your chin. Lift your buttocks from the floor. Then, slowly lower your buttocks, while at the same time, pushing your legs away. Your legs should be nearly straight, with your feet held two inches from the floor.

- Hip-Up
  (Assisting)

Hold a support with your hands, or place your hands on the floor at your sides to make the exercise more difficult. Keep your legs straight. Raise your hips off the ground and then slowly lower them. Make sure to push your legs slightly away from your face to make the exercise more effective.

- Side Push-Up
  (Assisting)

Lie on your side, with one foot on top of the other. Use your feet as a fulcrum. Place the forearm of your down arm flat on the floor, and the hand of your opposite arm in front of your stomach and on your fingertips. Push your hips straight up, using your arms for support. Variations of this exercise can be performed by turning your body more inward, so that more of your stomach is facing the ground. This step will shift the emphasis of the exercise from your side or oblique muscles to the intercostals around your front rib cage.

- Elbow Hip Dip
  (Assisting)

  Supporting your body on your elbows and toes, keep your hips off the ground. Hold this position for ten seconds, and then allow your hips to quickly dip to briefly touch the floor, before returning to the supported position. This sequence completes one repetition. This exercise is a great stabilizing activity for the lower back and torso.

- Elbow Tuck-in
  (Assisting)

  Assume the same starting position as for the elbow hip dip. Allow your chin to extend slightly over your hands. Begin the exercise by slowly exhaling as forcefully as you can, while at the same time, flexing your abdominal muscles. If the exhalation and abdominal contractions are forceful enough, your buttocks should rise to the ceiling. The motion of the exercise should feel as if you are doing a sit-up, upside down.

- Quarter Elbow Tuck-in
  (Assisting)

  This exercise is performed the same as the elbow tuck-in. However, in this exercise, you turn your hips slightly to the side, lifting one hip. This hip position is held in-between the flat position of the elbow tuck-in and the fully turned position of the side push-up. This positioning of the hips enables you to focus on the intercostals.

- Clock Work
  (Assisting)

  Lying on your back, hold on to a support, or spread your arm straight to your sides on the floor. Start with your legs held together, straight above your hips. Carry your legs side to side. Imagine your body being the points on a clock. Your head is at twelve o'clock, while your buttocks are at six o'clock. When your legs are carried to the side, they should point toward three and nine o'clock in order to maximize the exercise.

- Reverse Hyperextension
  (Assisting)

  Lie face down, with only your upper torso supported on a high bench or table. Your legs and hips should be off the bench, with your feet touching the ground. Grasp the sides of the bench firmly with your hands. Keeping your legs straight, lift your legs to a point parallel to the floor. Use your lower back and gluteal muscles to perform the lift. Then, lower your legs slowly to the floor to complete the repetition.

- Skydiver
  (Assisting)

  Lie face down on the floor. Bend your arms ninety degrees at the elbow, and spread your legs apart. Lift both arms and legs upward, using your lower back and gluteal muscles to perform the lift. Slowly return your arms and legs to the floor to complete the repetition. Never rest your arms and legs on the floor during the exercise. Just lightly touch the floor, using it as a point of reference for the movement.

- Hi Ya
  (Assisting)

  This exercise is a precursor movement to the sky diver and superman exercises. Lie face down on the floor. Extend your arms and legs fully. Keeping your feet in contact with the floor, alternate raising one arm at a time off the floor as high as you can. Contract your lower back muscles to help provide lift from the floor. Do not twist your body to go higher. You can push up slightly with your down hand to provide support during the exercise. Attempt to clear your entire chest and upper stomach from the floor before switching hands.

- Bye Ya
  (Assisting)

  This exercise is another precursor movement to the sky diver and superman exercises. Lie face down on the floor. Extend your legs fully, and start with both of them in contact with the floor. Place your hands flat on the floor beside your shoulders. Alternate lifting one leg at a time from the floor. You can push up slightly with your down leg to provide support during the exercise. Attempt to clear your entire upper thigh and hip from the floor before switching legs.

- Superman
  (Assisting)

  This exercise is performed like the sky diver exercise, only it is a more difficult version of that exercise. To make this exercise even more difficult, instead of the arms being bent and the legs spread, extend your arms fully in front of your body and keep your legs together and fully extended as well. This step adds more resistance on each end of your body, causing your lower back and gluteal muscles to work harder.

● Alternating Superman
  (Assisting)

This exercise is like the superman exercise, only it is performed with one arm and leg raised from the floor, while the other arm and leg remain on the floor. To maintain balance during the exercise, raise your right arm with your left leg and your left arm with your right leg.

● Scissoring
  (Assisting)

Sit on the floor with your legs fully extended in front of you. Lean back and rest on your elbows. Raise your legs off the floor about six to ten inches, and spread them apart to your sides. Bring them together, crossing one leg over the other at the mid-line of your body. Spread them back apart to complete one repetition of the exercise. Switch the leg on top each time you cross your legs.

● Fluttering
  (Assisting)

Assume the same starting position as with the scissoring exercise. Instead of spreading your legs apart, split them apart up and down, as if to flutter kick while swimming. Keep the fluttering motion short and rapid to create a more exhausting effect.

Cylinder #1	Cylinder #2	Cylinder #3	Cylinder #4	Cylinder #5	Cylinder #6
1) Quarter sit-up	1) Sit-up	1) Sit-up	1) Supported hanging ab	1) Hanging abs	1) Sit-up
2) Sit-up	2) Reverse sit-up	2) Reverse sit-up	2) Reverse sit-up	2) Ball throw	2) Butt row
3) Butt row	3) Hip-up	3) Hip-up	3) Hip-up	3) Hip-up	3) Scissoring
4) Sky diver	4) Clock work	4) Clock work	4) Side push-up	4) Elbow tuck-in	4) Fluttering
5) Hi ya	5) HI ya	5) Quarter sit-up	5) Butt row	5) Quarter elbow tuck-in	5) Elbow tuck-in
	6) BYE ya	6) Superman	6) Elbow hip dip	6) Hyperextension	6) Quarter elbow tuck-in
			7) Reverse hyperextension	7) Alternating superman	7) Hyperextension

Table 8.17. Sample cylinder circuits.

■ CALF EXERCISES

- Standing Calf Raise
  (Assisting)

  Perform a heel raise (i.e., come up on your toes), using some type of resistance. Figures 8.88a and 8.88b demonstrate the heel raise, performed using a Smith machine. Again, any type of resistance can be applied. If you do not have this machine, then choose another alternative. The important thing is to keep the knees locked and use only the ankle to fully emphasize the muscles of the calves.

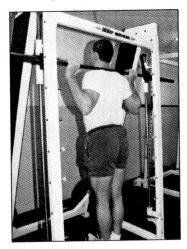 

Figure 8.88a   **Figure 8.88b**

- Calf Raise/Leg Press
  (Assisting)

  Perform a heel raise on a leg press machine. Allow your toes to rest on the bottom edge of the leg press platform, with your heels hanging off. DO NOT TURN THE PLATFORM SUPPORTS OUT OF THEIR LOCKED POSITION. If the platform were to slip off your toes, a serious injury could occur.

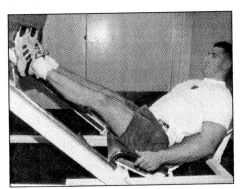

Figure 8.89

- BW One-Leg Calf
(Assisting)

This version of the heel raise is performed with one leg at a time, using only your body weight for resistance (Figures 8.90a and 8.90b). Again, keep your knee as straight as possible, using only your ankle to move your weight.

Figure 8.90a   **Figure 8.90b**

■ COMBO EXERCISES

Combo exercises are two or more exercises combined together. Combining the exercises requires you to use more coordination of movement. As a result, to a degree, these combo exercises are more beneficial to athleticism. Combining exercise is also a method of condensing your workout and saving time. These exercises can also provide a greater demand on your cardiorespiratory system, thereby providing a conditioning effect. The following pairings illustrate examples of combo exercises:

- Dumbbell Lunge/Dumbbell Upright Row
(Supercore)

Holding a dumbbell in each hand, step forward performing an alternating leg lunge. Upon pushing back from the lunge to a standing position, perform a dumbbell upright row. Remember to keep your elbows higher than your wrists during the row. One set can be performed with the same leg while always stepping to the front, and then a second set can be performed with the opposite leg stepping out.

- Dumbbell Snatch/Dumbbell Push Press
  (Supercore)

  After performing a dumbbell snatch, lower the dumbbells to your shoulders and perform a dumbbell push press. Then, lower the dumbbells to the sides of your body and reset for the next dumbbell snatch.

- Side Dumbbell Raise/Lunge
  (Supercore)

  Holding a dumbbell in each hand, perform a side dumbbell raise. Remember that the dumbbells should end parallel to the floor in a side dumbbell raise. Then, lower the dumbbells back to your sides, step forward, and perform a standing-in-place forward lunge.

- Step-Up/Shoulder Fly
  (Supercore)

  Holding a dumbbell in each hand at your sides, perform a step-up with one leg onto and off of a bench or box. Then, upon returning to the floor, perform a repetition of the shoulder fly. Remember that the fly should end with the dumbbells above your head. Then, step onto and off of the box again, but this time with the opposite leg.

- Backward Lunge/Dumbbell Upright Row
  (Supercore)

  Holding a dumbbell in each hand, step backward, performing a standing-in-place backward lunge. Then, upon pushing back up from the lunge to a standing position, perform a dumbbell upright row. Remember to keep your elbows higher than your wrists during the row. One set can be performed with the same leg while always stepping back, and then a second set can be performed with the opposite leg stepping back.

- Step-Up/Side Dumbbell Raise
  (Supercore)

  This exercise is performed the same as the step-up/shoulder fly exercise, except in this sequence, the dumbbells are only brought parallel to the floor during the side dumbbell raise.

- Side Lunge/Shoulder Fly
  (Supercore)

  Holding a dumbbell in each hand, perform a side lunge. As you lower your body to your side, allow the dumbbells to meet at the center line of your body at arms length. Upon pushing back up to a standing position, allow the dumbbells to move back to the sides of your body. Once at the sides, the dumbbells are lifted, and a shoulder fly is performed. One set can be performed with the same leg always stepping to the side, and then a second set can be performed with the opposite leg stepping out.

- Dumbbell Squat/Two-Arm Dumbbell Press
  (Supercore)

  Perform a dumbbell squat (dumbbell dead lift). The dumbbells can be held at shoulder level during this combo rather than at the waist. Upon standing up from the squat, press the dumbbells upward to arms length. If the legs are used to help perform the press above the head, it becomes a dumbbell push press, instead of a simple dumbbell press. However, this step may be necessary if the weight becomes too heavy as a result of fatigue.

- Squat/Press
  (Supercore)

  Use dumbbells or a light barbell to do a squat, as previously described. Once you come up from the bottom of the squat, press the barbell or dumbbells above your head. Return the resistance to a squat position to complete the repetition.

■ OTHER EXERCISES

- Around the World Legs

  This is a leg combination exercise that is performed on a basketball court that consists of a series of continuous activities (e.g., walking lunges, step slides, backward-walking lunges, deep-knee bends, or any plyometric exercise). One example of this activity might be to have the athlete perform 20 deep knee bends in each corner of the court, lunge the length of the court, and step slide the width of the court. You can create a combination in any order to fatigue yourself. Once around the rectangle completes one repetition.

- 21 Blaster (Bicep)

  This is an exercise technique to insure muscle fatigue rather than an actual exercise. You can use this technique while performing the straight bar curl, the preacher curl, or the EZ bar curl. You will be performing twenty-one repetitions during this technique, so the resistance must remain light enough to accomplish this number. Begin the sequence by performing seven half-repetitions from the lower portion of the movement to the halfway point along the range of motion. After the seventh half- repetition, move directly into doing seven more half-repetitions from the halfway point to the upper point at your chin. To complete the technique, perform seven full-range repetitions.

- Wrist Flex

  Hold a sand-filled bag or sponge and quickly squeeze the bag, 100 repetitions each wrist.

- Jump Rope

  Jump rope in the traditional rope-skipping fashion; any and all variations of rope jumping can being performed.

- Crabbing
  (Functional)

  Assume a push-up position, but spread your arms and legs wide apart. As if to walk to the left, move your left arm and leg out to the side at the same time. Shifting your weight to the left, then move your right arm and leg to the left. Repeat this pattern, thus walking the body along the floor for a given distance.

- Leg Dragging
  (Functional)

  If you're on a slick surface like a basketball court or a tile floor, you can place the feet on a towel or seat cushion. Moving dollies with wheels work well on rough surfaces. With your feet in the starting position, assume the up position for a push-up. Begin walking along the floor using your hands to a designated point, dragging your legs behind. Your legs will sway from left to right with each hand placement. This action will work your hips and lower back during the exercise.

Speed and Power Exercises

Explosive jumping ability, first-step quickness, and lateral and court speed are integral factors in helping players establish court dominance. If you have speed and quickness and an first explosive first step, you can usually out-run, out-jump, and overwhelm your opponent. The point to keep in mind is that if you want to be competitive on the basketball court, you must develop your speed and explosive skills. Perhaps your parents bestowed upon you a lot of fast motor neurons, which in turn will give you more fast-twitch muscle fibers. Truth be known, the best assurance of acquiring speed, quickness, and explosiveness is to be born with it. However, no true way exists to measure your exact genetic potential. All you can do is to work as much as you can to make sure you are not wasting whatever potential you were born with. Over the years, there have probably been many Michael Jordans in the world, but only one has maximized his potential to the fullest.

Power is the ability to move a resistance as quickly as possible from point A to point B. In order to move your body weight either horizontally, as in sprinting, or vertically, as in jumping, you must enhance your level of power. You can promote your power output by using both resistance training and specific power drills. The most important type of strength, with regard to power development, is reactive strength.

Improving Reactive Strength

Reactivity does not directly refer to reaction time (i.e., the time it takes to respond to a movement or signal). Relative to power production, reactivity refers to how fast the muscle can go from a stretched position to an active position (i.e., eccentric to concentric muscle contractions). During jumping, you crouch slightly prior to accelerating upward. As you crouch, the muscles of the legs stretch. Then, the muscles must rapidly contract to produce vertical height. If your muscles are stretched quickly, they can help to sling-shot you upward. It's like stretching a rubber band and letting it go.

One method of enhancing reactivity is through weight training. During the downward path of the bench press exercise, for example, you must apply an eccentric muscle contraction in order to decelerate the weighted bar. At some point along the range of motion, you must upwardly accelerate the bar from your body. If you can improve on the skill of rapidly decelerating, and then accelerating, you will increase your level of reactivity.

An athlete often performs at high speed. However, in the weight room, the speed of movement seems to be slower because the weights of the objects being moved are often a lot heavier than those of your body weight. In this way, the weight room serves its training purpose of providing an environment where overload is created. An overloaded level of resistance is more weight than you would normally encounter during an athletic event. This overload, therefore, makes your body weight seem less like a burden when you are performing on the basketball court.

A more athletically specific and highly reactive type of resistance training, called plyometrics, has become popular in recent years (Figure 9.1). The training effects produced by plyometrics are similar to that of heavy resistance training, with the exception that plyometric movements result in visibly greater limb speeds.

Figure 9.1. An example of plyometric training

Certain neural adaptations occur when methods of both speed and power training are incorporated into the workout program. These adaptations have been described as intramuscular coordination and intermuscular coordination. Intramuscular coordination refers to how effectively actions occur within the muscle (e.g., neural communication, cross-bridging of muscle fiber, chemical exchanges, etc). While intermuscular coordination refers to the coordinated actions that occur between separate muscles or muscle groups.

Both plyometric and resistance training contribute to power and speed development . One is not better than the other. By employing both methods into your training regimen, you will produce the highest gains. For example, both methods of training can be applied to enhance jumping ability. As you perform a traditional squat exercise with very heavy resistance, the movement speed may seem slow. However, the motor neurons are having to fire very rapidly in order to involve enough muscle fibers to efficiently control the weight.

Squatting, however, does not involve the ankle movements or the arm action used during jumping. Squatting then, may be an excellent intramuscular exercise to improve the internal workings of the muscles, while the high-speed act of jumping during a plyometric exercise can improve your intermuscular requirements.

Designing a Plyometric Program

It is important to consider your sport when designing a plyometric program. Basketball is a highly plyometric sport. You do not need to perform workouts consisting of repetitive jumping exercises to receive the benefits of plyometric training. All you need to do is play basketball and add a little extra jumping before or after you play, and on occasion incorporate a plyometric movement into a drill you are working on.

Many plyometric routines that are currently used by athletes and coaches are variations of routines that were originally created for track athletes. A track athlete trains for one specific event, like sprinting or variations of jumping and throwing. Therefore, a track athlete's training is relatively low in plyometric stress. In order to receive the benefits of plyometrics, a track athlete must have a slightly more structured plyometric routine added into their training.

In basketball, you are sprinting, jumping and performing many other combined movements, all of which provide plyometric benefits and stress. Also, you must consider the hard surface on which basketball is played. Because the basketball court is less forgiving, you are more likely to experience overtraining injuries. If plyometric movements are performed too often, on too hard a surface, or if they are performed incorrectly, overtraining of the nervous system can occur. This overtraining can result in diminishing your level of performance. Keep in mind that acceleration and deceleration techniques used in plyometric training are also applied during every other exercise within a sound training program. So, it makes very little sense to create a strenuous jump routine for yourself. In basketball, a little bit goes a long way toward helping you improve.

In this chapter, several packaged routines are provided with plyometric exercises incorporated into them. All factors considered, it is best for basketball players to blend their plyometric exercises in with agility and foot-speed drills. This recommendation makes more sense for basketball players, because basketball requires you to use your agility to break free from an opponent. Once you are free, you can shoot or grab a rebound. These final actions typically require the athlete to jump. Because of this blending of plyometric exercises with agility-type movements, overtraining with plyometrics while using the suggested workouts in this book, is very unlikely to occur. If you are inexperienced or not yet physically mature, however, overtraining can occur. For these athletes, their plyometric exercises may need to be reduced in volume, performed on softer surfaces, or performed off two feet instead of one. Some exercises might need to be totally deleted from the routine in order to reduce the athlete's level of orthopedic stress. If you are an inexperienced athlete, you should choose the plyometric exercises from the low-to-medium intensity packages presented in this chapter. Later as you become stronger, you can move up to the higher-intensity packages.

Plyometric exercise is stressful to the body. However, if the intensity of the plyometric exercise is increased slowly, the occurrence of injury or overwork is minimized. Like any exercise, plyometrics should be used in a periodization context, with both lower intensity training days and higher intensity training days occurring during the same training week.

Some plyometric exercises are easier on the body than others. Those that are easier on your body should be used to introduce you to plyometric training. These same exercises can be incorporated into the advanced athlete's training program as a means of providing a lower-stress training day. In periodization, the two main principles to consider are:

- As the exercise becomes more intense, do not perform as many sets of that exercise.

- If the exercise is less intense, you can perform more sets of that exercise.

Are You Physically Ready to Begin Plyometric Training?

Though many athletes on your team may be the same age and possess some of the same strengths, not all players may be ready for the same levels of plyometric training. Weaknesses in primary or stabilizing muscles signal a potential for injury. The Soviet coaches, who originally developed plyometric training, suggest that the athlete be able to perform a 1 RM squat with a weight one-and-a-half to two times his body weight. In his book, *Eccentric Muscle Training in Sports and Orthopedics*, physical therapist and athletic trainer Mark Albert suggests a series of one-legged squat tests performed statically (held in place). These tests seem much more practical, and can provide an athlete with more specific feedback about where his muscular weaknesses exist. Albert's recommended tests are as follows:

- Stand on one foot in place for 30 seconds with your eyes open. Repeat with your eyes closed. Switch legs.

- Stand on one leg and perform a quarter squat. Hold in the bottom position for 30 seconds. Perform once with your eyes open and again with eyes closed. Switch legs.

- Stand on one leg and perform a half squat. Hold in the bottom position for 30 seconds. Perform once with your eyes open and again with your eyes closed. Switch legs.

If you can perform the first test standing on one foot, and the second test, the quarter squat, without noticeable wobbling or shaking of your support leg (i.e., the leg in contact with the ground), then you are qualified to begin a progressive plyometric program. You should perform the half-squat test prior to the initiation of the program, and then again after you have trained for a while to measure improvement in your level of stability.

Guidelines for Performing Plyometric Exercise Training

Before beginning plyometric training, you should become knowledgeable of the following guidelines in order get the most out of plyometric training and to minimize the chances of being injured:

- Keep the exercises you do during training specific to the activities performed on the court.

- Use low-intensity exercises primarily during the off-season or other preparatory period. Use high-intensity exercises during the preseason or competitive periods of training.

- As the intensity of exercise increases, decrease the volume (sets and reps) of training.

- If you increase the intensity of the workouts, then allow more recovery time between workouts.

- Terminate the exercise when fatigue begins to occur, and you can no longer perform the exercise correctly.

- As the exercises become more difficult because they require more agility and coordination (complexity) to perform, reduce the number of sets and repetitions of that exercise.

- During the off-season, lower the complexity of the plyometric exercises.

- During the preseason and in-season, increase the complexity of the plyometric exercises.

- During the off-season phase of training, perform your plyometric workouts no more than three times per week. During the preseason and in-season phases of training, perform the plyometric workouts no more than two times per week. During the in-season phase of training, use discretion. Reduce your plyometric workouts to zero if you feel overtired.

- If the emphasis of your training program is on endurance, the resistance training intensity is low. In this case, perform the plyometric training before the resistance-training session. If the emphasis is on muscular power, then perform the plyometrics after the resistance-training program. If you choose to do the plyometrics after the resistance-training session, either choose a lower-intensity resistance training day to perform these plyometric exercises or choose to do upper-body plyometrics on a lower-body resistance training day, or vice versa.

- Keep the progression in plyometric-training intensity slow. More is not necessarily better. A conservative approach to training is always advised. The SAID principle (specific adaptations to imposing demands) restated means that you should allow your body to adapt to the stress; don't give it too much stress all at once.

- Use the one-leg squat test to assess your strengths. Use these tests before, during, and after a training phase to track your progress.

Determining the Intensity of the Plyometric Exercise

Several factors should be used to determine how intense you should perform a specific plyometric exercise, including:

- The type of exercise.
- The number of exercises performed during a workout.
- The increase in repetitions and sets of that exercise.
- The changes in takeoff and landing surfaces.
- The height of the objects jumped over or on to.
- The rest period between sets of an exercise.

Types of Plyometric Exercises

Some plyometric exercises are low in intensity, while others are more stressful, and therefore, are categorized as high intensity. In this regard, the following relative comparisons are examples of how plyometric intensity varies:

- Plyometric exercises performed on two legs are less intense than those performed on one leg.

- Movements in place are less intense than movements that cover distance (jump rope vs. triple jump).

- Jumps performed low to the ground are less intense than those performed higher off the ground.

- Movements performed primarily with single-joint involvement (e.g., ankle bounce) are less intense than movements performed with multiple-joint involvements (jumps).

- Upper body plyometrics are more intense than lower body plyometrics.

The National Strength and Conditioning Association (NSCA) suggests that exercises should be performed on a stress continuum divided into four levels (Table 9.1). Level I (the lowest intensity level), for examples involves exercises performed while standing in place. The exercises within each level get progressively more intense (from low to high). Some researchers suggest that the total number of foot contacts be considered as the measure of plyometric intensity during a particular phase of training. One of the leading researchers in plyometric training, Dr. Donald Chu, suggests in his book, Jumping into Plyometrics, that during the off-season phases of training, a beginner should only perform a total of 60-100 total foot contacts using high-intensity plyometric exercise. Dr. Chu suggests that an advanced athlete only perform 120-200 foot contacts. Most coaches and athletes are engaged in programs that have many more foot contacts than this in a single workout. This information attempts to stress the point once again that performing more in the case of plyometric training is not better, especially in the sport of basketball.

For basketball players, it is best to incorporate agility and foot-speed exercises with plyometric exercises. The agility and foot-speed exercises you employ in your training program should require you to push for increased lateral and court speed, while still allowing you to rapidly apply a vertical jump. In a later chapter of this book, agility drills are presented which focus primarily on coordination, balance, and quickness. In this chapter, some of the same movements are examined. These movements not only enable basketball players to move with grace and agility, but also to move explosively and with authority.

Intensity	Level I In-place	Level II Short response	Level III Long response	Level IV Upper body
Low	Ankle bounce Tuck jump Split jump Lateral bounce Skate bound Single-leg hops Spin jumps	Long jump stop Jump ups	Power skip	Overhead throw Chest pass
Medium	Lateral hops Ski jumps	Triple jump Zigzag bounds	10 or more bounds	Underhand backward throw
High			Hop Alternate leg bounds	Drop and rebound push-up Spider push-up

Table 9.1. Plyometric stress continuum

Lateral and Court-speed Training

Basketball is a sport that depends relatively little on pure linear speed. Most of the speed requirements of team sports like basketball are based around lateral speed or the ability to change your direction of movement in a purposeful manner (agility). For some basketball programs, the 40-yard dash is still a measuring tool of performance, even though the collegiate basketball court is just over 30 yards long.

In reality, it makes little sense to focus on a benchmark that has little bearing on the sport you play. In basketball, you are continually forced to step sideways and backwards to cut your opponent off or make him switch directions. If he gets by you, you are then forced to sprint. These sprints, however, are usually measured in steps, not in yards. Therefore, no need exists for sprint mechanics to be overly emphasized in this section. While it is always good to be aware of your running and sprinting posture to avoid injury and to save energy, in basketball, track-based sprinting techniques are not essential to success. If you feel, however, that you need additional information on starting stances, and increasing stride length and frequency, many books are available that discuss these subjects, including one by this author, *52-Week Football Training*.

By incorporating short-rapid sprints and lateral movements with changes of direction, followed by some type of jumping, you are simulating the requirements that are imposed while playing basketball. Also, the power you gain from these drills is more immediately usable because you are developing the movement cross bridges that exist between the speed and plyometric requirements of the activity.

The exercise packages presented in the following section are just a few examples that you might include in your training routine to develop your level of lateral and court speed. Each routine can be performed individually or as a group. If performed as a team or group, optimally, you should create stations of no more than four athletes at each basket. Such a number of athletes will provide just enough rest between the repetitions of each exercise to maintain a good work-to-rest ratio. Don't be afraid to use your imagination when training. If the plyometric and lateral-speed exercises in your training program are not to your liking, feel free to incorporate others in their place. Just remember to work hard and keep your training sensible by performing an appropriate (i.e., low) number of foot contacts during your plyometric training.

The Plyometric or Dynamic Warm-up

A plyometric warm-up should consist of a short course of minor jumping, hopping, and skipping drills. Such a warm-up should help prepare you for the other more strenuous, packaged drills. The following exercises should be performed together or in parts until you break a light sweat. For the very young or inexperienced athlete, the warm-up may be all the plyometric work you need.

■ Choose one of the following activities:

- Jump rope (on two feet) . . . . .50 turns
- Agility ladder . . . . .five drills
- Dot drill . . . . .two times at 15 seconds
- Quick feet drills . . . . .one time each at 15 seconds

■ Perform the following series of exercises to half-court and back:

- Skipping forward – Skip forward.
- Skipping backward – Skip backward.
- Carioca – Perform moving sideways. Alternately move your left foot in front and behind your right foot as you progress down the floor.
- Carioca skipping – Perform a carioca. Add a skip on each foot fall.
- Skipping sideways – Perform a step slide with a skip.
- High knee and arm running – Move forward bringing the knees as high as you can while at the same time pumping the arm in an exaggerated running motion.
- Alternate leg bounds – Run forward with exaggerated strides, as if to jump forward from leg to leg.
- Butt kicks – Move forward by alternately kicking your heels to your buttocks. Keep your knees pointing down to the floor.
- Back pedal – Run backward. Stay low and lean forward over your feet to help you maintain your balance.

■ Perform some very light stretching. Overstretching can reduce your level of power performance.

■ Perform two of the following (in one place):

Note: Young or inexperienced athletes, who choose to make the warm-up their plyometric workout, should perform two sets of each of these exercises. Softer surfaces, like gymnastics mats or grass, may be the best surface for these individuals to start training on.

- Tuck jump . . . . .5 times each
- Split jump . . . . .5 times each
- Hop (one leg) . . . . .10 times each leg
- Lateral hop . . . . .10 times each leg

Plyometric and Speed Packages

■ PLYOMETRIC PACKAGE #1
(Low intensity)

- *Lane Coverage:* Start at the low block on the three-second lane. Move in a rapid, almost horizontal, jumping step-slide to the elbow of the three-second lane. Fall to the floor on your backside as if to take a charge. Get up off the floor (no call!!). Jump off two feet as if to block a shot. Aggressively step-slide back to the low block and jump three times off both feet. Repeat two times on each side. The fall to the floor can be alternated to the front as if to dive for a loose ball. In this case, you would be falling and then do a drop-and-rebound push-up to clear yourself from the floor.

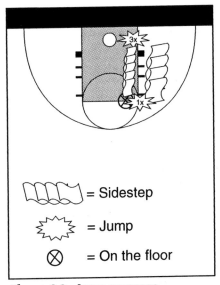

Figure 9.2. Lane coverage

- *Catch Up:* Begin by performing an ankle bounce at the free-throw line. Look down the floor toward the opposite free-throw line. Sprint sideways (looking over your shoulder) to the sidelines at half-court. Move from the sprint directly into a defensive stance at half-court. At this point, you should be looking at the free-throw line where you began. Step-slide backward as if jumping horizontally at 45-degree angles to the baseline you are facing. This movement is done as if to prevent someone from dribbling around you on the sideline. Step-slide back and reset. Perform the step-slides in this direction three times. After the last step-slide to the sideline, reset yourself at half-court. Now, move in the opposite direction from the sideline as if to force some one into a double-team. Perform each jumping step-slides three times in each direction. Finish by jumping vertically off two feet as if to block a pass. Perform the entire series twice to each sideline.

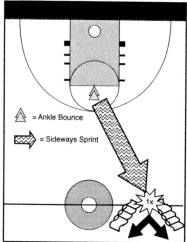

Figure 9.3. Catch up

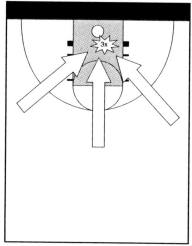

Figure 9.4. Trailers bounty

- *Trailers Bounty:* Sprinting toward the basket, jump off two feet as if to dunk. A ball can be passed to you, or you can catch a rebound coming off the goal for the put-back. Enter the three-second lane from both wings and from the center. Perform three times from each direction.

- *Inbounds Cutter:* Start on the left wing at the three-point line. Sprint rapidly into the three-second lane as if to lure your man inside. Then, rapidly change directions by sprinting sideways toward half-court. Turning to face the basket you just moved away from, jump off both feet as if to catch a high inbounds pass that is about to sail into the backcourt. Perform three times on each side of the basket.

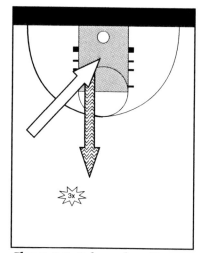

Figure 9.5. Inbounds cutter

● *Inbounds Ziggy:* Assume a defensive stance at the baseline with your back to the open court. Drop-stepping back with your right leg, perform three quick step-slides at a 45-degree angle to the baseline. Rapidly switch directions by dropping back with the left foot. Perform five changes of direction, and then jump to a stop. Finish by jumping off two feet as if to intercept an inbounds pass. A ball can be used. Perform this drill four times, twice on each side of the basket. Alternate the leg you begin the step-slide with each time.

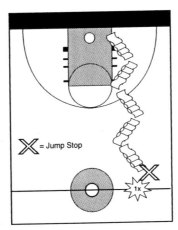

Figure 9.6. Inbounds ziggy

■ PLYOMETRIC PACKAGE #2
(Medium Intensity)

● *Jam Drops:* Assume a defensive stance on the low post block. Rapidly step-slide to the baseline and back six times at 45-degree angles. Rapidly drop step, turn and jump off two feet. A ball can be used, either to make a lay-in or a dunk, or to be caught coming off the backboard as if to rebound. Perform this drill three times on each side.

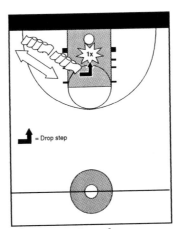

Figure 9.7. Jam drop

● *The Arrow:* Start on the baseline. Rapidly sprint to the elbow of the three-second lane, building out into a heads-up, defensive stance. Drop-step and perform three explosive step-slides at a 45-degree angle to the corner. Rapidly jump stop and then jump upward off both feet, as if to block a shot. Perform this drill three times on each side.

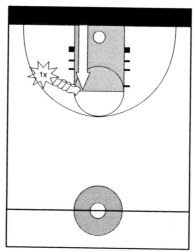

Figure 9.8. The arrow

● *The Disorientor:* Standing with your back to the basket on the free-throw line, spin jump 180 degrees, seven times. After spinning and landing, rapidly jump and spin back toward the direction you began. On your last jump, you will end facing the basket. Upon hitting the ground, sprint to the basket and perform a jump off both feet. A ball can be used, either to make a lay-in or a dunk, or to be caught coming off the backboard as if to rebound. Perform this drill six times, three times spinning toward your right shoulder and back, and then three times spinning toward your left shoulder and back.

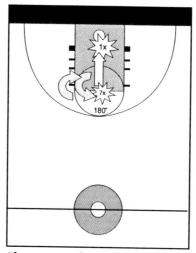

Figure 9.9. The disorientor

● *Rabid and Rapid:* Standing under the basket, quickly jump off both feet. As soon as you hit the ground, rapidly rebound to jump again. Perform five jumps, and then sprint to the three-point line. At the left wing, perform an immediate jump stop and ski jump from left to right five times. Drop-step and step-slide rapidly under the basket, and perform five more rapid rebounding jumps. Repeat twice on each side of the basket.

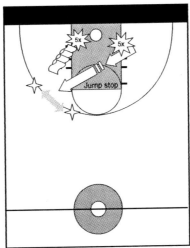

Figure 9.10. Rabid and rapid

● *Take-Offs:* Starting at the baseline from the corner, zigzag bound across the three-second lane. Jump to a stop on two feet at the low post, and then aggressively step-slide up to the high post. At the high post, skate bound six times. After the last bound, plant and take off on the leg closest to the basket. Turn and move toward the basket on the opposite side of the lane. Jump by taking off on one foot as if to catch an alley-oop back door pass. Perform three times on each side of the basket.

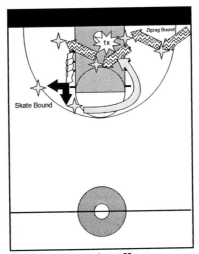

Figure 9.11. Take-offs

■ PLYOMETRIC PACKAGE #3
(High Intensity)

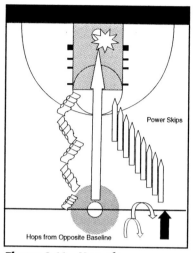

Figure 9.12. Hop along

- *Hop Along:* Hop (multiple times) as far out as possible from the baseline to half-court. You are trying to perform as few hops as possible before reaching half-court by hopping out as far as you can. Power skip from half-court to the free-throw line. Try to get at least 10 power skips within that distance, by going straight up and down. Step-slide backward to half-court as if lunging horizontally, at 45-degree angles to the baseline you are facing. Sprint forward to the goal, catch a pass or pick up a ball from the floor and lay it in or dunk it. Perform twice; hop on the opposite leg to begin the second bout of the exercise.

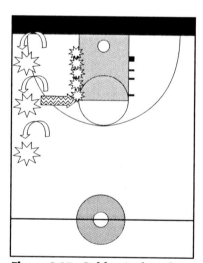

Figure 9.13. Spider, tuck and cover

- *Spider, Tuck and Cover:* Begin in the corner in an up push-up position. Rapidly drop into a down position. Explode upward, propelling yourself off the ground, sideways down the sideline, toward the opposite basket. Return to a down push-up position upon landing (spider push-up). Quickly get to your feet and then perform a tuck jump. After landing, drop to the ground and prepare for another spider push-up. Perform three sets of spider push-ups and tuck jumps. Upon landing after the last tuck jump, sprint sideways back to the high post and perform five quick rebounding jumps off both feet toward the low post. Repeat the drill twice on each side of the basket.

● *Rapid Fire:* Place three basketballs in a row on each side of the three-second lane. For the advanced athlete, medicine balls can be used. Begin by performing a lateral bounce in the center of the three-second lane. Rapidly step-slide sideways and pick up a ball. Step-slide back in toward the basket and jump off both feet to make a lay-in or dunk. If you choose, you can make your approach to the basket by dribbling the basketball (some medicine balls can be dribbled as well). Dribbling would allow for post moves to be incorporated

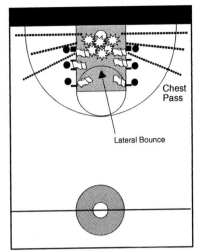

Figure 9.14. Rapid fire

before the basket is made. After the basket is made, catch your own rebound and pass the ball out, performing a two-handed chest pass or overhead pass. After passing the ball, rapidly slide to the other side of the three-second lane and grab another ball. Repeat the cycle until all the balls have been shot and passed out. Repeat this drill three times.

● *The Crusher:* Starting at the free-throw line, pick three heavy medicine balls up from the floor, one after the other, and explode upward performing an underhand backward throw. Make sure you begin each throw in a low-squat position with your back straight. After the final ball is thrown, turn toward the opposite basket and perform a triple jump. After your final landing, sprint toward the basket to receive a pass. Leave off one foot, jumping as high as you can and make a lay-in or dunk. Repeat the drill four times, thereby jumping off each foot twice to make the finishing basket.

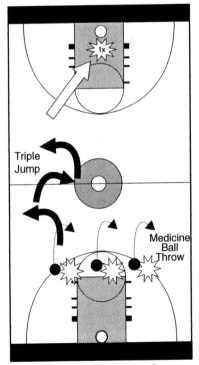

Figure 9.15. The crusher

Exercise Descriptions

■ BASKETBALL TERMS

- *Step-Slide:* The most common method of moving your body when playing basketball. Step-sliding is a low-level bounding movement. Assume a defensive stance with feet a little more than shoulder-width apart, knees bent and arms out stretched. If you are moving to the right, step out to the side with your right leg about 8-12 inches, while remaining a low as possible. Then move the left foot toward the right about the same distance. If you were standing on a line with both feet, one foot would never be off the line while the other was on. Both feet are always in line with one another. Your feet should always remain the same distance apart regardless of how fast you perform the movement. Never cross your feet to perceivably achieve more speed.

- *Jumping Step-Slide:* A fast and explosive version of the step-slide previously described. You are now covering the distance by quickly bounding sideways, while maintaining a position low to the ground. Your feet should always remain the same distance apart, regardless of how fast you perform the movement. Never cross your feet to perceivably achieve more speed.

- *Building Out:* How a defensive player approaches an offensive player with the ball. You aggressively rush to him, however, the closer you get, the more aware you are that he might try to drive by you. Building out is, therefore, a control sprint. Once with in arm's length of your opponent, you drop into a good defensive stance, with one hand up and the other at the level of the basketball.

- *Jump Stop:* Movement like a low-level long jump. You sprint to a spot, where you jump from the ground, and then land to a stop, on two feet, some distance ahead.

- *Sprint Sideways:* Like sprinting straight ahead with the exception that you are looking over your shoulder behind you. This is a common sprint posture when you are trying to sprint in front of an opponent who is just slightly behind you at your shoulder. With one more step, you could step in front of him and cut off his path downcourt. Of course, because not looking where you are running can be dangerous, you must be aware of what is ahead of you on the court before starting this type of exercise.

- *Drop-Step:* Performed by placing your feet approximately side-by-side, about shoulder-width apart. As quickly as you can, drop one foot straight back behind you as if to turn your body sideways to the direction you were just facing.

■ PLYOMETRIC TERMS

Several terms are used to describe plyometric exercises. Among the more common types of plyometric exercises are the following:

- *Jump.* A jump is performed off two feet and usually involves landing on two feet. Depending on the exercise intensity and objectives, a jump can be performed vertically, in-place, for height, or horizontally for distance.

- *Hop.* A hop is performed off one foot and, depending on the intensity of the exercise, you can land on the same foot or on two feet. Also depending on the level of exercise intensity, a hop can be performed vertically, in-place, for height or horizontally for distance.

- *Bound.* Bounds are hops performed by leaving the ground off one leg and landing some distance away on the opposite foot. Bounds can be performed laterally (to the side) or horizontally (straight ahead).

- *Bounce.* A bounce is used to describe a less-intense version of a jump, hop or bound. Usually, bounces are quick, low-intensity, rebounding movements that are employed to initiate a more intense action. Bounces are also used to provide a degree of "spring" in an action or movement.

- *Leap.* A leap is an action where after leaving the ground, you change your leg position in mid-air by swinging kicking or lifting.

Specific terms are also used to describe the intensity and/or the direction of a particular plyometric technique, including the following:

IN-PLACE LOW INTENSITY

- *Ankle Bounce.* Standing in place, use only the ankles to create upward, bouncing momentum. As soon as you touch the ground, rapidly rebound into another bounce. A pad can be placed on the floor to land on. Padded surfaces will prevent over stressing your body and make plyometric training less stressful for the beginner.

- *Single Leg Hops.* Standing in place, hop on one foot. As soon as you touch the ground, rapidly rebound into another bounce.

- *Tuck Jump (Leap).* Jump up and tuck your legs near your chest while suspended in air. To emphasize the tuck, loosely hug your knees. This hug must be performed quickly in order to not impede the landing. Upon landing on this exercise (and all plyometric exercises), allow your knees to give a little in order to absorb the landing.

- *Split Jump (Leap).* Jump up and bring your outstretched legs near your chest. While suspended in air, attempt to touch your toes. To improve your balance while you are in the air, lean as far forward as you can. To insure safety in the movement, make sure your lower back is completely warmed-up. This exercise can be a great activity to work the dynamic flexibility aspect of training into your plyometric routine.

- *Lateral Bounce.* Standing with your legs about shoulder-width apart, begin quickly bounding from one foot to the other. Perform this movement in-place. Your feet should leave and return to the floor in nearly the same place.

- *Skate Bound.* This exercise is an expanded version of the lateral bounce. The distance of the bounds is greater in this particular exercise. You must land further out to the side as you leave the ground. Bound laterally and low to the ground, leaving the ground with your left foot and landing on your right foot. Then, move back to your left, using your right foot.

- *Spin Jump.* Jump up. While in the air, spin your body around. You can start with a quarter turn and expand the spin into half and full turns. This exercise is a great developer of body control and awareness. It can also profoundly affect your level of balance.

IN-PLACE MEDIUM INTENSITY

- *Lateral Hop.* Hop on one foot from side-to-side. This action can be done over a line or an object of a predetermined height. As you become more advanced at performing the exercise, the distance that you hop laterally can be extended.

- *Ski Jumps.* Jump from side-to-side onto and off of both feet. The beginner can jump over a line on the floor. The more advanced athlete can jump over a raised object, like a low hurdle or cone.

IN-PLACE SHOCK

- *Depth Jump.* Standing on a box or other stable object, step off the edge and land on two feet. A cushioned mat can be used to reduced the initial stress of the exercise. Later, the mat can be taken away to increase the level of intensity. This exercise is stressful and should be used sparingly. It is important that you bend your knees on landing to absorb the impact, and allow your muscles to absorb the load. The loading on your muscles will benefit their reactive abilities.

SHORT-RESPONSE, LOW INTENSITY

- *Jump Ups.* Stand with your feet side-by-side. Hop forward and up onto a box or other stable object. After landing, move forward and step off the box on the opposite side. The height of the box can be increased over time.

SHORT-RESPONSE, MEDIUM INTENSITY

- *Triple Jump.* Stand with your feet side-by-side. Hop forward as far as you can onto your right foot. Upon landing, immediately bound forward as far as you can onto your left foot. After landing, immediately bound forward, landing on both feet in a jump stop. The action can be repeated for a given number of times or for a given distance.

- *Zigzag Bound.* Move forward while at the same time, bound from side-to-side. A line on the floor can provide a means of insuring that you jump from one side to another on consecutive jumps.

LONG-RESPONSE, LOW INTENSITY

- *Power Skip (Leap).* This exercise is called a leap. In some of the workouts included in this book, this exercise is also referred to as a power skip. To perform the exercise, pull your arms, as well as the knee of your non-support leg, upward quickly. At the same time, hop vertically up and off the floor, using your down (or support) leg. Land on the same leg you took off on. Upon landing, quickly pull your arms up again, while also pulling the knee of your opposite leg (the one that was the support leg) upward. This time, hop vertically upward off your new support leg. Repeat the action for a given distance or a given number of times. The emphasis should be on moving vertically as high as you can. In other words, while you are performing this exercise for a given distance, you should try to perform as many vertical Leaps as possible.

LONG-RESPONSE, HIGH INTENSITY

- *Hop (Multiple Times).* Jumping on one foot is termed a hop. The beginner may choose to jump off one foot and land on two. As your level of strength is improved, jumping off and back onto one foot will increase the intensity of the exercise. Hops can be performed vertically or horizontally to the floor.

- *Alternate Leg Bounding.* This exercise is used in the warm-up exercises and is performed like a hop. You hop off one leg, propelling yourself forward as far as you can, landing on your opposite leg. Repeat the action by hopping off the leg you just landed on. This exercise is like running with really long, jumping strides.

UPPER-BODY, LOW INTENSITY

- *Overhead Pass.* Stand with a medicine ball at arm's length above your head. Place one foot in front of the other to provide support. Keeping your arms straight and above your head, throw the ball. This exercise can be performed with a partner or a pitch-back device designed for heavy medicine balls. Catch the ball high above your head. Allow your arms to give in order to absorb the incoming weight of the ball.

- *Chest Pass.* Pushing with both hands at the same time, pass the medicine ball forward. This exercise can be performed with a partner or a pitch-back device designed for heavy medicine balls. When catching the ball, allow your arms to give in order to absorb the incoming weight of the ball.

UPPER-BODY, MEDIUM INTENSITY

- *Underhand Backward Throw.* Assume a squatting position with your back straight and your chin tilted slightly upward. Place a medicine ball between your legs, and grasp it with two hands. Rapidly extend your legs, and jump slightly off the ground. At the same moment, bring your arms upward above your head, arching your back slightly. At your body's fullest extension, release the ball so that it flies upward to its maximum height. The ball should land behind you. A partner or coach can time the length of how long the ball stays in the air to help maximize your efforts. Begin with a light medicine ball, and as you become advanced in the movement, use a heavier ball.

UPPER-BODY, HIGH INTENSITY

- *Drop and Rebound Push-Up.* This exercise involves the use of some device (e.g., a box) as a support. Assume a push-up position on the support. Allow your hands to drop free of the support and land on the ground. Upon contacting the ground, immediately allow your arms and shoulders to give in order to absorb the shock of the landing. Landing on a pad will also minimize the shock of the exercise. As your shoulder and arms bend to absorb the landing, continue lowering as if to go down into a push-up. Once at the bottom of the push-up, rapidly drive your arms upward. The object is to push yourself high enough to land back onto the supports. Be very careful as you initially drop from the supports. If the supports are too high for your level, you could be injured while performing this exercise.

- *Spider Push-Up.* Start in the up position of a push-up. Drop into the downs position, and then push yourself up rapidly so that your hands leave the floor. At the same time, kick one leg up so that your feet leave the floor as well. When you push up, push at an angle so that while in the air, your body moves sideways. When you land, land on both hands and feet, while simultaneously allowing your body to move downward into the bottom phase of the next push-up. Then, explode upward and sideways again. Remember this is an aggressive body movement, and some potential for being injured during this exercise exists.

CHAPTER 10

Basketball-Specific Agility Exercises

The way that you perform a particular movement may be completely different from how your teammates perform that same movement. However, the outcome can be the same. Every athlete's body is unique in the way it performs. You must, therefore, explore different methods of teaching your body to move. Effortless movements result from an appropriate amount of time invested in a sound workout program. Gifted athletes may not have to invest as much time to be good, but they would undoubtedly be better if they demonstrated the desire to improve and make the effort to keep practicing.

It is important to understand that sports-related movements are very complex combinations of smaller, simpler movements. The primary reason some athletes are better at performing certain movement skills is that they more easily bring together and coordinate all the smaller movements. Some athletes seem to be born with the gift of coordination. That might be true, but anyone can learn if he is taught in the correct manner and is willing to evaluate himself constructively. In any class, you have A students and D students. Through desire and hard work, however, many D students can reach the top of the class.

The drills presented in this chapter are designed to work the smaller or individual skills necessary for you to become more athletic. They allow you to concentrate on the individual movements that you might need while playing, without having to be responsible for all the movements of your position. Given the importance of the smaller component parts of movement patterns, let's investigate some of these smaller parts of movement, balance, foot-speed, and agility. Then we'll coordinate these smaller movements to explore combination movements and reaction and quickness drills.

Balance

Balance is critical to being able to move gracefully and quickly. Humans depend on the senses of sight and touch, and the faculties of their inner ear to achieve proper balance. Balance is a fundamental physical ability, and sadly, one of the most overlooked.

You can develop and improve your balance, as you can any physical ability. The drills presented in this section are designed to improve your balance during movement and while standing still. Most of the drills are performed on one foot. All factors considered, if you can improve your balance on one foot, you can more easily balance yourself on two feet. If your body is orthopedically sound, perform the drills barefoot. By performing the movements with your shoes off, you will force the small stabilizing muscles of your ankle and knee to work harder to maintain your balance. Working with your shoes off can also strengthen weak muscles in your ankles and knees, thus possibly preventing injury. If your knees and ankles are injured, then perform the movements with your shoes on. The shoe acts as a stabilizer and provides additional balance and support to your already balanced body.

Some balance exercises are performed with the eyes closed. Without sight, you are forced to depend more on the feedback from your muscles and joints. You can develop a higher level of kinesthetic sensory information (motor feedback) by relying more on how your body feels, and less on your other senses. The sense of sight helps you with balance. Accordingly, if you can develop a level of balance proficiency with the eyes closed, you will be more balanced in a sport's movement where your eyes are open.

Balance Packages

Perform each of these drills barefoot, on both your left and right foot.

■ BALANCE PACKAGE #1

- Stand on one foot with your foot flat on the ground for 30 seconds.

- Then, stand on the same foot on your toes for 30 seconds.

- Bring the knee of your free leg up and kick to the front. Remain on one foot. 10 kicks with each leg.

- Stand on one foot, hold your free leg out to the back for 30 seconds.

- Stand on the other foot, hold your free leg out to the front for 30 seconds.

■ BALANCE PACKAGE #2

- Stand on one foot with your eyes closed for 30 seconds.

- Stay on the same foot and make quarter turns, pausing for 10 seconds at each turn.

- Stay on the same foot and hold your free leg out to the side for 30 seconds.

- Bring your knee up, rotate your support leg and kick your free leg to the side for 10 kicks.

- Finally, stand on the toes of the same foot for 30 seconds.

■ BALANCE PACKAGE #3

- Stand on one foot and push your opposite leg behind (10 times each leg).

- Hop on the same foot. Do a three-quarter turn and kick to the side slowly (5 times each leg).

- Hop sideways.   After each hop, add a side kick (10 times each leg).

- Stand on one foot, perform a three-quarter turn and then kick slowly out to the side (10 times each leg).

■ BALANCE PACKAGE #4

- Hop on one foot sideways, maintain your balance, and reach down and touch the floor. Balance and hop again, trying not to double hop (10 times each leg).

- Stand on one foot, push your free leg out in front of you and lean back as far as you can without falling (10 times each leg).

- Stand on one foot, lean to the side, push your free leg out to the side, and then try to touch the floor (10 times each leg).

- Stand on one foot and then lean your upper body in all directions as far as you can without falling (5 times each leg).

Foot Speed

Everyone talks about foot speed and quickness. Everyone wants to know how he can get it. The question is, "what is it?" Foot speed is the ability to touch the foot quickly to the ground, while reducing the amount of time the foot is in contact with the ground.

Try tapping your hand on your leg. Slowly increase the rate of the tapping until it is as fast as you can tap. You'll probably find that you can tap faster if your hand makes light contact rather than contacting with a greater force. Now, try the same thing with your foot to the ground. You will probably find it more difficult to tap your foot as quickly as you tapped your hand. This is because the hand has a higher number of nerve fibers activating a smaller number of muscle fibers. The hand is designed for more delicate and faster work than the foot. Another reason that the foot cannot move as quickly as the hand is because it is seldom required to do so. What if the foot were trained to act like the hand regarding speed? The foot may never be as fast as the hand, but I would bet that you would see an increase in its agility.

The following drills are designed to address the smaller, more basic movement components of the hip, knee, and ankle to produce greater foot-speed. The drills are arranged to address the most simple of foot movements first, adding more complex foot movement patterns later. These drills are designed to help you perform more complex movements, with softer and faster footfalls.

Foot Speed Packages

This first set of foot-speed drills addresses the most basic of speed components: the cadence of the foot, ankle, knee, and hip movements. How fast you become is ultimately determined by how efficiently the joints of your lower body work with one another. You can facilitate faster joint actions by applying tapping routines to each joint area. Tapping is a synchronization exercise that you perform by tapping the floor or some other surface with your foot. You tap your foot by moving your ankle, knee, or hip.

In some cases an athlete's lack of movement coordination could be the result of one or more of his joints being out of cadence with his other joint segments. For example, if you are having trouble while sprinting at high speed, the problem may not be at the hip or knee. Instead, your ankle might be losing the ability to retain the higher-speed movement pattern. The tapping exercises may help correct this problem and improve your synchronization.

■ FOOT SPEED PACKAGE #1

Try to tap as fast as you can without losing rhythm:

- Sit in a chair. Moving only the ankle (let your heels remain in contact with the floor), tap your toes on the floor alternating legs. Tap for 30 seconds, three times.

- Sit in a chair. Moving only the ankle (let your toes remain in contact with the floor), tap your heels on the floor alternating legs. Tap for 30 seconds, three times.

- Sit in a chair. Moving only the ankle, tap the heel of one foot and the toes of the other foot on the floor in an alternating fashion. Tap for 30 seconds, three times.

- Sit in a chair one foot from a wall. Moving only the knee, tap your toes on the wall in an alternating fashion. Tap for 30 seconds, three times.

- Sit on a plyometric box with your the feet on the floor. Moving only the knee, tap your heels on the box in an alternating fashion. Tap for 30 seconds, three times.

- Lie on your back on the floor. Keeping your legs straight and moving only your hips, tap the floor with your heels in an alternating fashion. Tap for 30 seconds, three times.

- Lie on your stomach on the floor. Keeping your leg straight and moving only the hip, tap the floor with your toes in an alternating fashion. Tap for 30 seconds, three times.

The second foot-speed workout uses slightly more complex movement patterns. Also, this series of drills requires that you incorporate your entire body weight into the exercises. Managing body weight is the most critical aspect of athletic movements. In this package, you perform these exercises, which involve more cyclic, alternating, dance-like movement patterns, in a contained area. This "teaches" your ankles, knees, and hips to act naturally to a variety of situations, while at the same time, maintaining cadence.

■ FOOT SPEED PACKAGE #2

- *Wall running.* Stand facing a wall and place both hands on the wall for support. Stand on one foot. With your free leg, bring that knee up toward your chest. Then, push your free leg slightly out in front of you and down-ward toward the ground. When your foot touches the ground, slide it lightly backward and up as if you were a bull pawing the ground. Perform this movement in slow motion for the first few repetitions and then gradually increase speed without loosing the coordination of the move-ment. Perform for 30 seconds, three times each leg.

- *Russian hops.* Mark a straight line on the floor, six feet long. Stand on one foot on that line. Slowly begin to perform very small, short hops. As you move down the line, attempt to hop faster and faster with lighter contact to the floor. Attempt to perform as many hops within that six-foot margin as possible. Perform three times each leg.

- *Box running.* Place a small sturdy box, 6-to-12 inches high, on the floor. Place one foot lightly on the box, while allowing the opposite foot to remain on the floor as if to step up on a step. Quickly begin to alternate the position of your feet. The foot on the floor moves to the box, while the foot on the box moves to the floor. Attempt to keep foot contact, both on the floor and on the box, light and quiet. Perform for 30 seconds, three times.

Figure 10.1

- *Box shuffle.* Perform this drill in a similar manner to the box run drill previously described. Place one foot on the box and allow the other to remain in light contact with the floor. The foot on the floor moves up to the box, while at the same time, the foot on the box moves to the floor on the opposite side of the box. The motion is like stepping up on a step, sideways and back off again. Quickly alternate your feet back and forth. Perform for 30 seconds, three times.

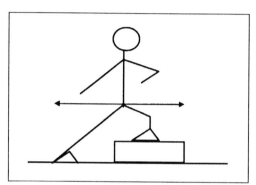

Figure 10.2

- *Quick-feet drills.* These drills consist of simple foot-movement patterns performed in place, using a line or rope on the ground. These drills are designed to help you improve your quickness by hopping or stepping over the rope. To make the exercises more difficult and to incorporate high knee action, you can suspend the rope a few inches off the ground. On all movements, hop as low to the ground as possible.

- *Side-to-side bounce.* Stand sideways on one side of a rope. Jump across the rope with both feet together, and then backward for an assigned period of time (e.g., 30 to 60 seconds). You may vary the drill by allowing one foot to hit first upon landing, followed immediately by the other.

- *Front and back bounce.* Stand facing the rope. Jump forward across the rope with both feet together, and then backward. Continue jumping for an assigned amount of time (e.g., 30 to 60 seconds). You may vary the drill by allowing one foot to hit first upon landing followed immediately by the other.

- *Single-side split bounce.* Stand over the rope so that one foot is on each side. Jump up (leap). While in the air, cross your leg so that upon landing, your left foot lands on the right side of the rope, and your right foot lands on the left. Next, jump back with both feet in their starting position. Alternate by crossing with your right leg behind and in front of your left leg. Continue jumping for 30 to 60 seconds. Try to achieve the switch in foot placement by staying as low to the ground as possible.

- *Three-sided square.* The three-sided square is a foot-pattern drill. Place three strips of tape on the floor forming a square with only three sides. The objective of the drill is to step in and out of the square in various patterns as quickly as possible. You can also form the square with string or rope raised slightly off the ground in order to force yourself to raise your knees higher.

  ✓ Two in, one out. Start by standing on your right foot. Step into the square with your left foot. Next, bring your right foot into the square, while simultaneously moving your left foot to the opposite side of the square. Your feet should rapidly touch the ground one after the other. Pick up your right foot, then put it back down into the square. Next, bring your left foot into the square, while moving your right foot to where it originally began. Keep repeating this one-two-three, one-two-three pattern for 30 seconds, two times.

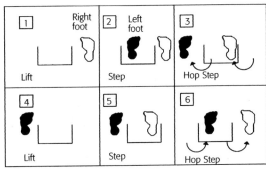

Figure 10.3

  ✓ Two in, two out. Start by standing on your right foot. Step into the square with your left foot. Next, bring your right foot into the square, while simultaneously moving your left foot to the opposite side of the square. Pick your right foot up and move it to the outside of the square beside your left foot. Next, bring your right foot back into the square, and then your left foot. Return your right foot to where it originally began. Follow this by bringing your left foot out of the square beside your right foot. Keep repeating this one-two-three-four, one-two-three-four pattern for 30 seconds, two times.

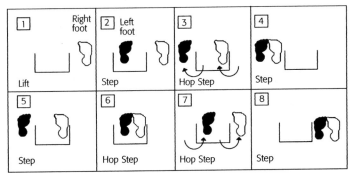

Figure 10.4

The third foot-speed workout involves even more complex movements by having you perform foot patterns, while at the same time moving forward (or backward) and laterally. Cutting drills are also included to provide you with lateral stability and transfer of balance, while still being able to rapidly change directions.

■ FOOT SPEED PACKAGE #3

- *Ladder drills.* These drills are performed on a five-yard long rope ladder that is lying on the floor. A variety of drills can be performed on both the three-sided square and the ladder. The previously mentioned drills are only a few. Use your imagination and create new drills for yourself. Ladders can be placed on the floor or raised a few inches off the ground to insure high-knee actions.

  ✓ Two in, one out. Move forward and backward, in and out of each hole created by the ladder. Perform the two-in, one-out pattern used in the three-sided square drills, one-two-three, one-two-three, and so on. Perform this drill three times, as quickly as you can, paying very close attention to the detail of the movement.

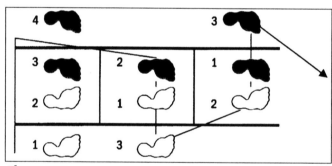

Figure 10.5

  ✓ Lateral two in, two out. Move sideways through the ladder, placing two feet in each hole and then stepping back out of the ladder with both feet, one-two-in, one-two-out, and so on, down the length of the ladder. Perform this drill three times, as quickly as possible, paying very close attention to the detail of the movement.

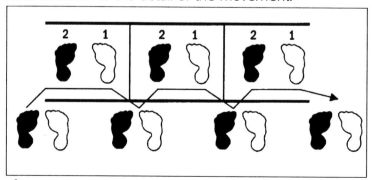

Figure 10.6

- *Additional ladder drills.* (These drills can be added into your routine or used in place of the two drills described in the previous section.)

  ✓ Quick run, sprint out. Move forward along the length of the ladder, stepping one foot after the other into the spaces created by the rungs of the ladder. Start with your left foot first. On subsequent runs, begin with your right foot. Once you are through the ladder, sprint to a set distance.

  ✓ Lateral quick run, sprint out. Moving laterally along the length of the ladder, step one foot after the other into the spaces created by the rungs of the ladder. Once you are through the ladder, sprint to a set distance.

  ✓ Two in, two out. Start by standing on the right side of the ladder at the first rung space. Step into the first rung space with your left foot, followed by your right foot. Step out on the left side of the ladder, first with your left foot and again followed by your right foot. Move forward along the length of the ladder, zigzagging in and out of the rung spaces.

  ✓ One in, three out, sprint out. Start by standing on the left side of the ladder at the first open space created by the rungs. Moving to your right, place your right foot into that first space, lifting your left leg slightly off the floor. Next, put your left leg back down on the floor where it originally began. Pick up your right leg and quickly bring it back beside your left leg outside the ladder. Move forward along the length of the ladder by stepping with your right leg into the next rung space. In this way, your right foot is always stepping into the ladder, and your left foot is always out. During this drill, you are always on one side of the ladder. On subsequent passes through the ladder, begin on the right-hand side. At the end of the drill, sprint forward.

- *Tiny hurdle drills.* Set 10 to 12 one-foot high hurdles two feet apart. These hurdle drills are designed to help you develop hip flexion and to improve coordination of movement at the hip joint, while you are moving in a horizontal direction. This action will be of great coordination and strength benefit during many sports movements.

  ✓ Quickly step over each hurdle, with each foot moving in a straight line. Step over 10 to 12 hurdles, five times.

  ✓ Moving sideways, quickly step over each hurdle with each foot. You should never cross your feet while performing this drill. Step over 10 to 12 hurdles, five times.

  ✓ Moving laterally, quickly step over each hurdle with each foot. Move back and forth for 30 seconds.

- *Cutting drills.* Cutting drills are designed to develop the ability to change direction rapidly while remaining under control.

  ✓ Transitional carioca. Perform a carioca movement. Upon command, rapidly change directions, back and forth for 30 seconds Coaches can give the commands at different intervals to keep the athlete guessing and avoid establishing set movement patterns.

  ✓ Sprint forward and pedal back. Sprint forward 10 yards and then rapidly change directions, backpedaling to the starting point. Perform three sets of 10 transitions.

  ✓ 30-second step slide. Use the width of the three-second lane on the basketball court. Try to maintain a regular rhythm and step slide from side-to-side for 30 seconds. Attempt to perform as many slides as possible. Each time you change directions is considered a repetition. Perform two-sets.

  ✓ Cutting inside and outside legs. Perform the drill by running up court at 45-degree angles to the sideline. Imagine another line running parallel to the sideline at half-court. Each time you reach one of the lines, cut back toward the opposite line, off your outside leg (leg nearest the line). One variation of the drill is to perform your changes of direction off your inside leg (the leg further from the line). This procedure will cause you to spin as you make your cut. Another variation is to cut off your outside leg on one line, and then cut off your inside leg at the other line. During this variation, the same leg will be doing the cutting for each change of direction. In this variation, you must switch legs and repeat the drill. Complete three sets of 10 changes of direction with each leg.

Agility

As you approach the basketball season, you should place more and more emphasis on performing even larger, more complex movements. Agility movements are an excellent method of increasing the specificity of your workout training sessions to basketball activities.

- *Agility packages.* The agility and reaction drills presented in Table 10.1, along with work on specific basketball drills, will help you learn how to use your newly developed muscular size, power, endurance, and speed.

Agility Package #1	Agility Package #2
• T-cone drill — perform five times, against the clock • Three-cone reaction drill — perform three times. • Dot drill — perform three times, for 30 seconds bouts. • Triangle-cone drill — perform five times, against the clock	• W-cone drill — perform five times, against the clock. • Ball-drop, reaction drill — perform five times. • S-cone drill — perform five times, against the clock. • Goalline tag — make 10 approaches to the goal.
Agility Package #3	Agility Package #4
• Snake-cone drill — perform five times, against the clock. • Box #1 cone drill — perform five times, against the clock. • Pick up the tag — play three or four games. • Dodge ball — play two games.	• Dot drill — perform five times, for 30-second bouts. • Box #2 cone drill — perform five times, against the clock. • Cops and robbers tag — play two or three games. • Sharks in the tank tag — play two or three games.

Table 10.1

• *Cone drills.* The most basic agility movements can be practiced by a series of drills, involving different cone formations (Figures 10.7 to 10.13). Timing yourself through the drills may be beneficial as long as you maintain good form. If you get out of control with your movements, you should slow down and concentrate on the quality of movement, rather than the speed. Your objective during these drills is to move as quickly as possible from one cone to the next, staying low and outside the cones on the turns. Placing your hand on the ground when maneuvering around the cones is allowed. Each drill should be performed twice, once in each direction (clockwise, counterclockwise, left or right).

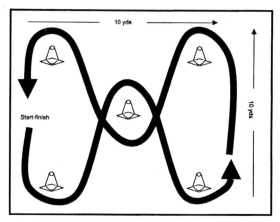

Figure 10.7. Snake-cone drill

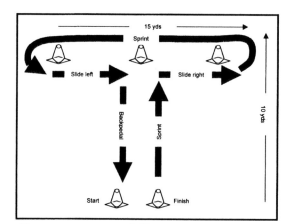

Figure 10.8. T-cone drill

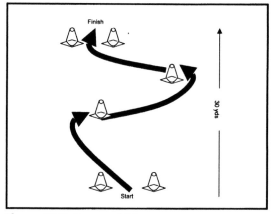

Figure 10.9. S-cone drill

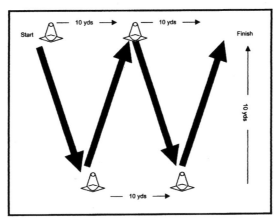

Figure 10.10. W-cone drill

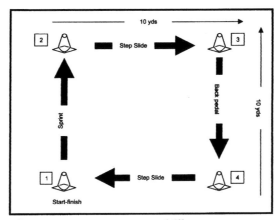

Figure 10.11. Box #1 cone drill

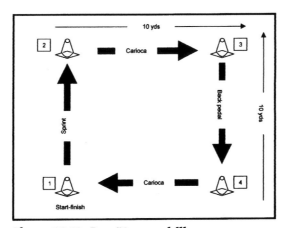

Figure 10.12. Box #2 cone drill

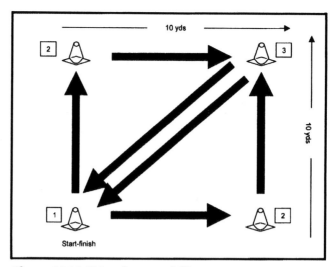

Figure 10.13. Triangle cone drill

Reaction and Quickness

Often your opponent does not beat you physically, he beats you with deception. He is able to prevent you from reading his intentions, causing you to either delay your reaction or to overreact. In either case, you'll find yourself a split second behind, and he has gained the advantage.

- *Reaction drills.* Once you have begun to perform the previously described cone drills more efficiently, you should then progress toward honing your ability to perceive movement and to react to that movement as if it were your opponent's initial step. The following drills are just a few such exercises to sharpen your reactive abilities.

  ✓ Three-cone reaction drill. This reaction drill is most often done with one athlete at a time, but it can be performed with three athletes by setting up three sets of cones. Each athlete is responsible for his three cones, numbered #1 through #3, arranged in a straight line in front of him, about 3-to-5 yards apart. Perform this drill by lightly bouncing on your feet, about 10 yards from the middle cone. When the coach calls a specific number or points to a cone, rush to the cone and tap it. If the coach calls another number, quickly move to that cone. If he doesn't call a number, then rush back to the starting position and resume bouncing and wait for the next cue. Be alert? You may also be ask to jump or hit the ground, as if to recover a loose ball.

  ✓ Ball-drop reaction drill. The ball-drop drill is the next drill in the progressive cycle of improving your reaction. Perform this drill by having a coach stand about five yards from the athlete. The coach holds a ball in each hand. The objective for the athlete is to attempt to catch the ball before it can take a second bounce. The coach can choose to drop the ball out of either hand, thus making the athlete's job more difficult. Several cues can be provided to the athlete. The main cues can be visual, like the sight of the ball dropping, or a corresponding blink of the coach's eyes, or the change of body position, timed with the drop of the ball. A verbal cue can be issued prior to the drop of the ball if an improvement in auditory reactions is a sport requirement. After each drop of the ball and successful catch by the athlete, the coach takes one normal step back away from the athlete's starting point. This will assist in challenging the athlete to push his first-step quickness to its highest level.

- *Games.* The next drills are actually games within themselves. These games are commonly played on the schoolyard, but still provide a sound base of "recognize and react" skill requirements. These games are the next step forward in the reaction development continuum. These games require that you react to an ever reacting opponent similar to that of the athlete's sport of basketball.

  ✓ Dot drill. While the dot drill does not develop perception and reactive skills, it can increase quickness through improvements in foot patterning. Five dots are painted on the floor in a square. Each corner should be one and a half feet apart. Another dot should be painted in the center of the square. Various patterns of the drill can then be preformed on one or both legs. The most common pattern is to stand on one side of the square with a foot on each corner dot. Hopping forward, bring the feet together and land on the center dot with both feet. Hop forward again to land on the opposite side of the square with the feet apart so that each foot lands on the corner dots. Now hop backward retracing the pattern you have just performed. Continue moving forward and backward as quickly as possible for a designated amount of time.

  ✓ Tag games. These next games have school-yard origins. Still, they require you to use and improve your "recognize and react" skills. These drills are the next step in the reaction continuum. Tag is an excellent method of working on cutting skills, reacting to an opponent, and changing direction and speed. These require athletic movements and involve hard work, but also are a great way to have fun. in addition to the tag games presented in this section, you can create others by using your imagination. For example, perform all games with boundaries. A square marked off with cones will do. If an athlete about to be tagged steps out of bounds, then he is out. The five following examples illustrate the variety and diversity of tag games that can be played.

* Dodge ball. Several variations of the game of dodge ball can be played. In one of the safest versions, you stand with your back against a wall as a coach or teammate issues a hand-tossed barrage of tennis balls toward you, one at a time. This drill forces you to dodge and spin to avoid the projectiles. Stop the play if you are tagged by a ball, or if the balls begin to gather dangerously under your feet. Of course, you can play the larger version of the game in which one athlete serves as the thrower and the others attempt to avoid being tagged by the ball. This version can quickly get out of hand, however, so use it only with small groups.

* Sharks in the tank. Try performing these games in a 15-by-15 yard square with five or six athletes being tagged by one individual, or in a 30-by-30 yard square with 10 or more athletes being tagged by two players. In this tag game, one or two people are "it," depending on the dimensions of the tank. The objective of the game is for the person who is it to tag everyone else. The game is complete when all players have been tagged.

* Pick-up tag. Try this games in a 30-by-30 yard square. Four to twenty paper balls are needed. Match one to three pickers with one to three taggers and blockers. One athlete is the designated picker, while another serves as a tagger. The picker's objective is to pick up assorted paper balls that are lying randomly on the floor or playing surface. The picker is guarded by a blocker. The blocker's job is to stay between the picker and the tagger. The tagger attempts to keep the picker from getting any of the balls by tagging him. The blocker can only shield. He cannot hold or touch the tagger.

* Goalline tag. The objective of this tag game is for the player to cross a goal-line without being tagged by the tagger. The goal-line should be about 20 feet in length so that the tagger will have to work hard to defend it. This is a one-on-one tag game. Players line up and the line moves forward as players who have run against the tagger become the next tagger.

* Cops and robbers. In this tag game, two people are designated "it." The "its" (taggers) are the cops. Everyone else is a robber.

The objective is for one cop to tag and jail all the robbers. Once tagged, the robbers must go to jail (typically a designated side of the playing area. The robbers can break into jail and free a robber by tagging him out, but only one at a time. They must however, get by the jailer cop, who is a goalline defender, both going into and coming out of jail. The jailer is assigned to a limited area, along the goalline (jail) and cannot tag a robber unless the robber enters the area or tries to enter or leave the jail. The game is over when all robbers are jailed.

- *Combination movement drills.* The agility drills previously described, along with foot-speed drills, can be combined to create movement courses. A movement course can help you improve your balance and movement strength, which, in turn, can ease your transition toward actual play. Movement courses are basically obstacle courses. Shifting from linear to cutting activities and from sprinting to jumping, movement courses do not have designated measurements. The courses can vary in size. They can be contained within the half-court or expanded to full-court. Naturally, the larger the course, the more stressful it will be. These courses can be undertaken as a team or done individually. They can be repeated several times to produce a conditioning effect. Timing yourself through the course can be beneficial to gauging your performance. It is important, however, that all of your movements are performed with good form. This requirement will help you avoid forming bad habits.

The point to keep in mind is that movement courses can be altered in a variety of ways. The following three movement courses are just starters. Design your own course by incorporating all the things you feel are important to helping you move better.

■ MOVEMENT COURSE #1 (Figure 10.14)

Equipment needed: Eight to ten low hurdles; four or five high hurdles; one agility ladder.

- Start by ankle bouncing in place.

- Then, sprint to a set of low hurdles.

- Begin moving sideways over the hurdles.

- After moving over the last low hurdle, quickly backpedal to a series of high hurdles.

- Face the hurdles and begin jumping over each hurdle, off of and onto two feet.

- Turn and quickly sprint to an agility ladder.

- Move through the ladder performing a two-foot in and one-foot out pattern.

- To complete the course, turn and sprint to the finish.

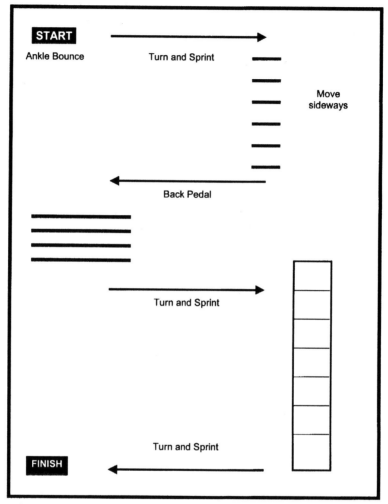

Figure 10.14. Movement course #1.

■ MOVEMENT COURSE #2 (Figure 10.15)

Equipment: Four or five high hurdles; two agility ladders; four to six cones; one basketball goal.

- Start by ankle bouncing in place.

- Then sprint to a set of high hurdles.

- Face the hurdles and begin jumping each hurdle, off of and onto two feet.

- Move forward and begin quickly step-sliding at angles from cone to cone.

- Perform a two feet in, two feet out (described above) on an agility ladder.

- Move quickly to a spot under a basketball goal and begin performing 8 quick vertical jumps.

- Step-slide rapidly to a cone and then turn up the course performing a carioca.

- Proceed through another agility ladder doing the same two feet in, two feet out pattern done in the previous ladder.

- Sprint to the finish.

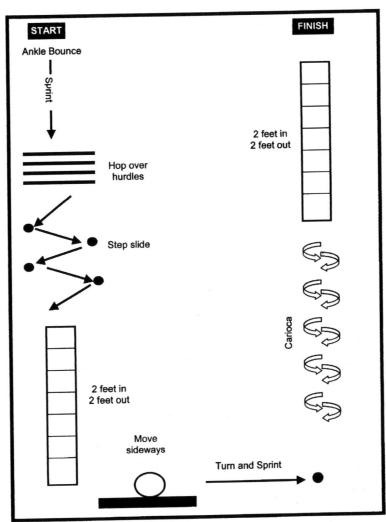

Figure 10.15. Movement course #2.

■ MOVEMENT COURSE #3 (Figure 10.16)

Equipment needed: Two agility ladders; nine cone; eight to ten low hurdles.

- Start by ankle bouncing in place at the start of a box drill.

- Begin the box drill moving left to cone #1, performing a carioca. Sprint to cone #2. Carioca right to cone #3. Finish the box by backpedaling to cone #4.

- Quickly change directions and sprint forward to an agility ladder.

- Perform a two-feet in, one-foot out pattern down the length of the ladder.

- Quickly move toward a line of cones. Step in-between each open space between the cones, and then step back out. Move sideways down the cones, addressing each opening. Turn and sprint out at the last cone.

- Hop over a series of low hurdles.

- At the last hurdle, begin to backpedal up the course to a cone.

- At the cone, begin to step-slide to the right to an agility ladder, where you again perform the two-feet in, one-foot out pattern.

- Once out of the ladder, move to a push-up position, and begin moving to your right in a quick crabbing motion. This simulates scrambling for a loose ball.

- Finish by sprinting to the finish.

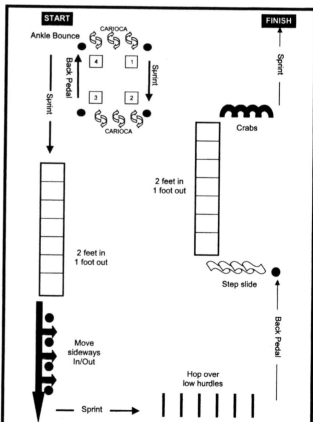

Figure 10.16. Movement course #3.

CHAPTER 11

Running and Cardiorespiratory Conditioning Drills

During a basketball game, you are continually moving when playing offense, defense, and transitioning up and down the court. This chapter on workout exercises presents several running drills. Running and other continuous forms of body movement enhance your cardiorespiratory conditioning. The previous chapters have addressed how to create bigger and more powerful muscles through resistance training.

Optimal levels of muscle are important for success in athletics. Muscle is what enables you to move with grace and speed. In athletics, however, working for added muscle alone is of little value. It is critical that you improve your heart and lungs (cardiorespiratory system), kidneys (renal system), sweat glands, and various other organs of the body (thermoregulatory and endocrine systems) to provide your muscles with the nutrients and oxygen necessary to keep them functioning well. While resistance training works these supporting systems, it places a lower demand on them such as more continuous activity, such as running, would.

Your body responds in different ways to different types of exercise or activity. During a basketball game, you may have to ask your body to respond in a variety of ways. For example, you may have trained very hard with resistance exercise in order to become stronger and more powerful, but you may have done very little running. When your first game comes along, you may be the strongest, most powerful athlete on the court. However, your heart and lungs are so poorly conditioned that you can't get enough oxygen to your muscles to keep them functioning. Even though you may be the biggest and "baddest" player on the court, you can't stay on the court long enough to help your team. What good is that? Accordingly, you must include cardiorespiratory conditioning exercises, like running, into your workout program.

Food for Energy

Being able to stay on the court for long periods requires energy. The longer you play, the more energy your body is going to demand. In order to understand how to best improve your level of conditioning, it is important to understand where energy comes from, and how your body uses it during different types of running or conditioning programs.

Sound nutrition is critical. However, it is often the most neglected and abused aspect of an athlete's training program. Food determines the maximal levels of muscle growth and energy gained for athletic use. It is impossible to effectively gain muscle tissue without a proper protein intake. Energy levels will plummet without proper levels of carbohydrates. Cell membranes, steroidal hormones, and prostaglandin production would not be possible without sufficient levels of fat.

Eating food is something that human beings not only need to do, but most individuals love to do as well. Eating has evolved into a celebration of life itself. Most of our social interaction involves the ingestion of some type of food or beverage.

Figure 11.1. Sound nutrition is essential for an athlete.

Vitamin and Food Supplements

Companies touting the undocumented benefits of their foodstuffs generate almost a billion dollars annually by selling their products to eager, yet often unsuspecting, customers. Countless articles appear everyday in newspapers, magazines, and books, each telling their own version of what foods or supplements are best and why. With so much information being offered, it is easy to become confused about your dietary plan. Fortunately, the true basics of nutrition remain the same as they always have:

- Eat a wide variety of foods to insure all the vitamins and minerals are obtained.

- Take in a sufficient amount of calories to match your energy and body-weight needs.

- Moderate your intake of saturated fat, simple sugars, and salt.

- Drink plenty of water. The amount you need to drink will depend on your body size and weight.

Even though hundreds of quick-fix, fad diets are devised and promoted each year by unscrupulous, misguided individuals, this section has no intention of adding to that confusion. Clarifying what foods are best for an athlete is the goal in this section. As such, an overview is presented of the basic structure of the foods you eat, and the amounts of energy and muscle those foods can provide to you.

Regardless of all the different types of food, each food can be classified as having three basic components or macronutrients. These macronutrients are called carbohydrates, proteins, and fats. Each of these macronutrients is displayed on a food's packages. The label on the package usually describes how much of each macronutrient is present in a serving size of that food. Some foods are composed of primarily carbohydrates. Others are composed of primarily protein, or mostly fat. It is from these carbohydrates, proteins, and fats that you derive your energy for activity.

Figure 11.2. Breads are an example of starches.

Carbohydrates

Carbohydrates (CHO) are foods that are composed of sugars. You might be thinking of pies, cakes, and ice cream as carbohydrates because of the sugar in these foods. However, many other foods that do not taste as sweet as those are considered carbohydrates as well. Carbohydrates exist in two major forms – sugars and starches.

Sugars may only consist of one molecule. A single molecule of sugar is called a monosaccharide. Those sugars that consist of two molecules are called disaccharides. The white powdered sugar and the table sugar you put in coffee, cakes, and pies are examples of a disaccharide. Other mono and disaccharides that you consume most often are found in foods like milk (galactose) and fruits or fruit juice (fructose). Starches consist of many monosaccharides that are linked

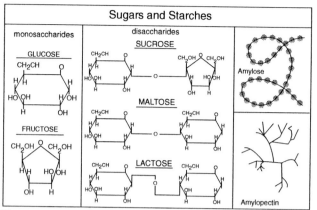

Figure 11.3. Molecular breakdown of sugars and starches.

together in a chain-like formation to form a polysaccharide. A starch is a very complex carbohydrate. Starches involve foods like potatoes, pasta, and breads.

Once a carbohydrate is eaten, it is digested by the body and broken down into glucose molecules. Glucose is another type of monosaccharide. These glucose molecules are either used for the body's immediate energy needs, or are stored in the muscle and liver as a polysaccharide called glycogen. Both glucose and glycogen are the body's primary source for providing energy during strenuous activity or work.

Proteins

A lot of athletes are hooked on including excessive levels of protein in their diet. Over they years, the literature has identified protein as the building block of muscle. As a result, many athletes jumped right on that idea and began consuming large quantities of supplemental protein. In fact, protein is the building block of muscle. In fact, muscle is protein, meaning your own body's muscle is considered stored protein.

High in protein, meat is usually the main course in most American diets. Dietary proteins are available in various grains and vegetables as well. When you eat animal products (meat, eggs, milk products) or other foods with proteins, your body eventually digests the proteins into molecules called amino acids. For a number of years, vitamin and supplement companies have been selling amino acids to the athletic-minded public by the truckload. In the 1960's and 70's, these companies sold protein powder. Currently, they choose to call these products amino acids. However, regardless of the name, you are still just buying protein. Other supplements on the market that are created from combinations of individual amino acids purport to take on specific roles in the body to provide energy and act to decrease the breakdown of muscle.

Currently, the most popular of these substances is called creatine. Creatine is created from a combination of the amino acids methionine, arginine, and glycine, and acts as an energy substrate by the body in the form of creatine phosphate. Creatine is used for quick and immediate energy needs. The human body manufactures a certain amount of creatine daily from the food you eat. Some individuals supplement that amount by taking creatine (orally or intravenously) that is widely available through a number of sources. Keep in mind that as you turn the pages of this book, you will most likely be using creatine phosphate to supply that energy.

Whether you are obtaining the protein in the food you eat or buying it in a vitamin type supplement, it is important that all nine of the essential amino acids are present. Without the nine essential amino acids, the body cannot efficiently use the ingested protein. Some proteins can be created by the body. These are called the non-essential amino acids. The essential amino acids, on the other hand, cannot be created by the body (refer to Table 11-1). Therefore, they need to be introduced to the body through the food you eat.

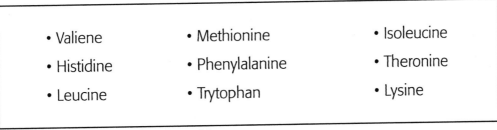

• Valiene	• Methionine	• Isoleucine
• Histidine	• Phenylalanine	• Theronine
• Leucine	• Trytophan	• Lysine

Table 11.1. Nine essential amino acids.

Most meat and animal products provide high-quality proteins because they contain substantial levels of the essential amino acids. On the other hand, because most plants and grains do not provide adequate levels of the essential amino acids, if you are a vegetarian, be sure to combine certain foods together in order to supply all nine essential amino acids. One excellent food combination for vegetarians is a combination of grains and beans, like navy beans and rice. Tofu or other soybean-based products, like soy milk and cheese, is another excellent way of insuring you get the nine essential amino acids. Whether or not the nine essential amino acids are present is another method of checking the quality of a protein supplement. If all nine essentials are not present in a supplement, you are probably wasting your money.

Once eaten, protein is digested into its building block components, or amino acids. The blood carries these amino acids throughout the body. Because you use your muscles to move your body, muscle cells can become damaged. Amino acids help to repair and replace enzymes and damaged cells. In regard to energy supply, muscle is broken down and used less often than stored carbohydrates and fats. The body would prefer to spare your muscles so that you can move to the table and eat. Your body will, however, use muscle for energy during extended periods without food. After about 24 hours without food, or a period of weeks without proper intake of carbohydrates, fats, and protein, the body will begin to degrade muscle tissue for energy. The body can also use

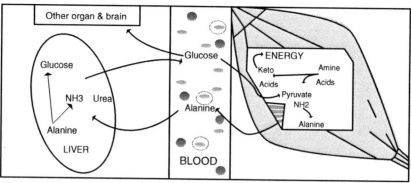

Figure 11.4.

muscle for energy during long, strenuous exercise, like marathon running. This use of protein for energy is called gluconeogenesis. Muscle is broken down into the individual amino acids via the removal (deanimation) or the transfer (transamination) of the amine groups within the molecular structure (refer to Figure 11.4).

The non-essential amino acid, alanine, does not play a large role in the building of muscle tissue. But when muscle is broken down for energy, alanine plays a major role. Alanine is carried back to the liver and chemically converted to a glucose molecule. Glucose is what the body likes to use most to provide energy. In turn, this glucose-like protein serves the body's energy needs. The key point to keep in mind is that consuming protein in the form of a supplement is not necessary. What is important about building muscle is to not lose muscle, a process that is best accomplished by eating the proper number of calories and by keeping enough carbohydrates in your diet to provide sufficient energy. If you adhere to these two essential steps, your body will not have to break down muscle for energy. If you are a vegetarian who eats the correct food combinations, or if you are a meat eater and are eating well, then you are probably getting all the protein that you need.

Endurance athletes: 1.8 grams protein per kilogram of body weight

Athletes: 1.2 to 1.6 grams per kilo body weight

Infants and children: 2.0 to 2.4 grams per kilo body weight

Late childhood: 1.2 grams per kilo body weight

Adolescence: 1.0 grams per kilo body weight

Adult: 0.8 grams per kilo body weight

Table 11.2. Approximate daily protein requirements.

Fats

Fat is a "dirty" word in today's fit-conscientious society. Some dietary fat, however, is necessary in an individual's diet. As such, fat should make up about 20% to 30% of your daily caloric intake. Fat provides your body with the basic building material for cell membranes, prostaglandins, and steroids. Fat also provides energy during endurance activities.

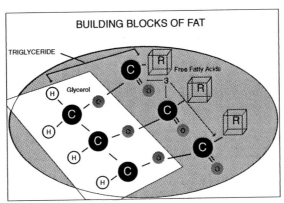

Figure 11.5. Building blocks of fats.

Fat is obtained from animal products, nuts, seeds, and vegetable oils. The fat-soluble vitamins A, D, E, and K are provided by dietary fat. In the body, fats are digested and reduced to molecules called triglycerides, phospholipids, and cholesterol esters. These molecules, plus the fat-soluble vitamins, are bonded together to form a chylomicron. The chylomicron is then moved out of the stomach where it is picked up by the blood stream and carried to all parts of the body.

The individual parts of the chylomicron are released wherever they are needed. The triglyceride portion is picked up and used by the cells to repair cellular membranes, or is taken in and used by the cell (muscle cell) for energy. The phospholipids and cholesterol portions of the chylomicron are also removed and used by various cells. If the fat components of the chylomicron cannot be used, they are stored in the body at various fat depots. The depots are located under the skin, and around the internal organs of the body. Small quantities of this fat are stored within the muscle cell for future energy needs.

Your body will use fat for energy when the conditions are right. From a fitness perspective, that is what you would like most of all. If you can deplete the stored fat from under the skin, you will appear leaner and have a more athletic appearance. The loss of body fat also benefits you because fat does not move itself like muscle does. If fat weight can be reduced, then the muscle does not have to work as hard to move your body. Keep in mind that fat is not only stored in fat depots, but excess protein and glucose can be stored there as well. If you are eating more carbohydrates and protein then you can use for energy or convert to muscle, your body can chemically change and attach the excess glucose and protein to triglycerides, sending them into fat storage areas. In other words, regardless if the food you ingest is a fat, a protein or a carbohydrate, if you eat too much, you're going to get fat.

Simple Bioenergetics

Bioenergetics is the study of how your food is converted into usable energy. Your muscle cells have two dominant chemical refineries that are used to produce adenosine triphosphate (ATP). ATP is the fuel your cells use to create movement. Glycolysis is the chemical refinery where glucose from carbohydrates you have eaten is converted to ATP. The Krebs or citric acid cycle refines glucose, fat, and sometimes protein into ATP. The body prefers to change glucose and fat into ATP, and only uses protein (amino acids) if needed. The amount of fat or glucose used to make ATP depends on the type and intensity of exercise you are performing. Using fat to create ATP, requires that oxygen is present in high quantities in the muscle cell. With oxygen present, the Krebs cycle can begin using more fat and less glucose to produce ATP energy.

Higher-intensity exercise requires more ATP. This is like being in your car, and pressing harder on the gas pedal. The harder the engine has to work, a greater amount of gasoline is burned. During a high-intensity exercise, like stop-and-go or sprint training, you will need high levels of ATP energy. Suppose, however, that you were told by your coach to run as fast and far as you could without stopping. You would start very fast, but after a few seconds, you would begin to lose speed. You try hard to increase your speed, but it's no use. You still begin to slow down. Eventually, your muscles will no longer work, and you will be forced to stop all together. This process is similar to the concept of momentary muscular failure (MMF) that was discussed in the chapter on resistance training.

So what happened to make your muscles stop? First, the sprint activity used all the available ATP that was stored in the muscle cells. Next, the chemical refineries (glycolysis and Krebs cycle) in the cells began to quickly manufacture additional ATP from your stored food (fat, carbohydrates, and protein). The muscle's demand for ATP, however, was too great. Glycolysis and the Krebs cycle simply could not produce ATP fast enough to meet the energy demands of the exercise.

Two factors that reduce the production of ATP are the production of lactic acid and a low level of oxygen availability at the muscle cell. Lactic acid is a waste product created from refining glucose into ATP. Like the gasoline exhaust coming from the tail pipe of your car, lactic acid is the glucose exhaust resulting from glycolysis. Lactic acid is responsible for the burning sensation that you might feel in your arms or legs when performing strenuous exercise. High intensity exercise results in greater levels of lactic acid production.

When glucose is refined to produce ATP, it goes through several chemical changes. If oxygen concentrations are high in the muscle cell (during rest or low-intensity exercise), the Krebs cycle can begin using some of the chemicals created by glycolysis to produce additional ATP. If oxygen levels are low (high-intensity exercise), glucose is turned into lactic acid. During an activity, if the exercise intensity lessens, some of the lactic acid can slowly be changed into ATP. If not, the lactic acid will eventually cause the exercise to stop.

With question, considerably more information could be included concerning diet and nutrition for the athlete. Such a review is simply beyond the basic scope of this text. Keep in mind that nutrition is equally, if not more, important than the workout you perform. Also, remember that proper nutrition is a form of recovery. Recovery is when you build your body, making it stronger in order to perform better during the next bout of exercise or activity.

Types of Cardiorespiratory Training

As a rule, you can do two general types of cardiorespiratory conditioning, depending on whether you are training for power or endurance.

- *Anaerobic* (also referred to as sprint or stop-and-go training). This type of conditioning concentrates on using elements of speed or power. Basketball players need only to include stop-and-go work in about one-half of their cardiorespiratory training. Basketball is a stop-and-go sport. However, very little opportunity exists for rest during time-outs and momentary breaks in the action. A basketball player must be able to stop and go, time and time again. Therefore, endurance can also have a substantial impact on an athlete's success.

- *Aerobic* (endurance training). Basketball players should engage in aerobic-type conditioning during the second half of their training. Preferably, this half of training should involve more combination, endurance training (i.e., sprints followed by lesser intense movements), rather than long- distance, continuous running.

Different types of cardiorespiratory activities, like the varying styles of resistance training, use different types of muscle cells. Sprint training involves the fast acting FG cells or fast-twitch muscle cells. During an all-out sprint, the chemical refining of glucose and glycogen occurs primarily within the FG muscle cells. During less intense exercise, such as a 30-minute run, the refining of fat and glucose occurs in the SO, or slow-twitch muscle cells. The extent to which the

FOG muscle cells are utilized is contingent on the intensity of the activity. Remember that the FOG muscle cells possess the capacity to assist either FG or SO cells, depending on the sprint or endurance requirements of the activity. Each of the different cell types can perform glycolysis and the Krebs cycle. Even though FG fibers can perform chemical activities that require oxygen, they are better at performing glycolysis. The reverse is true for the SO muscle cells. They can perform glycolysis, but they don't do it as well as the FG cells.

The design of an athlete's conditioning program should depend on the needs of the individual. Most sports require a combination of both aerobic and anaerobic conditioning. The elements of power versus endurance are always of concern when planning a conditioning regimen for the body, even one that includes a cardiorespiratory-conditioning program.

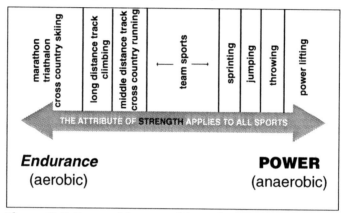

Figure 11.6. An aerobic-anaerobic, task-specific continuum.

Because some sports are similar in their cardiorespiratory requirements, they place similar physical demands on the body. The point to keep in mind is that if you play two different sports, you run a greater risk of not being as physically prepared for one sport as you are for another, unless the physical requirements of both sports are similar. Soccer, lacrosse, and basketball are closely related in their cardiorespiratory requirements. Football and some track and field events, on the other hand, have vastly different cardiorespiratory requirements than sports such as soccer, lacrosse, or basketball. This is not to say that a multi-sport athlete cannot perform well in all of his sports. But differences in the physical demands among sports mean that a multi-sport athlete may have to work twice as focused (i.e., smart) as the single sport athlete in physically preparing himself.

Adjusting Suggested Running Times

Basketball is played at a variety of skill and age levels, by both men and women. The running workout times suggested in this book are based on the abilities of the college-age male basketball athlete who is performing on a 94-foot college court. Of course, for the high school athlete who plays shorter games on smaller courts, these distances might need to be adjusted. Most college woman basketball players, because of their skill level, may not need to adjust the running times in this book. On the other hand, similar to their male counterparts, adjustments may need to be considered for women basketball players at the high school level. As the distance increases, a female athlete may need more time to complete the run. The smaller female body and shorter stride length can result in less ground being covered during the time allowed.

One step that can be taken to insure the safety and recovery level of the high-school athlete could be to keep the suggested running times the same regardless of the length of the court. Some individuals might feel that a high-school player needs to achieve faster times to insure a proper conditioning effect, because he or she plays on a 84-foot court. On the contrary, the lower skill level and physical abilities of the "typical" high-school athlete, however, might justify allowing more time for the running to be completed. After a week or so, if the athlete is easily running the final sprints in the workout, then the times can be shortened to insure a proper training intensity. Among the factors that coaches can consider in adjusting the running times of their athletes are the following:

- For the college female and both the male and female high-school athlete, if the running times become too easy, drop one-second off.

- For the college female and both the male and female high-school athlete, if running times are too difficult, then add one-second to that particular exercise.

- If the exercise continues to be too difficult for athletes of either gender or at any competitive level, then begin adding additional rest between the bouts of exercise, in five seconds increments, until the running times are achievable.

In fact, adjusting the rest time between bouts of exercise is not the best method for correcting a sprint's intensity. However, during actual activity, a second is a very long time, and a tremendous amount of ground can be covered. Dropping or adding more than a second on a sprint can make the sprint far too difficult or too easy.

Anaerobic Training

Anaerobic training (also commonly referred to as stop-and-go or sprint training), is exercise that is performed at 85% to 125% of your maximum oxygen uptake ($\dot{V}O2$ max), or that which pushes your heart rate to around 90 percent of your maximum heart rate. An approximation of your maximum heart rate in beats per minute can be determined by subtracting your age from 220.

Anaerobic means without oxygen. During anaerobic-type exercise, the intensity at which the muscles are working prevents them from properly absorbing and utilizing oxygen from the air being breathed. Anaerobic training can improve the efficiency of your body's anaerobic energy-producing systems and can improve your level of muscular strength and your tolerance to the muscular discomforts caused by lactic acid.

During sprint training, energy is supplied mostly through glycolysis when your body chemically converts glucose and stored glucose (called glycogen) into ATP. The demand for ATP by the muscles is very high during this type of training. Oxygen levels in the muscle cell may be low during intense exercise. This state occurs because you cannot physically breathe enough air into the lungs, or move enough oxygen into the cells from the air you breathe. In other words, intense exercise requires more oxygen than the lungs can deliver. During low-intensity exercise, on the other hand, you can breathe more regularly and absorb more oxygen into the cells, thus producing enough ATP to meet the body's demands.

When sufficient oxygen is lacking in the muscle cells, lactic acid levels increase rapidly. The body attempts to reduce the discomfort caused by lactic acid by chemically buffering it with hydrogen carbonate (HCO3). This method is similar to taking an antacid tablet to ease the pain of acid indigestion caused by a spicy meal. When you first begin a sprint-training program, you may find the demands imposed by the exercise very difficult. Your breathing may seem out of control, causing you to stop the activity all together. Lactic acid causes hydrogen ions to be released into the blood. This situation causes the blood to become more acidic. HCO3 is released, resulting in water and carbon dioxide being produced. Remember, carbon dioxide (CO_2) is the stuff you breathe out. In grade school, you learned that plants love CO_2. When CO_2 begins to build up inside your body, your lungs begin to work harder. You begin to breathe faster to not only get needed oxygen, but also to get rid of CO_2. Lactic acid also hinders muscle contraction. The body eventually gets better at stop-and-go training by improving its ability to produce HCO3. Also, the body becomes more efficient at changing lactic acid into ATP for energy. As a result, your muscles work better, and your breathing is controlled.

Basketball is a stop-and-go sport. However, in basketball, very little time is allowed between periods of activity. Basketball players do not cover the total distance they run in a basketball game in a single explosive burst. Instead, they perform numerous explosive bursts, followed by lesser intense movements. During a basketball game, it is difficult to determine what is considered sprint activity. If you sprint down a 94-foot college court (31.3 yards) or an 84-foot high school court (28 yards), you can considered that yardage as a base measurement for an anaerobic conditioning workout. On each end of the court, however, you typically have to engage in offensive and defensive tasks, which might also be performed with sprint-like efforts. A sprint-like effort in basketball will probably never be maintained for more than 35 to 45 seconds before you'll either reduce your level of intensity or stop altogether.

A 35-to-45 second time period is equivalent (time-wise) to around a 300-yard sprint or running up and down the court 10 times (a college court) without stopping. A basketball player usually covers his performance yardage over a series of continuous trips up and down the court. You must consider the work totals during an actual game to properly design and perform your stop-and-go conditioning program. For the best conditioning results, you should consider the total yardage run in any one play or moment in the game, the total yardage run during the game, and the amount of recovery needed during timeouts or during pauses in play.

A conditioning program for a basketball player may need to have longer and slightly slower sprints, with less recovery time between them. Also, it is important to conduct as many of your sprint workouts as possible on the basketball court, rather than on a track. The deceleration and acceleration required when changing ends of the court requires more energy than running straight track distances. For basketball, controlling recovery during stop-and-go training is most important. Considering all these variables, you can better create a conditioning environment that simulates game situations.

- **Intervals**

Interval training refers to sprint bouts that cover a given distance and must be completed in a given amount of time. These sprints are usually followed by moments of complete rest. Your total workout yardage can be divided into a series of sprints, based on the amount of yardage you might cover during a game. Rest is allowed after each sprint or a group of sprints. The rest between sprints should also be based on game situations. All aspects of conditioning should be relative to a game situation. This type of exercising is usually intense. You can regulate the intensity level in three ways:

- Increase the total number of sprints, or increase the yardage each sprint covers. The best way to do this is to establish the total number of yards covered in a game situation. Let that amount of yardage be your goal. Gradually, over a period of weeks, add more and more yardage or additional sprints until you reach your total yardage goal.

- Reduce the amount of rest between exercise bouts. This approach, however, is a less effective method of increasing your intensity level because during a game, the amount of rest is relatively constant. The amount of time the players are on the court and the rest taken during time-outs, losses of ball, and foul shots are about the same each game.

- Increase the speed of the sprint by reducing the time allowed for its completion. As a rule, this method of increasing intensity is not advised, because you can only adjust the speed a sprint so much without making the sprint too easy or too difficult for an athlete. Adjusting the time allowed for the activity works better for longer distance running. Another argument for not adjusting the speed of the sprint is the psychological effects that success and failure have on an athlete. If the time allowance is too difficult to achieve and the athlete fails repeatedly, he may be more likely to get discouraged with either himself or the conditioning program.

- **Crosses**

All of the interval runs in the workouts, which are performed on the basketball court, are termed court crosses. Each time you run down the court, you are performing one crossing. For example, four court crosses means you will go baseline-to-baseline four times. Table 11.3 provides an overview of how much yardage you will cover, depending on the number of crosses you perform on either a high-school or a college court.

	84-foot court		94-foot court	
32 court crosses	896	yards	1001.6	yards
10 court crosses	280	yards	313	yards
6 court crosses	168	yards	188	yards
4 court crosses	112	yards	125	yards
2 court crosses	56	yards	62.6	yards

Table 11.3. Total yardage covered for specific number of crosses.

- **50-yard crosses**

Fifty-yard crosses are performed in the same fashion as the crosses previously described on a basketball court. One major difference between the two types of crosses, however, is that 50-yard crosses are done on a 50-yard section of a running track. It is acceptable to perform 50-yard crosses on the track for their full measured distance. Running 50 yards, however, and then turning to run back forces you to decelerate and then reaccelerate like you would on a basketball court when making transitions. Some of your workouts can contain both court crosses and 50-yard crosses. If you must perform your 50-yard crosses on a track, then measure off the court distance on the track and designate that area by cones. This step makes it easy to move directly from the 50-yard distance to the shorter court distances. Table 11.4 details how much yardage you will cover, depending on the number of 50-yard crosses you run.

6	50-yard crosses	300 yards
4	50-yard crosses	200 yards
2	50-yard crosses	100 yards

Table 11.4. Total yardage for a specific number of crosses.

- **Sideline crosses**

Sideline crosses are performed like the 50-yard crosses previously described, however, they are done by running the width of the basketball court, sideline to sideline, rather than running the length. Because all basketball courts are 50-feet wide, this run will be the same at every age level. For example, if you run four sideline crosses, you will cover 200 yards total.

- **Ladder runs**

Ladders, once commonly referred to as suicide runs, involve a series of sprints that originate from a common starting point. When performing ladders, you sprint to a particular spot on the court or track and then sprint back to the starting point. Immediately, you turn and sprint again to a different point (usually farther away than the first), and then back to the starting point again. This action, like climbing up and down a ladder, continues until all the spots are touched, and you've finished by sprinting back to the original starting line.

- **Double-court ladder**

This exercise involves a type of sprint that is performed on the basketball court by using the baselines, free-throw lines, and half-court as the rungs (spots) in the ladder. You begin by sprinting from the baseline to the nearest free-throw line and then back. Next, you sprint to half-court and back, followed by a sprint to the opposite free-throw line and back. You then sprint to the opposite baseline and back. Repeat this entire process twice to complete one repetition of the exercise. Table 11.5 shows how much yardage you will cover when you perform one repetition of a double-court ladder, depending on the type of court you run on.

	84-foot court	94-foot court
One double-court ladder	280 yards	313 yards

Table 11.5. Total yardage for one repetition of a double-court ladder.

- **Gassers**

A gasser is another type of ladder where the athletes step-slide to the free-throw line and back, ten times. Gasser are not timed. Rather, you should perform them as quickly as possible.

- **20-yard shuttle**

A 20-yard shuttle is similar to a ladder. Primarily, it involves a movement where the focus is on lateral quickness. Place two cones 10-yards apart on a straight line. Begin by standing in a marked spot between the two cones. As quickly as possible, sprint to the cone on your left. Stay very low by placing a hand on the ground and circling outside the cone. Rapidly sprint to the opposite cone, circling it in the same way. Finish by sprinting back through the spot where you began the drill. Repeat the drill, this time by starting to your right.

- **Game-simulation sprints**

The game simulator is a method of increasing the specificity of the conditioning session. The simulator is based on the number of transitions up and down the basketball court that a player might experience during a game. The simulator consists of a series of sprints from one end of the court to the other, followed by step slides to simulate defense and jogging to simulate offensive. Light jumping is included to represent battling for a rebound. Each bout of activity is called a flurry and is representative of a typical number of transitions that might be made during a game situation before a stop in play occurs. Rest is allowed between flurries to represent time-outs, loss of ball, or committed fouls.

During the course of a college game, with consideration to substitutions, stolen balls, and half-court transitions, the average guard will run a little over 3000 yards. This distance is equivalent to over 96 full transitions on a 94-foot court. Forwards will run about 2700 yards, and centers about 2200 yards. The numbers drop off for each position, because guards and forwards often lead fast breaks, and centers do not always make full transitions on breaks. Furthermore, guards and forwards cover more distance when playing offense and defense. Because the simulator is often more intense than a real-game situation, only 2000 yards will be simulated. To perform these game simulations effectively, create two groups of six-to-eight athletes. On command, the first group will begin their initial flurry. The athletes sprint down-court to the opposite baseline and begin to simulate defense by performing step slides from the baseline to the free-throw line. The numbers of suggested defensive and offensive movements in a 2000-yard simulation are designated in parentheses in

2000 yards + 56 transitions on a 94 foot court + 38 movements at the end of the court
Number of transitions before a rest (number of movements at end of the court)

Group 1		Group 2
8 (4)		4 (6)
	Foul / Foul	
4 (6)		8 (4)
	Foul / Out of bounds	
4 (6)		4 (6)
	Foul / Foul	
10 (4)		6 (4)
	Time Out / Foul	
6 (4)		10 (4)
	Foul / Time out	
12 (2)		4 (8)
	Time Out / Foul	
4 (8)		12 (2)
	Foul / Time Out	
8 (4)		8 (4)

Figure 11.7.

Figure 11.7 (each flurry has a different number). Before sprinting up the court on offense, the athlete must perform three strong vertical jumps, as if to rebound. On the offensive end, the athletes jog from baseline to the free-throw line. One senior athlete should lead the pace on the offensive and defensive ends of the court. After the first group completes a flurry of activity, a time-out is called, and the second group begins their flurry.

- **Uphill sprints**

Sprinting uphill is a high-speed resistance training exercise. By using the intensity created by a graded incline, you can build leg strength in a way that is very specific to the act of running. The steeper the incline, the more work you will perform. Do not use these hill workouts very often, however, because they can possibly shorten your stride length, due to the shorter chopper steps you must take when attacking the slope of the hill.

- **Combination training**

Combination training involves using techniques that attempt to incorporate both sprint (stop-and-go) and endurance training. The different types of combination work can be used to keep the workout fresh, in order to reduce the level of boredom for the athlete. Combination training can help you train at a higher intensity for longer periods before fatigue causes you to require a rest period.

Considered a moderately intense form of exercising, combination training can be used during the week after a really intense running session to provide a type of active recovery. During the sprint portion of combination training, you are working at a very high level of intensity, thereby stressing your anaerobic energy systems. During the less intense endurance portion, you can partially recover from the sprint portion of your training by making it easier for your body's cells to absorb oxygen, thus benefiting your aerobic energy systems. Seldom in athletics is it possible to run slowly. Competition most often demands that you push yourself to maximal muscular limits. Combination training provides an effective way of developing the ability to exercise for longer periods at the highest possible intensity.

• Ventilatory breaking points and combination training

Ventilation is simply breathing. As the exercise becomes more difficult, you begin to breathe deeper and more rapidly. The ventilatory breaking point is a time during exercise when your breathing increases. Ventilation has two breaking points. Figure 11.8 illustrates approximately where your two break points occur.

The first breaking point was once termed the aerobic threshold. This breaking point occurs when the level of lactic acid in your blood reaches two millimoles per liter of blood (mmoles/l). At this point, your breathing increases and then levels off. Usually when this occurs, your heart rate is around 130 to 150 beats per minute (bpm), and your cellular rate of oxygen absorption (VO2 max) is about 40-to-60 percent. The second, and more drastic rise in breathing rate, occurs when the level of lactic acid in your blood reaches four-

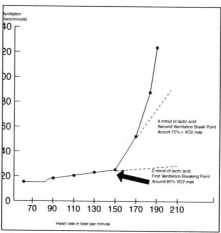

Figure 11.8. The two breaking points in ventilation.

mmoles/l. This point is called the anaerobic threshold, or the second ventilatory breaking point. At this stage, your heart rate is around 160 to 180 bpm, with a VO2 max of 65-to-90 percent. Simply put, when you work harder or longer and become fatigued, you breathe harder. You breathe harder because muscular work is producing lactic acid. The breakdown of lactic acid produces carbon dioxide (CO_2). You must get this CO_2 out of your body, so you breathe harder.

Combination training can help you train a relatively high level of intensity, thereby allowing you to push closer to the point where the body is relying on FG muscle fibers-cells to do some of the work. Remember, FG muscle cells produce more lactic acid when they're active. If lactic acid is at four-mmoles/l, you're working too hard (i.e., your heart rate is 160 to 180 bpm). Your heart rate is the best indicator of your exercise intensity. If you are in good condition, you may be able to allow your heart rate to go as high as 180 bpm before lactic acid reaches the four mmole/l mark. If your level of physical conditioning is relatively poor, you may only be able get as high as 160 bpm before fatigue sets in.

Previously, it was stated that lactic acid could be chemically altered by the body to create additional ATP for energy production. The mitochondria of the SO muscle cells have the ability of converting lactate to pyruvate. This conversion of lactate reduces the levels of lactic acid. If your level of lactic acid is reduced, your body can effectively buffer or neutralize the remainder with HCO_3. Training at, or near, the second ventilatory breaking point can improve the SO muscle cell's ability to convert lactate to pyruvate and also improve buffering of any lactic acid already formed. As a consequence, an athlete can perform longer at a higher level intensity before fatigue sets in.

- **Fartlek training**

Fartlek is Swedish for speed play. This particular training method was developed by Gosta Holmer, who ran his athletes on paths in the Swedish forest. When possible, the athlete ran fast, and when the terrain became too rugged, the athlete ran more slowly. Fartlek training uses the idea of intermingling higher intensity surges with slower running. Running at regular speed, you can choose to sprint on impulse for a given amount of time (e.g., 10 to 60 seconds), or you can design to sprint between marked areas (e.g., 25- to 100-yard burst) Once the sprint is completed, you then return to the regular running speed.

- **Two- and four-section fartlek**

Two- and four-section fartleks are fartleks that are performed on a track with either two or four 25-to-50 yard designated sprint sections. When the exercise is first introduced, you should keep the length of the sprints you run low. As you become more conditioned, you can increase the sprint distance.

- **"Indian running"**

The term "Indian running" was given to the type of exercise once performed by Native Americans at gatherings and ceremonies. This running technique involves a game, as well as a test of endurance. The running would continue until all the participants retired due to exhaustion. The participants would begin running in a single-file line at a moderate speed. The last runner in the line would sprint past all the others and take his place at the front of the line. Each runner, as he became the last person in the line, would sprint to the front, and the process would continue. This type of running is continuous, with bursts of sprinting mixed in. Indian running involves fartlek training, with a twist.

• **Hill training**

If you live in a hilly area, you are in luck. You can achieve the same type of cardiorespiratory work as fartlek or Indian running by running hills. As you run along at a moderate pace, you build your endurance capabilities. But as you begin to run up a hill, you increase the demands on your muscles. This situation is much like the added demand that increased speed places on your muscles. By running a trek over hills, you can simulate a fartlek run. Hill training should not be confused with hill sprints, discussed in the stop-and-go section. In hill sprints, you are moving at high speed. In hill training, you are moving at slower speeds.

• **Endurance training**

Endurance training (also referred to as aerobic—with oxygen—training), involves activity that is not as intense as sprint training, but it continues for a longer time. Because the intensity of the activity is relatively low, the muscles do not have to work as hard. The muscle's demand for energy is lower. The demand for ATP by the muscle is also lower. Therefore, muscle cells easily take up the oxygen you breath. Because the level of oxygen is high in the cells, lactic acid does not accumulate. Lactate can be changed to pyruvate and then to ATP energy by the cells. Simply put, endurance exercise is not as intense as stop-and-go training. Because the intensity level is lower in the two-mile run than in a sprint, for example, you can perform it longer before becoming exhausted. A practical definition of endurance training is exercise that can be performed for 20 to 30 minutes nonstop each day. You can perform endurance-training exercise three to five days per week, at an exercise intensity of 60 percent of your maximal oxygen uptake (VO2 max), or around 65 to 70 percent of your maximal heart rate.

Although basketball is a stop-and-go sport, it is stop-and-go, over and over again with little rest allowed between the actions. Therefore, it borders on being a semi- endurance activity. As such, endurance training should be included along with combination training to achieve maximum benefits from your basketball con-

---

• 1/4 mile – Run the prescribed distance for time

• 1/2 mile – Run the prescribed distance for time

• 2-mile fun run – Run two miles for time

• 12-minute run – Performed on a 440-meter track, attempt to run as many laps as possible during a 12-minute period.

Table 11.6. Examples of basic endurance runs.

ditioning efforts. You can also use endurance activities to maintain level of fitness, while reducing the stress associated with stop-and-go work.

Similar to resistance training, cardiorespiratory conditioning can result in fatigue and overtraining. Lesser-intensity conditioning days are necessary to promote positive overall gains in conditioning. If you perform an intense stop-and-go session on Monday, and perform some type of lower-body resistance training on Tuesday, you can be assured that your legs will be tired. Remember, you do not gain from the workout — you gain from the recovery after the workout. Endurance training can keep the muscle active, keeping the circulation of blood to the legs at a higher level. That higher rate of circulation can further promote healing of over-stressed muscle tissue, and thus, enhance recovery.

Endurance training can also improve your level of body composition by reducing your level of body fat. This factor would greatly benefit most athletes, because being too fat can hinder performance. Table 11.6 illustrates four examples of basic endurance runs.

- **Alternative forms of endurance training**

  Heavy play. Heavy play involves running on a basketball court, while wearing a 2-to-6 pound weighted vest. Run up and down the court, as many times as possible, for three minutes. Use a basketball and make lay-ups at each basket. Over time, the level of weight worn in the vest can be increased. Do not dunk on this exercise. Too many dunks can reduce the effectiveness of your plyometric program and lead to possible injury. If you have a partner, you can pass the ball out after making your lay-up, and after transition, receive a return pass for your next lay-up. Perform three or more three-minute bouts during the workout. You should attempt to cross the court between 22 to 26 times (on a 94-foot court). After each bout of exercise, rest one minute.

  Shadow-boxing bouts. If you're tired of running, or if you have a lower body injury, try shadow boxing for three-minute bouts. Begin each bout by moving your arms easily. As you warm up, punch more forcefully. Box your imaginary opponent for three minutes, then take a one-minute break. Perform three or more three-minute rounds. During each three-minute round, you should attempt to punch 150 or more times. After each bout of exercise, rest one minute.

  Jump-rope bouts. Jump-rope bouts are similar to the shadow boxing previously discussed. Jump rope for three minutes, then rest for one minute. Sometimes during the resistance training workouts, you are asked to jump rope. When you jump rope during your resistance training efforts, you are usually required to jump for a given number of times (turns).

The Heart of the Matter

Even though basketball has endurance requirements, you must still be able to rapidly accelerate to steal a bad pass or cut a man off on defense. The conditioning programs for basketball should mimic the sport. Often, recovery may have to be made during a period of lesser-intense activity. Because basketball is a stop-and-go activity, the base of your conditioning program should center on stop-and-go or sprint-type training. For your conditioning program to be successful, it is essential that you consider how you will recover during the exercise, with complete rest between bouts of exercise or during less intense periods of exercise. This stage is where you can apply your sense of creativity to make your conditioning program both fun and productive.

Basketball Shooting Games and Applied Skills

Basketball is a sport that requires a high level of skill. Raw athletic ability alone will not determine your success. You must spend as much time as you can developing specific basketball skills. This is not to say that you should neglect to do your daily conditioning routine. For every hour you dedicate to basketball, you should spend approximately 15 minutes conditioning yourself and the other 45 minutes should be spent working on applied basketball skills.

The primary purpose of this book is to provide you a means of conditioning yourself for basketball. It does not attempt to coach you on improving your skills as a basketball player. If your coach has a more effective approach for developing your essential skills, then you should do the drills that he suggests rather than those included in this chapter. It is important, however, to be as fundamentally sound at every basic basketball skill, regardless of your position. You never know when you may be called on in a game to rebound, shoot, dribble, pass, or play defense. As such, the following drills and games presented in this chapter are very basic. Properly performed, however, they can help you develop and refine your skills.

SHOOTING GAMES

■ Game #1: At Least 20 in 30 or Less

The objective of this game is to score at least 20 points in 30 or less shots. You must shoot at least five shots from behind the three-point line, five free throws, and five two-point shots. If you make every shot of the first fifteen attempts, you will score thirty points. However if you miss a three, you must subtract three points from your score. If you miss a two, subtract two points. If you miss a free throw, subtract one. At the end of the first fifteen shots, if you have twenty points you win. If you have less then twenty points, keep shooting. The hardest thing about this game is keeping score. If you have a partner, let him keep your score, and you keep up with the number of shots taken. Play this game at least three times to get enough shots accumulated for that day's workout.

274 Total Basketball Fitness

■ Game #2: Beat the Pro to 20

The objective of this game is to score 20 points. You can shoot two's and three's, but no lay-ups. Each time you make a basket, you get one point. However, each time you miss, you give the imaginary pro two points. If you miss ten shots, the pro wins. Play this game at least five times to insure getting enough shots for that day's workout.

■ Game #3: First to 20

The objective of this game is to score 20 points. You can shoot two's and three's, but no lay-ups. You shoot, and then your opponent shoots. Each time you make a three, you get three points. Each time you miss a three, subtract three points. The same rule for two-point shots. The first person to make 20 points wins. The first person to reach a negative 10 points automatically loses. Play this game at least three times to insure getting enough shots for that day's workout.

■ Game #4: Around the Whole World

This game requires eight numbered spots to be designated on the floor; you can choose the spots. A point where you might shoot from during a game is preferable. Start at point #1. Before you can move to point #2, you must hit three of five shots. To win, you must hit three of five from all eight spots. After three unsuccessful attempts of trying to hit three of five from any spot, then you must go back to spot #1 and start over. This game can be made more difficult by making all the spots behind the three-point line, or by requiring that you make four of five shots at a particular spot before you can advance to the next spot.

BASKETBALL APPLIED SKILLS: WORKOUT #1

■ Passing Drills

Whenever possible, work with a partner when practicing your passing skills. A pitch back device or a wall will be needed if you're working alone. Incorporating both two-handed and one-handed passes (refer to Tables 12.1 and 12.2). These drills are examples of how to structure a basketball-skills workout. Try creating your own workout if you desire. Just like any conditioning or skill-development routine, in order to become better, you must create a degree of structure and consistency in your workout routine. Inconsistent practice leads to inconsistent play.

All passes should be performed quickly, but under control. Backspin is a must on every pass in order to make the pass more easily catchable. At the end of each pass, your arms should be fully extended with your hands facing palms apart. This factor will insure proper backspin. Try to visualize game situations when making a pass. The higher your skill level, the less time you need to spend at each beginning passing station. However, some time should always be spent at each station, regardless of your skill level.

✓ Chest pass	
	Beginners perform . . . . .20 each
✓ Overhead pass	Intermediate players perform . . . .15 each
	Advanced players perform . . . . . .10 each
✓ Bounce pass	

Table 12.1. Examples of two-handed passes.*

*These are the passes you should use during a game situation whenever possible. Generally considered the most dependable type of passes, two-handed passes typically result in fewer turnovers, compared to the more creative passes.

✓ Baseball pass	
	Beginners perform . . . . .20 each
✓ Behind the back pass	
	Intermediate players perform . .15 each
✓ Over the shoulder pass	
	Advanced players perform . . . .10 each
✓ Underhanded flip or shuttle pass	

Table 12.2. Examples of one-handed passes.**

**These are the passes you should not use during a game situation unless forced to by the situation. One-handed passes are commonly thought to be less dependable and more likely to result in a higher number of turnovers compared to the more basic (two-handed) passes. Working on these passes can provide a higher level of target perception, better ballhandling ability, and additional mobility and dexterity to escape from tight situations.

BASKETBALL APPLIED SKILLS, WORKOUT #2

■ Ballhandling Drills

Whenever possible, work with a partner when performing these drills. The following examples illustrate one way to structure a basketball-skills workout. Try creating your own workout if you desire. All ballhandling drills should be performed relatively quickly, but under control. Each drill should be performed with each hand. Add 15 seconds to your weaker hand on each drill. The higher your skill level, the less time you need to spend at each beginning ballhandling station. However, some time should always be spent at each station, regardless of your skill level. Do not watch the ball. Instead, work on developing your sense of touch. You cannot develop touch if you always use sight to follow the ball. Perform each of the following drills for 30 seconds to one minute.

- **Revolutions** – Circle the ball around your body by moving the ball from hand to hand.

- **Ball swimming** – While dribbling at knee level in front of you, move your hand so that your palm opens and closes, as if moving back and forth in a pool of water, thus pushing the ball to the left and then right. Next, perform the same hand motion, but from front to back on the outside of your leg.

- **Tiny dribbles** – Start dribbling the ball and then gradually shorten the height of the dribble until you can hardly keep the ball bouncing. Start with the ball in one place. As you become more advanced, dribble the ball in and around your feet.

- **Behind-the-back dribble** – Stand in one place and dribble the ball back and forth, from one hand to the next behind your back. As you become more advanced, move forward and back side-to-side, while still dribbling the ball behind you.

- **Two-ball dribble** – While standing in place with a ball in each hand, bounce one ball, then the other. Next, bounce both balls together. As you become more advanced, move forward and back side-to-side, while still controlling both balls. Ball swimming can also be performed by the more advanced player.

■ Game-Specific Ballhandling Drills

Perform each of the following game-specific drills six times up and down the length of the court. Force yourself to use your weaker hand more than your stronger hand. Both drills can be employed as heavy play training by wearing a weighted vest.

- **Zigzag** — Use any dribbling style against a defender, while attempting to maintain ball control. The defender attempts to slow the dribbler's advancement down court, while the dribbler attempts to break free and score. Use the cross-over, inside out, reverse dribble, etc.

- **Game scenario** — Dribble against imaginary or real defenders, using full-speed, straight-ahead dribbles, sudden stops, backing up, reverse dribbles, cross-overs, and inside-outs, as if trying to single-handedly break a press, or run a delay game.

BASKETBALL APPLIED SKILLS, WORKOUT #3

■ Ballhandling Penetration Drills

Whenever possible, work with a partner when performing these drills. The following examples illustrate one way to structure a basketball skills workout. Try creating your own workout if you desire. Just like any conditioning or skill-development routine, in order to become better, you must create a degree of structure and consistency in your workout routine. Inconsistent practice leads to inconsistent play.

All ballhandling drills should be performed relatively quickly, but under control. Each drill should be performed with each hand. Add five additional attempts with your weaker hand on each drill. The higher your skill level, the less time you need to spend at each beginning ballhandling station. However, some time should always be spent at each station, regardless of your skill level. Do not watch the ball. Instead, work on developing your sense of touch. You cannot develop touch if you always use sight to follow the ball. Perform each drill five times on each side of the basket, with the left side being penetrated with left hand.

- **Cross-over #1** — On the left side of the basket, using your left hand, catch the pass; square to the basket; establish your left foot as your pivot; swing the ball up and down in a rounded sweep clockwise to your face; pick up your right foot as the ball passes your right leg; cross your right leg in front of the defender; turn your right side to him; dribble baseline with your left hand. Repeat on the right side, using your right hand.

- **Cross-over #2** — On the left side of basket, using your right hand, catch the pass; square to the basket; establish your right foot as your pivot; swing the ball up and down in a rounded sweep counter clockwise to your face, pick up your left foot as the ball passes your left leg; cross your left leg in front of the defender; turn your left side to him; dribble right with your right hand. Repeat on the right side, using your left hand.

- **Jab step** — On the left side of the basket, using your left hand, catch the pass; square to the basket; establish your right foot as your pivot. Head fake a shot; bring the ball back to your left hip; make a short jab step with your left leg; then make a long step, dribbling baseline with your left hand. Repeat on the right side, using your right hand.

- **Reverse dribble** — On the left side of the basket, using your left hand, catch the ball with your back to the basket; back into the defender, dribbling with your right hand; turn your left shoulder slightly into the defender as if to go right, then reverse dribble to your left hand, spinning around the defender; dribble baseline left handed. Repeat on the right side, using your right hand.

- **Reverse dribble with a behind-the-back or a between-leg cross over combo** — On the left side of the basket, using your right hand, catch the ball with your back to the basket; back into the defender, dribbling with your right hand; turn your left shoulder slightly into the defender as if to go right, then reverse dribble to your left hand, spinning around the defender. If he successfully cuts you off, cross over using your body as a shield. Dribble behind your back or through your legs to your right hand. Dribble right. Repeat on the right side, using your left hand.

- **Use your imagination** — Invent your own combination of dribbling maneuvers and work on that move.

BASKETBALL APPLIED SKILLS, WORKOUT #4

■ Defensive Drills #1

Whenever possible, work with a partner or partners when performing these drills. The following examples illustrate one way to structure a basketball skills workout. Try creating your on workout if you desire.

All defensive drills should be performed relatively quickly, but under control. Most defensive activities require tenacity and endurance. These drills should be performed aggressively, while maintaining a low, straight-backed defensive stance. These drills are designed to help you develop strength in your defensive stance. In turn, that additional strength should enhance your level of speed and quickness.

- **Stance builders** — Begin in a low defensive stance. Keep your back fully straight at all times, with one hand face high and one hand on the ball. Start in one corner of the basketball court. Have your body facing the opposite basket. Begin a slow and meticulous step-slide diagonally across the court. When you reach the sideline, make your inside foot your pivot foot. Pivot so that your back is now facing the opposite direction. In this way, the same foot will always be your pivot foot. Make about five diagonal crosses up the court. Then, come back down the court for another five crosses. This time, the opposite foot should be your pivot foot. Make this drill last three minutes total.

- **Zigzag** — The offensive player uses any dribbling style to maintain ball control. As the defender, you attempt to retard the ballhandler's advancement down court, while the dribbler attempts to break free and score. You must use a good defensive stance and step-slide to continually slide into the ballhandler's path and make him change directions. Perform this drill down the length of the court five times for each player.

- **Build-outs** — This drill is designed to help you approach your man once the ball has been passed to him. If the ball is passed to your man on the left-wing position, then you must rapidly run toward him with a degree of caution. Your left foot should be in front. This position is assumed in order to force the ballhandler to his left toward the baseline. The ballhandler can attack the defender's approach by going baseline, which would result in the defender having to step-slide to slow him down. Or, the ballhandler can attack the defender's front foot, which would result in the defender having to open his stance by dropping his left foot back, and then step-sliding with the ballhandler. If the ballhandler is on the right side of the basket, then you should approach with your right foot forward. If the ball is at the top of the key, you should approach with either foot forward. Each player should perform this drill five times on each side of the goal and five times from the top of the key.

BASKETBALL APPLIED SKILLS, WORKOUT #5

■ Defensive Drills #2

Whenever possible, work with a partner or partners when performing these drills. The following examples illustrate one way to structure a basketball skills workout. Try creating your on workout if you desire.

All defensive drills should be performed relatively quickly, but under control. Most of defensive activities require tenacity and endurance. These drills should be performed aggressively, while maintaining a low, straight-backed defensive stance. These drills are designed to help you develop strength in your defensive stance. In turn, that additional strength should enhance your speed and quickness.

- **Power backs** — After the pass has been made to the wing and you have successfully made your build-out, then you must turn up the pressure by crawling into your man's space. If he raises the ball as if to make a lob pass, go belly-to-belly with him. At the first indication that he might bring the ball down, power back a step, dropping down into a defensive position with the appropriate foot in front to force to the ballhandler toward the baseline. Your front hand should remain face-high, while your backhand should reach low toward the ball. Each player should perform this drill five times on each side of the goal and five times from the top of the key.

- **Man on ball** — This drill can be performed with up to four people. If you are by yourself, you can imagine the three ballhandlers that you are supposed to be defending. One ballhandler is at the top of the key, and two others are on each wing. One of the wingmen is your man. You can choose which. Start under the basket. As your man is passed the ball, you build-out and defend, forcing your man toward the baseline. Once your man passes the ball, for example to the top of the key, the ball is only one pass from your man. Then, overplay your man to prevent the pass from coming back. If your man passes the ball across the court to the other wingman, then the pass is now two passes away. You should sag back toward the basket with at least one foot inside the lane to a help position. Perform this drill for one minute, moving the ball back and forth. Each man should perform the drill four times. This drill can be made more difficult by having the ballhandlers move. This causes the defender to be always aware of whether his man is one or two passes from the ball.

- **Screen at point** — This drill can be performed with two other players and yourself. You are guarding your man, while the third player acts as a passer and screener. Once the pass is made to your man, then you must build-out. Play tight defense and power-back if necessary. The passer, after allowing you to come out and play defense, follows his pass toward your man, and proceeds to set a rear screen. Once you are made aware of the screen, either by self-awareness or in a game situation, your teammate who is guarding the passer should alert you. Prepare to fight through the screen, as if you had no help. This is done by stepping into the screen and putting your forearm against the screener's chest. Once he sets the screen, by rule, he can't move to retard you any further. If your man decides to use the screen, then push into the screener to create a gap or cushion. As your man attempts to go around the screener, take your other forearm and lay it on your man and ride around the screen with him. If he decides not to use the screen, then step-slide with him to defend. Each player should perform this drill five times on each side of the basket.

BASKETBALL APPLIED SKILLS, WORKOUT #6

■ Defensive Drills #3

Whenever possible, work with a partner or partners when performing these drills. The following examples illustrate one way to structure a basketball skills workout. Try creating your on workout if you desire.

All defensive drills should be performed relatively quickly, but under control. Most defensive activities require tenacity and endurance. These drills should be performed aggressively, while maintaining a low, straight-backed defensive stance. These drills are designed to help you develop strength in your defensive stance. In turn, that additional strength should enhance your level of speed and quickness.

- **Rebound** — This drill is performed with three players. One player acts as the shooter, another player is an offensive player attempting to rebound, and your job is to successfully box the rebounder out. Remember, successful rebounders have a instinct for getting great position, both on the ball as it come off the goal, and on their man. First and foremost, you must get between your man and the goal to perform a successful box-out. To box out your man, you must find him, touch him, and turn sideways to him as the ball is in flight. While maintaining contact with your man, try to find the ball with your peripheral vision. At the last moment when the ball hits the goal, quickly turn, putting your backside on your man. Do not lose contact with him. Maintain a low stance, while keeping your arms slightly down and out to your sides. Do not allow your man to push you under the goal. You must try to stay three to four feet out from the goal, regardless of what happens. The ball rarely ever drops straight down under the goal off a rebound. If he slides around you and goes under the goal, then that is his misfortune because now he is out of position. Perform this drill 15 times with each player.

- **Switching** — This drill is similar to the screen-at-point drill and is performed with four players. You are guarding your man, while the third player acts as a passer and screener. Once the ball is passed to your man, you must build-out, play tight defense, and power-back if necessary. The passer, after allowing you to come out and play defense, follows his pass toward your man, and proceeds to set a rear screen. Once you are made aware of the screen either by self-awareness or by your teammate who is guarding the passer, prepare by stepping into the screen and putting your forearm against the screener's chest. Once he sets the screen, by rule he can't move to retard you any further. If your man decides to use the screen, then push into the screener to create a gap or cushion. As your man attempts to go around the screener, allow him to do so. Step back. Now, your man is the screener. Your teammate switches and picks up the man coming off the screen. If the ballhandler decides not to use the screen, then you would keep him as your man and just step-slide with him to defend. Perform this drill five times on each side of the basket for each player.

- **Three-on-three** — At this point, it's time to incorporate all your defensive skills into the art of playing. The defense plays a helping man-to-man by using build-outs, power backs, switching on screens, boxing out and rebounding on shots, and by maintaining good man-on-ball relationships. If the offense scores, they maintain possession of the ball. As a consequence, working hard on defense will get you on offense. If you're lazy on "D," you stay on "D." Play two games to five points (each basket counts as one point).

ABOUT THE AUTHOR

Ben Cook is Manager of Exercise Programming for Carolinas Sports Performance Center and co-founder of the LINK Exercise and Evaluation System.

From 1990-1994, Cook was the assistant strength and conditioning coach for the Tar Heel football team at the University of North Carolina, where he helped 27 players reach the NFL. From 1994-2001, he was the head strength coach for Tar Heel men's basketball, whose teams made four Final Four appearances during his seven seasons.

Cook holds a master's degree in exercise and sports science from UNC and is a CSCS and NSCA-CPT with the National Strength and Conditioning Association. Cook lives in Harrisburg, North Carolina.

COACHING BY THE EXPERTS SERIES

 Coaching the Fast Break:
By the Experts
Bob Murrey, Editor
2002 • 108 pp • ISBN 1-58518-336-9 • $16.95

 Coaching Match-Up Defense:
By the Experts
Bob Murrey, Editor
2002 • 112 pp • ISBN 1-58518-335-0 • $16.95

 Coaching Zone Offense:
By the Experts
Bob Murrey, Editor
2002 • 120 pp • ISBN 1-58518-524-8 • $16.95

 Man-to-Man Defense:
By the Experts
Bob Murrey, Editor
1999 • 120 pp • ISBN 1-58518-243-5 • $16.95

 Practice Planning:
By the Experts
Bob Murrey, Editor
1999 • 152 pp • ISBN 1-58518-247-8 • $16.95

TO PLACE YOUR ORDER:

TOLL FREE: 888-229-5745
MAIL: Coaches Choice
      P.O. Box 1828
      Monterey, CA 93942
FAX: 831-372-6075
ONLINE: www.coacheschoice.com